Hannibal Muhammad

Copyright © 2021 Hannibal Muhammad

All rights reserved. No part of this publication may be reproduced, distributed, or transmitted in any form or by any means, including photocopying, recording, or other electronic or mechanical methods, without the prior written permission of the publisher, except in the case of brief quotations embodied in critical reviews and certain other noncommercial uses.

If you purchased this book without a cover you should be aware that this book is stolen property. It was reported as "unsold and destroyed" to the publisher and neither the author nor the publisher has received any payment for this "stripped book."

ISBN: 978-0-578-83953-0 (Paperback)

Library of Congress Control Number: 2020921704

Book design by Brother Hannibal LLC.

Printed in USA

Brother Hannibal Publishing
P.O. Box 374
Laveen, AZ 85339-0374

www.hannibalmuhammad.com

Publisher's Cataloging-in-Publication Data
provided by Five Rainbows Cataloging Services

Names: Muhammad, Hannibal, 1984- author.
Title: In my fathers' steps : self-reflection and lessons in my journey to Allah / Hannibal Muhammad.
Description: Laveen, AZ : Hannibal Muhammad, 2021. | Also available in ebook and audiobook formats.
Identifiers: LCCN 2020921704 (print) | ISBN 978-0-578-83953-0 (paperback)
Subjects: LCSH: Self-help techniques. | Self-actualization (Psychology) | Conduct of life. | BISAC: SELF-HELP / Motivational & Inspirational. | SELF-HELP / Personal Growth / General.
Classification: LCC BF637.S4 M84 2021 (print) | LCC BF637.S4 (ebook) | DDC 158.1--dc23.

TABLE OF CONTENTS

FOREWORD i
OPENING PRAYER vii
SALUTATION ix
IT'S TIME TO SAVE OUR YOUTH 1
FAMILY 29
DO WE TAKE THE TEACHINGS OF THE MOST HONORABLE ELIJAH MUHAMMAD AS A JOKE? 53
UNDERSTANDING VARIABLES OF LIFE 85
RESPECT FOR LIFE IN THE SPIRIT OF GOD'S WORD 107
PAIN AND POWER 117
CORRUPTED BY OUR OWN M.O. 139
LIVING OUR BEST LIFE PART ONE 161
LIVING OUR BEST LIFE PART TWO 189
DEFENDING FARRAKHAN 207
WHY I WALK WITH FARRAKHAN 217
GREATER IS HE THAT IS IN ME 239
PUT ON THE NEW MAN 259
ALLAH'S SAVIOUR IN OUR MIDST 269
DEDICATION 281
ACKNOWLEDGEMENTS 293

FOREWORD

"And I heard a loud voice saying in heaven, Now is come salvation, and strength, and the kingdom of our God, and the power of his Christ: for the accuser of our brethren is cast down, which accused them before our God day and night. And they overcame him by the blood of the Lamb, and by the word of their testimony; and they loved not their lives unto the death."--Revelation 12: 10-11

I am so honored that Brother Hannibal Muhammad, my dear brother, friend and fellow soldier in the ranks of The Nation of Islam, under the leadership of The Honorable Minister Louis Farrakhan, would ask me to write the foreword to his book.

It's more than a book.

It's a personal testimony of someone getting on the witness stand to testify of the Divine Power of The Teachings of The Most Honorable Elijah Muhammad, Taught to him by his Teacher, Master Fard Muhammad.

Out of a profound love for His Teacher, The Most Honorable Elijah Muhammad always bore witness to Who raised him and taught him. There are no articles, books, table talks or recorded addresses by him where you won't find him bearing witness and testifying of his Teacher, The Saviour, Master Fard Muhammad.

It has been the same with the Honorable Minister Louis Farrakhan for over 65 years. He always lets his audience know that he is a student of The Most Honorable Elijah Muhammad. He never shies away from elevating his Teacher or Master Fard Muhammad.

This profound love affair and example of the student raising up his teacher reminds me of what is written of in John 12:32 *"And I, if I be lifted up from the earth, will draw all men unto me."*

i

So many of us, including the author of this book, are products of the highest level of love displayed by Master Fard Muhammad, The Most Honorable Elijah Muhammad and The Honorable Minister Louis Farrakhan.

That love, sweet love, should compel us to want to get on the witness stand and testify—in our own unique way—to let the world know what the Teachings of The Most Honorable Elijah Muhammad through The Honorable Minister Louis Farrakhan has and is doing for us.

What would cause one who has such testimony to hesitate on sharing it? What would cause that one to shy away from letting the world know about The One Who raised and is raising them from mental and spiritual death? What would cause one to run away from the witness stand?

During The Honorable Minister Louis Farrakhan's address to the Nation of Islam's Student Laborers on February 20, 2020, he asked a piercing question:

"How Deep Is Your Love?"

Days later he repeated that very same question, "How Deep Is Your Love?", during his Saviours' Day 2020 keynote address on February 23, 2020 in Detroit and again during his March 1, 2020 address at Mosque Maryam titled, "Jesus is the Key".

Interestingly, just four months prior in Phoenix, Arizona, The Honorable Minister Louis Farrakhan flew out to speak at the Janazah services for Brother Hannibal Sirboya Muhammad, Sr. on October 5, 2019. I was blessed to be among those present to witness such a transformative experience in honor of a man whom I referred to as "Pop" and to support a family that I love and admire.

In his opening words, The Honorable Minister Louis Farrakhan marveled at the fact that love was talked about so much by those who spoke before him. He said, *"I thank Allah for our Teacher, The Messenger, Messiah, The Honorable Elijah Muhammad. I thank Allah for this service and all who came and all who had something to say. Your words were powerful. Your words were from the heart and the one word that was the strongest word spoken by all was the word 'Love'."*

The Honorable Minister Louis Farrakhan continued, *"The Bible puts it very simple. God is Love. 'He who has not love has not God. He who has not love has not yet come to life.' Love is a forgotten thing in a world like this. Where when he told his brother, "I love you brother," his brother had to stop a moment and, "What is this?" Because love is strange. Love comes in as a stranger in a world where Satan is the ruler. Love is strange in a world like this. We talk about it all the time. We sing about it. We tell our friends, "I love you." But the test of love, Jesus said, "Greater love has no man than he lay down his life for his friend.""*

The Honorable Minister Louis Farrakhan would then ask for Hannibal Muhammad, Jr. and said to him, *"It was your letter that touched my heart. Because I've been to a lot of funerals and a lot of painful days and I wasn't sure that I was going to come. But when I read your letter, my heart was moved and we summoned the troops to get me to Phoenix on time. I want to thank you Brother Hannibal from the depth of my heart and I want to thank Allah for moving my heart by your words to get on a plane with several members of my staff and here we are."*

It was in that moment, with tears in my eyes, I said to myself, "Oh Allah. This is major. What was in that letter? What was in Brother

Hannibal's mind, heart and spirit in the moments of writing that letter that would touch The Man of God in such a loving way?"

* * * *

I love and value reading, hearing and watching personal testimonies from people, especially the members of The Nation of Islam. I love learning more about them. Even those whom I think I know, I constantly find myself learning that there is so much more depth to what Allah (God) has placed within them. I especially love to read and hear people, even outside the inner ranks of The Nation of Islam, share spiritual accounts of how Allah (God) intervened in their affairs to give them a triumph in the midst of severe trials and tribulations; how Allah (God) guided them to turn their pain into a purposeful mission and how at their lowest moment He gave them the spirit to bounce back through seeing what was being done *for* them versus what was being done *to* them.

In witnessing what Brother Hannibal Muhammad, Jr. and his family has gone through and is still going through since his father made his transition, I have marveled at his spiritual evolution that Allah (God) is guiding him through. It has produced a different kind of witness bearing and testifying from him that's of a deepening love born out of trying times, self-reflection and an unforeseen journey.

Since I've known Brother Hannibal Muhammad, Jr., we've had a shared love for going out into the streets to testify of The Teachings of The Most Honorable Elijah Muhammad. When he lived in Houston, Texas, we always looked forward to leaving the Sunday meeting at Muhammad Mosque No. 45 to go and get on the witness stand at an all-mens drug rehabilitation center located in Northeast Houston. Along with other Nation of Islam brothers, I was inspired by watching him be transparent with those men and give them hope by lifting up our Spiritual Father, The Honorable Minister Louis Farrakhan.

Now, years later, I am excited that Allah (God) has inspired him to further document his testimony in book form, in hopes that it will inspire other witness bearers to come out of the shadows, deepen their love and testify more of what The Teachings of The Most Honorable Elijah Muhammad through The Honorable Minister Louis Farrakhan has and is doing for them.

Abdul Qiyam Muhammad
Houston, Texas
February 1, 2021

OPENING PRAYER

In the name of Allah, the Beneficent, the Merciful. Praise be to Allah, the Lord of the worlds. The Beneficent, the most Merciful. Master of the Day of Judgement in which we now live.

Oh Allah, I come to you. I ask that you remove me and my impediments. Oh Allah, use me as an instrument. Allow the words found in this book to be a healing to the reader. Allow the words to create change in the mind, spirit, and physical being. Oh Allah, I thank you for granting me the opportunity and desire to start this process of fulfilling my purpose in life. Allah, please forgive me for any mistakes I have made as it was not intentional, but it is a continued learning process for me. I pray I can become a better servant of yours and be more dutiful towards the upliftment of the masses.

Oh Allah, I pray that this is pleasing to you, the Most Honorable Elijah Muhammad, and the Honorable Minister Louis Farrakhan.

Thank you so much.

Ameen! Allah-u-Akbar!

SALUTATION

In the name of Allah, the Beneficent, the Merciful. I bear witness that there is no God but Allah Who came in the person of Master Fard Muhammad, the Great Mahdi. I thank Almighty God Allah for traveling 9,000 miles from the comfort of his own being, to not just find a people, to not just study a people, but to raise them up from the lost knowledge, the lost wisdom, and the lost understanding of self. He came so that the Black man and woman of America can learn who they are and whose they are.

We, the Black man and woman here in America, have been blessed that God Himself would come to comfort us. Think about that for a moment. He didn't send a messenger. He didn't send a prophet. He didn't send His son. He came Himself in the person of Master Fard Muhammad. He went to the worst part of America, which is called Black Bottom, Detroit, and he started the work of building a Nation out of the worst-conditioned people in America.

Master Fard Muhammad raised up a Georgia-born Black man, who is the son of a preacher and the grandson of a preacher. Almighty God Allah took this man who had not been beyond the 4th grade of schooling and taught him for 3 ½ years. He taught him night and day. Allah gave him His mind and exalted him as the Messiah and living Christ. I am speaking of the Messenger of Allah! A god sitting at the right hand of Allah! A god in control of the weather. I am speaking of the Most Honorable Elijah Muhammad!

I would not know Almighty God Allah who came in the person of Master Fard Muhammad and His messenger the Most Honorable Elijah Muhammad if it were not for this man. This man has opened my eyes. This man has been born again in the spirit of the father. He has lined his mind up with the Most Honorable Elijah Muhammad, which means he has lined his mind up with Almighty God Allah who came in the person of Master Fard Muhammad. This man is the father to the fatherless, the truths of all truths, the Messiah the world has been waiting for, the divinely guided one, the crusher of all evil, and much more. I am speaking of Jesus the Messiah, who has been in front of our eyes this whole time. I am speaking of the Honorable Minister Louis Farrakhan.

"We thank the Originator for setting into motion the universe with the thought to perfect it and Himself. He wanted perfection of Himself. People will argue that God is already perfect. Of course!

Whatever stage of development He's at, He is perfect. He is present now to perfect. There will be soldiers to create a perfect kingdom of perfect peace with unlimited progress. We thank Him for seeing something in us. There is no way we could have seen it in ourselves. His sight and His love was so perfect that He chose us to make us the heirs of the kingdom and to make us heirs to Himself. A nation of Gods!

Brothers and sisters, we are on a continued journey. This journey that you are on is a journey of continued demand. What will you give? And sometimes you may be overcome by duty. I can't do that. I don't have time. You may not have anything in your pocket. That is not what God is asking.

He is asking and demanding of us to perfect ourselves. The perfection of ourselves is the perfection of God. Hidden Deep in our DNA is the Original Man, the Original God Himself." ~The Honorable Minister Louis Farrakhan

I greet you with the greeting words of peace, in our original language of Arabic:

AS-SALAAM ALAIKUM!

1

IT'S TIME TO SAVE OUR YOUTH

"There will be no new Kingdom without youth. They must engage in the study of the knowledge of Self to bring in a new world."

The Honorable Minister Louis Farrakhan

Taking up any subject is always nerve-racking. I'm being honest with you. Any time any one of us are blessed to give a message to the people, we enter into a trial, a test, by Almighty God Allah. What are you going to say? How are you going to say this? Are you going to speak in vain or in the name of Allah? We're all being challenged.

Another subject I wanted to focused on was the head becoming the tail and the tail becoming the head. You and I as the Black man of America are the tail that is becoming the head, that we would be the standard for the world. But as I was driving home one day, I started praying to Allah in the car. And I said Allah, I want to make sure whatever the subject is, I can touch the youth.

As I pulled up to my home, I noticed a young brother who was raised in Islam who stepped away from his home as a young teen, out on the block, flamed up with some brothers. I pulled over, got out the car and started talking to this brother. And as I'm looking at him in his eyes, you can see he is far away. He's trying to get home. That caused me to reflect on all of the brothers and sisters I grew up with in the city of Phoenix where it was to the point that this room used to be full of youth.

I'm like, "Where's my brothers and sisters?" I said, "Oh, Allah, you just gave me my subject. **'It's Time to Save Our Youth.'**" It's that time. The Honorable Minister Louis Farrakhan teaches that time dictates the agenda. What time are we in? We are truly in the time of the departure of the Messiah that you read about in the scriptures. We are in the time when you and I will feel the chastisement of Allah after his departure. How does it feel to know that this chastisement is coming and our own children are not safeguarded with us?

Whose time is it? It's yours and mine. It's our time to separate ourselves from the one who has kept us in bondage. We may not be physically in bondage anymore, but we are psychologically and mentally and even spiritually at times in bondage to America. They didn't free us. They gave us liberty under their freedom and under their ideology. We are at the point where we have to separate, because if we do not, as Allah turns them to the tail, we will become the tail with them.

The one word in my title is 'save.' When you go into the church, you come up to that pit and that pastor wraps you up and brings you to that water and dips you down. And at that point in time, we are considered "saved," but it means nothing if the work is not being executed after submitting ourselves to that devotion.

Who and/or what are we saving our youth from?

One, we are saving them from themselves. We've all been in that situation where as we started getting older, we started feeling ourselves. "I'm grown! I'll close the door if I want to." What bills you pay in this house? If you're grown, you can go out on your own. But look, some are even eager to do that, to prove themselves as being grown.

We're also saving our youth from a condition that this enemy is trying to put on us. There's something that we learn about a needle getting put into the brain of the babies! Well that needle is a representation of America's policies. It's a representation of Satan's work coming straight to us, and wanting to turn us inside out to the point that we become him.

We have lost the knowledge of self. How did we get into this situation that we require saving? Some days I wish I was around in the 60s and the 70s. Some people say, "Hannibal, you got an old soul." It's not that, but when you read history and you learn what sacrifices took place during that history, sometimes you wish you can walk it with them and give your life with them. And when I look at our condition now, it's so disrespectful. Oh, Allah. We are saving ourselves from him who has made us into America. When you take a look on the back of your shirt, it has a tag on it. The tag lets you know who made the shirt. On the back of our neck, we have a tag, too, that shows that we've been branded by America and America's ways. Now we're fighting America's ways and God's way.

That brother, who is having a hard time with his own parents that he decided he wants to go on and do his own thing, is another youth lost that we have to now save. I reflected on the times when there were issues in the household and the child would go stay with his aunt or his uncle. He would go stay with his grandparents until he became a certain age where he would have reason to return to his parents. Something has happened where we do not think nor operate that way anymore. We have, as parents, instilled fear in our children. Not fear in a way of devotion, but fear in a way that if I don't do this, I'm going to be punished.

Have you seen the movie Fences with Denzel Washington? It's a pretty good movie. Not a great movie to see on your anniversary, but a really good movie. The character Denzel Washington played was this great baseball player who actually made it to the league. But at the end of his life, he was a normal blue-collar labor employee. That's how he saw himself. And he had a son who really admired him, who really wanted to be so much like his father, that he was very talented in sports to the point where the coaches were recruiting him to the school and said you have a chance to go to college on a full scholarship. But Denzel did not want his son to be anything like him, because he was not proud of himself. He allowed his frustration of himself to come out and transfer to his son. When his son made an agreement so he could still play sports, he said, "No. Why aren't you home cleaning up or doing your chores? Every Saturday morning, we should be doing this." The son was so frustrated that he joined the White man's army. We've lost a lot of our youth to this military, because they don't see nor feel the love that they need, the support that they need, from their own family.

We forget that we were once in their shoes. Sometimes we find ourselves being hypocritical. I'm speaking about myself right now. We find ourselves being hypocritical, because we forget that we were once in our children's shoes. We're so quick to judge the decisions of our children, like we weren't just doing that 20 years earlier. We were not listening to the same music. We were not doing the same dance. We become so holy, in our mosque or in our church, but we forget how we got there. If we forget, how we can support and guide them to the right course?

1st Corinthians 10:13 says:

> *No temptation has overtaken you except what is common to mankind. And God is faithful; he will not let you be tempted beyond what you can bear. But when you are tempted, he will also provide a way out so that you can endure it.*

We find ourselves in trials and tribulations, and we go seek guidance from everyone else but Almighty God Allah.

Look at how Allah was involved when the brother drove into the school. The women and children could have gotten frustrated and went and attacked the brother. There's a lot of things that could have happened. but if you look at the glass half full instead of half empty, you will see how Allah will guide you through the circumstances. Our goal is to put our youth, our children, on our shoulders so that they can go beyond our measures and take on our future. Denzel did not put his son on his shoulders to go beyond where he was in baseball. He could have taught his son finances so that he didn't make the same mistake. Then, when the son leaves, he will actually be in a better position, and he wouldn't have to take on such manual labor.

This is nothing new. I was born and raised in the Nation of Islam. I was born in 1984, but I did not get registered until 2007. Something happened. I was born and raised in this, but I didn't get registered until 2007.

I love my upbringing in the Nation, because when you're a certain age, parents do anything they can to appease the child. You'll come to the mosque and they set up things for the younger children to keep them occupied, keep them busy. But once you start coming into that preteen age, we start to become a lost cause to the point where you don't want to come out anymore. I'm being straightforward with you. I was bored out of my mind.

I wasn't bored. I'm young, energetic, hyper. If you know me, I'm really hyper. That's why I don't drink coffee. I would be here jumping off the walls all day, but then you want me to sit in the seat from two to four plus hours. And this is the time when the mosque meeting was on Sunday at 2pm. Imagine, I might have to get up and go to church first then come to the mosque. We didn't end on time, so you went from two to three to four to five. My mother's the student captain, so she had to stay behind as well. Oh man! I wanted to go home and play video games—it was more exciting—or go meet up with my friends and play basketball or football.

We are actually in a fight right now to keep our youth because we expect them just to sit down in a pew and listen. We are dealing with a generation that wants to be involved in whatever is taking place, but we do not involve them. We tell them to sit still and listen. Well, at what point in time can you take what is coming into you and apply it into your everyday life? This is what drove me away. Can we do youth Sunday? Can we set up a whole different area for the youth to teach in? Can we have youth study group? Sometimes certain subjects may be above the head of the child, so there's a disconnect now. We have to find a way to keep them involved.

I ran to the clubs, to parties, to basketball games, to video games. It was to the point where I would call a friend; I didn't have to like that friend.
"Yo, bro, what you doing this weekend? Can I spend the night?" Just because I did not want to sit in the pew all day. And I bet if most of us went and asked our children why they don't like to come out to the mosque or to church, you'll find a lot of the same answers.

When I say this mosque used to be packed, it was normal to see a family with three or more children. That was the norm in the city. It was to the point we had to set up a whole 'nother room for the children because after we would fill up the mosque, there would be no room for the guests. If I'm saying that was my upbringing and I'm one of the only ones still around, when I see one of my brothers who I'm always happy to see, that's scary.

We've already lost one generation, and we're at the cusp of losing another. The world is very, very enticing. I'm gonna be honest with you. We all came from it. I know none of us came floating down with wings on. We all came from the world in some form or fashion until we were developed and mature enough to understand what God was giving to us to bring us home. But when you compare what's happening to a mosque and a church, compared to what you get every single day of your life in the world, there's really no comparison. We're fighting, but we're not really fighting.

I love dancing. I mean, that was my thing. I wanted to be a background dancer for music videos. I wanted to be a choreographer and stuff. And it was really good. When I was in high school and we saw the movie 'Save the Last Dance,' everybody was like, you remind me of that one guy. That was the conversation. I was little Usher running around my school. I love dancing. I love music. But if we're not playing our own righteous music, that means those seeds that are being planted from the worldly music is now programming my mind to want to join into their cause. Same thing if our friends are outside influenced. We are now going to pick up their attributes, their way of thinking, their way of operating. Same thing when it comes to sports, movies, the whole nine yards, television, girls. Girls. I loved me some girls. Y'all heard Jay-Z, "Girls, girls, girls, girls, girls, I do adore." If you ask anybody who knows my father, he was a charmer in college. That apple didn't fall too far from the tree. I got in a lot of trouble with girls. But I didn't have that male figure around me at the time to help guide me on how to handle that properly, so I found myself making mistakes.

The new era of music right now is trap music. Trap music. Trap music is truly trapping our youth. It's trapping them. It is now glamourizing trap. What is trap? Trap is selling drugs, hustling and setting up shop somewhere. It's that lifestyle. And what's happening is it's being glamorized to the point that if you do this, you will be successful. They don't talk about the repercussions that come once you get caught chasing fast money. Now, we're finding our youth getting caught up in trap music. They're putting out videos where they're actually carrying guns and pointing guns at the camera, even though they may have never shot a pistol before a day in their life. But they want to live that style. When you go and see them in prison, the young ones, you ask them one simple question: Were you listening to your favorite song before you made that decision? And 9 out of 10 of them will say, "Yes! That was my jam. It hyped me ups, so I decided to make that move."

The music that is considered the opposite from what they're listening to is not enticing or cannot compare to what they're getting every single day of their life and what is being promoted on the radio. They can go online to listen to it. You can see it on TV. We are losing right now. I am not saying this to beat us up. I just want you to know that.

I wish I can go back to the 60s and 70s, because in this beautiful book, Supreme Wisdom—it's a very profound book. But guess what? You can't get it until you get in. You have to get in to be able to understand the true meaning that lives within this book. But I want to read something from our lessons.

"Question and Answer No. 8: Why does the devil keep our people apart from his social equality? Answer: Because he does not want us to know how filthy he is and all his affairs. He is afraid because when we learn about him, we will run him from among us. Socialist means to advocate a society of men or groups of men for one common cause. Equality means to be equal in everything."

Is that different now? Actually, it is. We're now part of his social equality. We're so engulfed in his social equality that we have now become part of his filth; all of his affairs. He didn't just bring it straight out to us. It was through phases.

Here's one: Once upon a time, the TV shut off at a certain time. Now the TV is 24 hours. Once upon a time, certain words were censored on TV. Now you can say it. It's all in phases. You didn't see same-sex marriage or same-sex activity on TV. Now you see them. This is his society. It's not ours. But these are things he did in phases, so he'll try something out by planting a seed. He might do a man-on-man kiss out of nowhere. Are you shocked? But then you might see it again later, so now the mind is becoming numb. First, it was shock. Now we're becoming comfortable with seeing it. It's the norm. Just like when the dean in Morehouse had to put something out saying the men can't wear heels on campus. That shows that there's something happening. Oh Allah!

Our mind has become Americanized. We have an American mind. We no longer have God's mind. And that's all by design. This is what he wants. If the enemy knows he's going down. His goal is to take as many of us with him. It's like someone getting caught and they're going to prison. "We'll give you a deal. Who else was involved?" "I'm snitching."

That's exactly what's happening. He's trying to bring as many of us down with him. This continues to happen as we as parents chase after their life and their likeness, which means we're not chasing after God's life and God's likeness. We're chasing after America's likeness. We were surprised at what they had, and we're so enticed on what they have that we're chasing after it.

If you watch the real rich Americans, they're moving out of the big fancy houses and moving into smaller homes. And what are we doing? Chasing the big fancy houses. Gentrification is happening right on the south side that we used to own. We owned the south side. Where do we live at now? Laveen, San Tan Valley, Scottsdale Chandler, Gilbert, etc. The south side is part of District 8. What is District 8? District 8 is downtown's district, so that means the south side and downtown combined together makes the heart of Phoenix. And people did not want to drive to the games because they knew they had to come through the south side.

So what they did was they built homes away from the south side, giving us the enticement or the excitement to live just like they've been living. I've never seen so many cyclists on the south side until now. That wasn't the norm. And maybe two or three every here and now have the same shade as me. We don't cycle. Not that we can't and I'm not saying we shouldn't but that wasn't a sport you normally saw us involved in.

We are moving away chasing after something, and by us chasing after something, we are abandoning our own children. Now, we're no longer part of God's life nor His likeness, because we are deviating from what he wants of us. He did promise us good homes, friendships in all walks of life, riches, money. We're going to get that, but He doesn't want us to go this route to get it. It's to the point where we're trying to build a Nation, but we won't have our future for it.

We get mad when our children are not fulfilling their potential, but when was the last time we spent true time with them, actually educated them, developed them and watched over them? While we're away from home, our children's minds are being programmed at home. Our own children are becoming zombies. What's a zombie? A person or a reanimated corpse; a corpse that has been turned into a creature capable of movement but not of rational thought; a person who is or appears lifeless, apathetic or completely unresponsive to their surroundings. Does that not sound like our youth nowadays? They're lacing the drugs. We do not know what's going on in our own homes. We barely even see them.

That's what we saw in the movie Get Out. They're trying to tell us: Get out! At the end of the day, when their time comes and God brings His wrath and He's addressing Satan, Satan will be like, "I gave them warnings. I told them who they were." He's not going to blatantly come out and say, "Hey, you know you are the man of God? You are the children of the Most High God. Do you know you're in His image and likeness?" No! But he's going to throw all the subliminals in books, which they say we don't read, and movies and cartoons and television. They want to drop the seeds to see if we grab it and understand it. They test that out to see how we respond to it. Are we zombies? And how we respond determines how they maneuver their next trap. That part of the needle in the brain of the child is really getting to us. know this does not sound good to have to hear this, but we as parents are aiding them in putting that needle in the brain.

Our children spend eight hours a day, 40 hours a week in school, and most of them are in public school, so that's eight hours right there we don't spend with our children. Then they spend another four to six hours a day, 30 plus hours a week watching television or on the internet. We are part of the reason why they are becoming zombies. When we get home, on average, we spend anywhere from 30 minutes to an hour with our children. We literally give them 70 plus hours a week to someone else to influence our own children, and then we get mad when they abandon us. We get mad when they walk away from us. We get mad when they go astray or deviate from the path that we say we want for them. But we only give them 30 minutes to an hour of quality time. That doesn't add up. That's like going to school expecting to get an A but you only go once a week, once a month. You show up to take the final and the midterm, but then we get mad when we don't get an A because attendance was part of our grade as well.

Our children are becoming zombies. Social media is helping to reduce our children's social skills. This is part of the reason why they become zombies. I have nothing against social media. I enjoy social media, because there's so much in social media we can grab, learn and elevate ourselves from. But most of us aren't doing that on social media. Our children's loss of social skills impacts the communication between parent and child, because if I ask most of the parents in this room, social media came after your phase. Social media really came when your children were around, so now when you try to have a conversation with your child, there's a disconnect there. There's no patience there. You're used to going outside and doing certain things, socializing and laughing.

At one point in time, you didn't have caller ID, so when the phone rang, you didn't know who was on the other line. You was hoping it wasn't a bill collector. You didn't find out until you answered the phone. Now when the phone rings, you have the chance to see who it is and who it is not. "Do I want to answer? I'm good. That's the lieutenant right there. Imma call him back later." "Aw they want some more charity at the church." "They want me to come help clean and cook." Now we're in a phase where we're able to see and make our own decision before actually communicating and learning about one another. Sending a text message does not create social skills. And as you see, most of us in this phase, we barely even communicate. We could be standing right next to each other. "As Salaam Alaikum." "Walaikum Salaam." You're standing right next to him and you shoot him a text message.

Now the parent who may not be tech savvy, who may not be on social media, who may not be able to communicate that way, there's a disconnect, because the child loves it. So when the mother or the father goes extreme in the eyes of the child and says, "Put your phone away. Give me your phone. I'm locking it up," that results in more animosity between the parent and the child, because there's no medium here. You don't like what I'm doing because you don't understand what I'm doing, which in the mind, you don't understand me. Now, the parent has taken the phone away, and that did not create social skills. It actually caused more of a problem. That means there's a point where the mother or the father has to get on social media or get involved in tech so that the child can communicate. But then it also has to be a part where the parent can get the child to put the phone away and they can have a simple conversation, which opens up communication in the children.

Simon Sinek was interviewed about millennials and social media. This is what he had to say.

> *We know that engagement with social media and our cell phones releases a chemical called dopamine. That's why when you get a text, it feels good.*
>
> *We've all felt a little bit down. You're feeling a bit lonely, so you send 10 texts to 10 friends and you get high, because it feels good when you get a response.*
>
> *It's why we count the likes. It's why we go back 10 times. ... If our Instagram is going slower, we wonder if we have done something wrong, or if people don't like us anymore. The trauma for young kids to be unfriended is too much to handle. We know when you get the attention, it feels good. You get a hit of dopamine which feels good, which is why we keep going back to it. Dopamine is the exact same chemical that makes us feel good when we smoke, when we drink and when we gamble. In other words, it's highly, highly addictive.*
>
> *We have age restrictions on smoking, drinking and gambling, but we have no age restrictions on social media and cell phones. Which is the equivalent of opening up the liquor cabinet and saying to our teenagers, "Hey by the way, if this adolescence thing gets you down, help yourself."*
>
> *An entire generation now has access to an addictive, numbing chemical called dopamine, through cellphones and social media, while they are going through the high stress of adolescence.*
>
> *Why is this important? Almost every alcoholic discovered alcohol when they were teenagers. When we are very, very young the only approval we need is the approval of our parents, and as we go through adolescence, we make this transition*

where we now need the approval of our peers. Very frustrating for our parents, very important for the teenager. It allows us to acculturate outside of our immediate families and into the broader tribe. It's a highly, highly stressful and anxious period of our lives and we are supposed to learn to rely on our friends.

Some people, quite by accident, discover alcohol, the numbing effects of dopamine, to help them cope with the stresses and anxieties of adolescence. Unfortunately that becomes hard wired in their brains and for the rest of their lives, when they suffer significant stress, they will not turn to a person, [but] they will turn to the bottle. Social stress, financial stress, career stress, that's pretty much the primary reasons why an alcoholic drinks. But now because we are allowing unfettered access to [the dopamine-producing] devices and media, basically it is becoming hard wired and what we are seeing is [as] they grow older, too many kids don't know how to form deep, meaningful relationships. "Their words, not mine."

They will admit that many of their friendships are superficial, they will admit that they don't count on their friends, they don't rely on their friends. They have fun with their friends, but they also know that their friends will cancel on them when something better comes along. Deep meaningful relationships are not there because they never practiced the skillset and worse, they don't have the coping mechanisms to deal with stress. So when significant stress begins to show up in their lives, they're not turning to a person, they're turning to a device, they're turning to social media, they're turning to these things which offer temporary relief.

We know, the science is clear, we know that people who spend more time on Facebook suffer higher rates of depression than people who spend less time on Facebook.

These things balanced, are not bad. Alcohol is not bad, too much alcohol is bad. Gambling is fun, too much gambling is dangerous. There is nothing wrong with social media and cellphones, it's the imbalance.

If you're sitting at dinner with your friends, and you are texting somebody who is not there, that's a problem. That's an addiction. If you are sitting in a meeting with people you are supposed to be listening and speaking to, and you put your phone on the table, that sends a subconscious message to the room [that] "you're just not that important." The fact that you can't put the phone away, that's because you are addicted.

If you wake up and you check your phone before you say good morning to your girlfriend, boyfriend or spouse, you have an addiction. And like all addictions, in time, it will destroy relationships, it will cost time, it will cost money and it will make your life worse.

Simon Sinek

A social gap has been created between parent and child. The gap will continue to grow because we're not there to keep them social. Why are they losing social skills? Because we're not home. We're at work all day, and when we come home, we only got 30 minutes to an hour to spend with them. But we're so tired. "I've been on the road all day. I've been talking to people all day. Can you stop bothering me?" We push the child away. And believe it or not, the child actually wants to develop social skills. They want to communicate with their parents, but after being pushed away numerous times, I'm not coming to you. You learn in that household that that means when mommy or daddy gets home, go to your room. Go find something to do. Don't engage in conversation with them, because they don't want to be bothered. So then who do you find to start communicating with? Your friends. Social media. Text messages. The internet. So now you're communicating. You're getting that gratification or that excitement, that part of social skills from someone else, but you're not truly developing it, because there's really no person-to-person communication. That's all by design.

Me being in banking, I get to meet a lot of different people, and one of my clients is a chiropractor. I talk to him a lot. And one day I asked, "How's business?" He said, "I'm going to be in business for a long time." I said, "What do you mean?" He said, "Because everyone's on their phones all the time, it actually causes problems to the neck, which means at some point in time, that person has to come and see me, which means we're becoming unhealthy."

We actually are developing this right now and don't even know it. I bet if every single one of us went and saw a chiropractor tomorrow, they'll say, "Yeah, you're on your phone a lot, huh, or you have a sit-down job where you're looking at a computer, so you're leaning." And the head weighs an average of 30 pounds. We're supposed to sit straight up, but now we're pushing it to about 60. We're putting more weight on our back to hold our head up, because we're leaning forward so much.

This has an impact on our relationships, because we're still disconnecting from one another, and we find ourselves communicating through social media. I enjoy social media, because it allows me to be part of the Farrakhan Twitter Army. I get to drop good seeds and get to communicate with people who I may never have seen a day in my life, but I can help uplift them through social media. I can also promote business through social media.

I'm speaking on this for a particular reason, because we need to look in the mirror. I know we don't like looking in the mirror at things, and this may not be easy to have to really think about, but we have to look in the mirror. It's like looking at our credit score sometimes. We only look at our credit score once a year, and then we get mad when our credit score is so low because we're afraid to address our credit. But if we actually address our credit, we can fix it. If we look in the mirror, we can find out what's wrong with it and we can work on it. The same applies to life.

My sisters stand in the mirror for hours at a time getting ready to go out. They switch outfits over and over and over because it's not the right one. It's the same thing. Why are you in the mirror? Because you want to make sure before you walk out this door you don't look crazy. I don't have sleep in my eye. I might have drool on my face. My lashes might be wrong. I might have a piece of hair sticking out. That's important.

We have to look in the mirror to see how we are functioning when it comes to our children. Because if we're not looking in the mirror, we think we're doing something, but for some reason when our child becomes an adolescent, they automatically go the opposite direction. That means there's been a disconnect for a while and we just didn't see the signs, because we actually wasn't paying attention to them, because we don't want to be bothered, because we've had long days at work and our children are bothering us, so we want them away from us. So when they get the opportunity to get away from us, what do they do? They get away. They don't come home. They go spend time with their friends.

We can't build our Nation for our future if we're not including our future. Our future is the children. We can't say, "I want to see the Hereafter. I want to build heaven on earth." What's the whole point of building this heaven if we don't have somebody to give it to? That means we did all this work for nothing. That means there has to be some vanity in there. If I do all this work to help build this Nation, but for some reason, my children are not reaping the benefits of my labor, I did something wrong. There was a disconnect. And we can't build a nation if we do not separate ourselves from our enemy, who has no respect for us. And he will never have respect for us.

We can't build a nation if we're constantly working a nine to five, helping somebody else build their company and we're not building our own company. See, there's a longevity in us building our own companies. Here's an example. Imma go back in the day to traditional family structure. The man has a job. He has a business. He's building his business; the son gets out of school; the son goes home or the son goes to business? The son goes to business. So from school the son will come and spend time with the father learning the business, which now allows the son to grow and develop, and the business can be handed over to the son. The son's responsibility is to make sure the siblings are taken care of as the parents go on with their life. But if we're building someone else's business, when our children become of age of being able to learn responsibility, we don't have anything to give them so they can learn how to run their own business. So we get mad at them. We say do for yourself, start a business, but we're not being the best example for them to start their own business. So now we're pointing the finger, and we get mad when the finger gets pointed back at us, because we're not truly helping our children like we should.

This enemy doesn't love us. I went and looked up the Black Panther Party, and I found an Atlanta Black Star article written March 25, 2015 titled "Eight Black Panther Party programs that were more empowering than the federal government programs."

The first one was the breakfast program. The free breakfast for schoolchildren program was set up and was served in 19 cities under the scholarship of the national headquarters and 23 local affiliates. More than 20,000 children received full, free breakfasts consisting of bread, bacon, egg and grits before going to their elementary or junior high. Some of us have to work. Some of us have to work for someone we don't want to work for. But if we don't have something in place for the child to still be connected to, we have abandoned them.

They had health clinics. The clinics were called People's Free Medical Center, PFMC, and eventually were established in 13 cities across the country. They offer services such as testing for high blood pressure, lead poisoning, tuberculosis and diabetes, cancer detection, screening, physical exams, treatment for cold and flu and immunization against polio, measles rubella, and diphtheria. Well, we don't do immunizations, but at least if we're able to test for certain things with our own family, we know that their getting certain things put into them.

We know we're not dealing with vaccines, because we know they're putting something into our children that's going to cause a negative effect down the line.

They had what's called the Youth Institute. The Black Panther Party established the Youth Institute in January 1971. Their goal was to get children to learn to their highest potential and to strengthen their minds so that one day they will be successful. They have Seniors Against a Fearful Environment – SAFE, which is a nonprofit corporation started by the Black Panther Party at the request of a group of senior citizens for the purpose of preventing muggings and attacks upon the elderly, particularly when they go out to cash their social security checks or their pension checks. Prior to approaching the Black Panther Party the seniors had gone to the Oakland Police Department to request protection. There, the seniors were told that they should walk close to the curb in the future. According to the Panther Report by David Hilliard, who served as the party's chief of staff, the program offered free transportation and expert services to the residents of the satellite senior homes and residential complex for the elderly in Oakland, California.

We should be patrolling our community and controlling our own environment, as the Honorable Minister Louis Farrakhan has been on us about. He has asked us to prevent the killing of our youth. They're taking our youth, killing them, because we're not here to protect them. Then they're taking their organs and selling them.

They're taking our children, because we're not home with them. We're not in open communication with them. We don't know where they're at. So now they're taking our children and they're putting them in sex trafficking. We have sisters missing in DC, and that's not a concern of theirs. They haven't put out an amber alert. But the question is, is it a concern of ours or are we really a part of their socially equality that we don't see anything wrong with this?

We are always reacting. When we're always reacting, we are always chasing after something after it already happened. That's not how we're supposed to be, especially not as parents. We're supposed to be the proactive ones. We need to practice the preventive method: preparing for things to happen and planning out to minimize major negative results. We plan out so we know our children are okay. There was a post on social media that asked, "Do men not love their children that they would leave them at the bus stop by themselves to catch the bus to school? My wife and I had a nice long conversation about it. And it's a challenge, because there's no unity in the community. We have programs out there, but the programs out there are not being funded by us. We're not supporting the programs that would help to offset some of these issues we're running into.

The Black Panthers had the People's Free Ambulance Service.

They had a free food program. This program provided free food to Black and other oppressed people. The intent of the free food program was to supplement the groceries of Black and poor people until economic conditions allowed them to purchase good food at reasonable prices. The free food program provided two basic services to the community: one, an ongoing supply of food to meet their daily needs, and two, periodic mass distributions of food to reach a larger segment of the community than can be serviced from the ongoing supply. The community was provided with bags of chicken, milk, potatoes, rice, bread, cereal, and so forth. A minimum of a week's supply of food was included in each bag.

Does that remind you of something? That sounds like the 10,000 Fearless a little bit right there, right?

They had the Black Student Alliance, which was founded in May 1972 when several Black student unions in the Bay Area pulled together with the goal of creating concrete programs on the campus that would unify the student body and Black students with the Black community. In order to make the Bay Area colleges better serve and be more responsible to the surrounding poor and oppressed communities, the Black Student Alliance instituted a program for free books and supplies, a free transportation program, childcare services, a financial aid program, a food program serving good, nutritious food at a reasonable price, and the initiation of relevant courses along with the demand for better instructors.

We have work to do. We can't build a Nation if we're not building our family. We can't build our family if we're not with our family. We can't build our family if we have abandoned our family and left them to raise themselves.

At the Saviours' Day graduation, the Minister talked about a book by our dear Sister Delores. Sis. Delores worked with the Messenger of Allah the Most Honorable Elijah Muhammad. But one thing I love when I was going through this book is that she talks about how the young brothers would be with the older brothers. The older brothers would mentor them, spend time with them, teach them mechanics and teach them farming and different things like that so that they could have life skills to be able to survive and do what they need to do as they get older. And the sisters would spend time with the sisters, learning different crafts, learning how to study, learning how to cook and clean, learning how to make decision and learning how to keep home.

Something has happened. We are to build a Nation within a nation. But we can't build a Nation within a nation if we have abandoned our children. I'm excited to say, though, that there are some of these programs out there, and I love seeing them. I love seeing them. A couple weeks ago, some brothers took a couple of brothers up north and took them camping. There was a brother the other day who decided to do a father-daughter photo shoot in the park. But does everyone know about these? Is everyone involved in these and supporting these programs? There's a group who does a cash mob. They go and focus on making sure we know about our Black-owned businesses. We go and support them so that our children know, and we're able to show our children, look out for your own before you look out for someone else. But the problem is we're still divided. We're running into the same programs and competing with one another instead of unifying together and making the program bigger and better.

So parents, I got an assignment for you. I want you to grade yourself just like Imma grade myself. How have you been as a parent for your child or children outside of the normal necessities like food, shelter and clothing? That includes being actively involved in their education enhancement, their life skills and their maturity development, teaching responsibility, teaching unity, teaching love, teaching patience, building trust and openly communicating. It also includes their level of community outreach and wanting to get involved with something that gives a bigger purpose in life, their ability to live on their own as they become adults, their finances and credit and their supporting of family. I want us to grade ourselves in those areas. Are we sitting somewhere close to an A, a B, a C or a D? Are we failing in those areas? Because our results will show how we're really doing. We can't afford to lose another generation. We all have areas of opportunities to work on. I'm speaking on myself right now.

We were taught that the natural order is Allah God, man, family, Nation. If we are not in oneness with Allah, then we're not developing self, and if we're not developing self, we can't develop family. If we're not developing family, how can we expect to have a Nation or a community of our own? So we first have to develop that connection to Almighty God Allah, which causes us to separate ourselves from our enemy's social equality. You can't love your wife or your husband or your family if you don't love yourself, first. You can't love a nation or a community if you have not taken the energy and devotion to raise and develop your own family. Because at the end of the day, you'll have a nation or a community, but you won't have your family in it.

I love driving home. I see all these children outside playing. I see a few fights here and there. I see a lot of police patrolling because it's us over there. And then I thought about it. I said, wow, I see this LA Fitness over here. We have another fitness place over here on 35th and Southern, but we don't have a community center for the youth. That's interesting, because they don't want us to be successful. So now the children are getting out of school. Like I mentioned, parents are at work, and then they're left out in a community to survive. We get mad when they get trapped, but we don't have anything lined up for them.

The closest community center is probably the Boys and Girls Club on Seventh Avenue and Southern, but I live on 51st Avenue and Baseline. You know how far of a drive that is for our children. And most of them don't have cars. So Now we have to figure out how they would even get to these programs so that they can reap the benefits, which keeps them out of trouble and minimizes their use of social media, helping to develop social skills.

Not all of our children are going to go off to college or go to that four-year university, so we still have to prepare for their future.

As I was doing some studying, I came across foster care. In foster care, many of America's child welfare systems are badly broken. Children can suffer serious harm as a result. Some are separated from their siblings. Others go from one foster care place into another, never knowing when their lives will be uprooted next. So there's no stability. Too many are abused in the system that are supposed to protect them. And instead of being safely reunited with their families or moving quickly into adopted homes, many languish for years in foster homes or institutions. On any given day, there are nearly 428,000 children in foster care in the United States. That's a lot. In 2015, over 670,000 children spent time in foster care. On the average, children remain in state care for nearly two years, and 6% of children in foster care have languished there for five or more years. Despite the common perception that the majority of children in foster care are very young, the average age of kids in foster care is nearly nine years old. So we have children coming up without getting real love, without stability and without family.

We're out doing everything we can to provide for our children. I understand that, but we're leaving children to survive for themselves. While most children in foster care live in family settings, a substantial minority, 14%, live in the institutions or group homes. In 2015, more than 62,000 children whose mothers and fathers parental rights had been legally terminated were waiting to be adopted. In 2015, more than 20,000 young people aged out of foster care without permanent families. Research has shown that those who leave without being linked to forever families have a higher likelihood than youth in the general population to experience homelessness, unemployment and incarceration as adults.

We have to save our children, man. While states should work rapidly to find safe permanent homes for kids, on any given day, children available for adoption have spent an average of nearly two years waiting to be adopted since their parental rights were terminated. These children don't belong to us. They belong to Allah. Imma say that again. These children don't belong to us! They belong to Allah! Allah has made us agents in His place. We are God to them in their early stages before they learn of themselves. That's why the first words that come out of the mouth is mama, dada, because anything they need, we answered their prayers. But when they become of age and they go away and they are not successful, we've done something wrong for our children, which means we have failed God, if God has put us in place to oversee His children. That's something to look in the mirror.

We've abandoned our children to public school, and there's always been an argument on whether public school is better than homeschooling, or more or less you could say a private school that we are involved in as parents. American public school by the numbers according to National Assessment of Educational Programs: only 13% of American high school students are proficient in US history. If you look at the homeschooling by the numbers, over 2.04 million students are now learning at home, a 75% increase from 1999. I wonder why that's the case. 73% of parents who schooled at home cite dissatisfaction with American school system as the reason. Students' progress and graduation rates have been stagnant since the 1970s, even as other nations advanced. Out of fathers who homeschool, 17.3%, are accountants or engineers, 16.9% are professors, doctors, lawyers, and another 10% are small business owners.

We hand our children off because we have to go to work. We have to pay bills, and we expect them to get a great education in the public school system, where they're coming out pretty much at average; and we say we don't want to take our children out of this enemy's school system.

Homeschoolers are less affected by external factors. This goes back to us protecting our children right. Household income. Their scores are largely unaffected by household income. Certifications. They did well whether or not their parents were certified teachers. You don't have to be certified. What makes you a great teacher is your love for your child. You want the best for your child, so you're going to do everything you can to give them what they need. Students of certified parents come in at the 87 percentile. Students of non-certified parents come in at the 88. Parent spending - they succeed, no matter how much money was spent on their education. Parents who spent under $600 on the students come in at 86 percentile. Parents who spent $600 or more come in at the 89. So even if you spend less money, we're actually able to educate our children even better. When they get to college, students keep on succeeding. They have higher GPAs. The one that frightens parents is the question, "But are homeschoolers a little odd?" Studies say no. In a study measuring communication, daily living skills, socialization and maturity, homeschoolers outscore public school kids on every level, but our concern has always been if we don't put them in public school, they won't have social skills. Excuses! We just broke that myth right there.

The studies show that homeschoolers are more mature. Why is that the case? Because we are actually spending the quality time developing our children, compared to putting them in a public school where there are 30 or more children to one teacher. So they may be communicating, but they're not learning real social skills. They're being taught to sit still in a chair for eight hours of the day. When you homeschool, your child is getting to spend time with you learning day in and day out. The school doesn't end at three o'clock. That might be the time the session ended, but afterwards you're taking them to do something else. You say, oh, remember we talked about this today? They're still learning. And then you put them into the club activities, which still allows them to be around people to socialize.

Working in the banking industry, I see a lot of this. Parents from Asia, including India and Arab countries, and parents from Africa sacrifice everything for their children's education while saving children's college money. I'm constantly getting students opening accounts, getting 40 to $100,000 wired into their accounts so they can go to Arizona State University. They're paying four or five times what we pay here locally to go to that university, but they're coming out with GPAs of 3.4 and 4.0 and higher grades. They're getting their master's programs. We're barely getting our children into college because we're expecting someone who doesn't care for children to develop our children. Like I said, I'm not saying this to beat us up, but I need us to look in the mirror. Because if we don't look in the mirror, we'll think that everything's gravy. Then when our children come of a certain age, we try to figure out why they ran from us. Why they're not home. Why they seem to lack self-love and unity that Allah has promised us we would get. We're not getting it because of the lack of self-love and unity.

There's a video where a brother named Ibn Ali Miller stops a brawl between two Atlantic City, high-school aged boys. The brother wasn't asked to step in and intervene. He didn't know if they were carrying anything on them, but him doing that, he actually was honored by the city. Afterward, he said, "I would like to first and foremost give God all the praise, all the recognition ... and after that I'd like to thank my mom. When I was young, I grew up in the projects."

Let's give him a round of applause. Allah-u-Akbar. His mother planted seeds into her son. So even as he became an adult, he got to talk about the trials he was going through and how he found himself coming back to that path, because the world can be a distraction and an enticement. His mother was a gardener in his life. She nurtured him so that he could be the man that he is today. He wasn't looking for 15 minutes of fame, but God Himself will make angels for situations. As long as we're doing the work in Allah's name, Allah will bless us. We don't have to seek praise. He didn't go there to say, "I'm gonna stop this fight so I can be on TV." He didn't want to see any more damage happening to this generation.

There was a parable of two men. One promised that he would do the work of the father and did not do the work. There was another one who said he would not do the work of the father and wound up doing the work. So just because you get saved, that you get registered, that does not mean that you're going to do the work of the Father. But the work is in the streets. The work is in our community. As we build our own children up, we have to build the children of the community up, and we have to help build our people up so they know how to build the children up.

We have to plant the right seeds into our children, so if and when the day of deviation comes, because it's going to come. It's going to come to our doors. They do not stray far from the path, because it's gonna be hard to stay on the right path, but at least if they deviate from it, they're not too far into the shore that they can't even get a lifeboat out there to 'em. It's not going to be easy in every area for us to plant that seed of the proper development of our children. But we have to be willing to sacrifice that so that we can build the right development, and the right encouragement, and the right upliftment of our children.

When I was growing up, I remember days I would stuff and my mother would get on me and get on me and get on. And I remember being at the house running up her bills, and she would come home so mad. It's the middle of the summer in Phoenix, and I got the AC at 60 degrees. It's hot; come home from school, listening to Jay-Z, playing **NBA Live** in one room, cooking in another room, and she coming home, rahraharahrarrrar! And then I remember going off to college and her coming to visit me, and me finally living on my own and her planting all these seeds in me. And I would call my mother out of nowhere to say thank you. And she's like, "For what?" "I get it! I understand what you were trying to put in me. I get it!" So when she came to visit me at college and she got the light on in one room, she's cooking in another room, she got the TV on in another room and she got the AC blazing, I'm like, "Yo yo yo what you doing, ma, for real! This bill a hundred something dollars." And she starts to laugh. "Now you know how I felt, don't you?" LOL.

We're not going to be able to be at every single place our children go, but if we instill what we need to instill in them properly, if we really give our all to our children, when the time comes, they will praise you. If they don't even say your name as they're praising you because of the seeds that we plant in our children, they're praising God.

Isaiah 41:10 says, *"Do not fear, for I am with you. Do not be dismayed, for I am your God. I will strengthen you and help you. I will uphold you with my righteous right hand."*

These walls count for nothing if we're not willing to help save the future who lives outside of these walls. These walls count for nothing if we're not going to save a life. These walls are a safe haven. This is the neutral ground for people to be able to come to and feel comfortable so that they can get away from that environment. But we have to go to them. We have to go to them and show them that we love them. They may not open up to us, because they've been abandoned. We talked about how long they sit in foster care and group homes.

We have to build their trust. We have to show true love like the Honorable Minister Louis Farrakhan shows them. After everybody that has turned their back on him, yes, he still shows love. After everyone has said nothing but negative stuff about him, he still stands firm and shows his love. We have to use that as our example for our future. When we're in the community, they don't always open up to us, because they are afraid. I don't want to get too close, or you'll treat me like the other ones did. But we have to stay firm in this and protect our children.

Our open enemy doesn't want life, light or a future for us. He wants us to fight one another, because that fighting will create disunity. That brother who broke up the fight just created unity. Youth are looking for proper examples to look up to. We must create tangible examples, not just speak on them. Be the example you desire to see.

2

FAMILY

"We have to make a perfect family. And it starts with perfect love and total commitment."

The Honorable Minister Louis Farrakhan

No matter what subject we tackle, it's not always easy, as you are striving to the best of your abilities to remove your personal self out of the way that Almighty God Allah can use you as a vessel. So I pray that Almighty God Allah uses me as an instrument that can play a fine tune that will tickle the air of each and every one of us, that will dig deep into us, that will wake us up and that will open up that direct connection to Almighty God Allah Himself.

My baby sister, was in town. I am older than her by two years, and she's the baby of the family. We have what you call the love-hate relationship. I'll be honest with you today. I love my sister, but I cannot stand her.

She always got whatever she wanted. Now, if you all got siblings like that you know what I'm talking about, or you might be that sibling that the family can't stand. Let's be honest. But one thing I love is that I'm the overprotective brother. So that was one of the reasons why she couldn't stand me. When we were in school, if a brother liked her, the other boys would say, "No, you can't talk to her. That's Hannibal's little sister. That's little Hannibal right there." By the time I started high school, I was only 4'11". I was less than 100 pounds, but I had a true big-man syndrome. I thought I was 6'10", 275, just yoked up, because you couldn't tell me nothing. I didn't care who you was. And I wouldn't let you talk to my little sister. You got two words: back up, or you got a two piece. Oh, I'm serious. I love my sister, but she was so spoiled. You talk about being rotten.

When we were working, we both worked together at the airport, because we had to get a job. I was being taught responsibility, which meant I had to get a job and pay for my own things. With her, no! She got the job, took the money and was able to keep it in her pocket. My mother would still take her clothes shopping, get her new jewelry, get her new shoes. And then we walked up to the register and she paid for her stuff. I'm looking at my mom like you got me, too? She's like don't you got a job! Oh man!

But I love that girl. We were laughing because I want to let you know how much I couldn't stand her. I want to let you know how much I couldn't stand my little sister. I'm gonna be honest with you. That's all I can do is be honest with you. Let's be transparent. She was telling me a story as we had lunch that day, and she's like, "Do you remember that time you were so mad at me that we were driving home and it's nighttime and you pulled over in the middle of the road and put me out?" I was like, "For real? I did that?" She was like, "You did that. We was only half a mile home, but you put me out and said you got to walk the rest of the way."

And she said she was so frightened because it was a dark area that she started running home. When she got home she went and yelled to my mother, "Mama, mama. Hannibal put me out, and made me walk home!" Oh, I sure did that, didn't I. But that was our relationship. You can't choose who your family is, and none of our families are perfect. But I know my dysfunctional family, and I thank Allah for them, as much as we may argue and bicker and want to fight. But I'm telling you when you caught us outside, you wouldn't even know we argued.

I was raised to don't put hands on a woman. When I was in high school, this girl and I used to crack jokes at each other, and I said something inappropriate. She slapped me in class. I mean, literally cocked back and got one of those good slaps on me. You could feel the tingling on the cheek when it happened, man. So I got up. I knew I couldn't hit her. I grabbed my backpack, and I went on and sat in front of my sister's classroom until she got out of class. You already know where I'm going with this one. She was walking. I grabbed her by her leg. "Yo." I ain't going to say the girl's name. You might know her.

"What's her name hit me." "What!?!" And she already didn't like the girl. Oh, that made it so much easier. So what she did was she went and found that girl. This is the conversation. "You hit my brother?" "He—" boop boop boop boop boop boop. Bow!! And I'm standing like yeah! That's right! Then I saw security come, and everybody surrounded. I grabbed her and ran off.

This is my dysfunctional family. We all got that in our family. My family loves to fight. I can't lie. If y'all know my older sister, Sahirah, you can see it in her demeanor. I remember I got into it with my ex-girlfriend, and I was just venting. "Man, this, this, that, and she did this." "She still live in that one house that look like...?" I'm like, "Sahirah no! No. No. No." "You sure?" "No! Because then I got to deal with that later."

But that's my family. And we all have family that does things that we may or may not agree with. In the Holy Bible, Acts 10:2 says,

> *"He and all his family were devout and God-fearing; he gave generously to those in need and prayed to God regularly."*

I'm talking about fighting, but I'm talking about giving to the ones in need.

One thing I can say is this: parents want for their child what they were not able to get for themselves. And that's not always easy. That's not always easy to sacrifice some of your own dreams, your aspirations, your own desires to pick up two or more jobs, just to make sure you can have ends meet, and then trying to still make time for your child.

Hmm. I'm talking about fighting. And during this time, my mother is a Student Captain of Muhammad's Mosque Number 32, but we're getting into fights at school because my mother is making sacrifices for our future, though we may not see it as children. As a child, you rarely understand the sacrifices that your parents make. Even if you have two parents, the sacrifices they make—but imagine just a single parent. Because there's someone who's absent. There's someone who was absent.

I love my mother. I love preaching about my mother, who has made many sacrifices just so I can be where I'm at today. This is the same mother—that when I went off to college, I would call her and say thank you. Because though I didn't understand then when she was making sacrifices, or she was demanding more of me and more of my sisters, when we had to grow up a little bit sooner, because she wants to make sure that the household was taken care of. And I would say thank you, and she would laugh and say, "What are you thanking me for?" And I would say, "I understand now what you meant by this. I understand now why you did this for us."

That's not easy to do. And now I'm becoming a parent, I'm seeing even more of those sacrifices. In Exodus 20:12, it says, "*Honor your father and your mother so that you may live long in the land the Lord your God is giving you.*" I took that different when I was growing up. I took it as, "She gonna take me off the planet Earth if I ain't honoring her right."

It is the same thing. But now I understand it. If you're honoring your parents, if you're actually taking your time to study them and what they do to sacrifice for you, it lines you up with them so that they can carry you to the next phase of your life so that you're able to move forward and help set the pace for your children.

If your parents are in the room right now, I want you to look at them and say thank you. I'll wait. If they're not in the room, I want you to take out your cell phones and send them a text message right now and just say, "Thank you." I'll wait. My father just walked in. "Thank you!"

Thank you, father. I honor you. Man. (emotional pause) I may not always show it. I may not always show it. I may let situations that have transpired cloud my judgment. But if you and my mother did not come together, I wouldn't be here. If you and my mother didn't see value in this, I wouldn't know who God is. I honor you. You see how Allah works? You see how He works? We started talking about honoring our parents and what happens? My father walks right through the door.

This is family. I'm blessed! Both of my parents are alive right now. I can call them at any given time. Some of you were adopted, abandoned, separated. Some of us have such a beef with our parents right now that we don't even converse or talk with them, because we're angry at situations. But then when someone is gone, when that pain and hurt hits us, then we want to start repenting for what we could have done before. There is no one that is perfect right here in front of us, but Allah brings perfection out of the trials!

Parents are constantly showing us different values, the different do's and the different don'ts in their lives. If we are to just study them, watch them, question them in the right way, we will see what it is that Allah's trying to show us, because not all of their trials are just for them! We don't know the sacrifices that a parent makes for the betterment of a family, because as a child, we are selfish.

All Praise is Due to Allah. This has been on my heart for a while. Oh Allah. And He's been sending me signs, and it just clicked. I was trying to fight it, but I can't fight it no more.

When I see love, and I see a father-son relationship, the closest one and the best one I see is when you hear the Honorable Minister Louis Farrakhan speak of his father, the Most Honorable Elijah Muhammad. That's not his biological father. But the person who gave birth to you doesn't make that person your father. It is what a father does to take the child and lift that child up and teach them how to be a man, teach them how to be a father, teach him how to be a protector of his wife and children, that makes a person a father. And when you have a father like that, it's easy to remove yourself, so you can line up in oneness with your father, because you see your father is guiding you. We want to be like that, when we want to be in oneness with Almighty God Allah, that's the God that we're looking to. But He gives us messiahs and messengers that we can line ourselves up with, who guides and drives us right to the father!

When I say the Minister is my father, that means this man has helped raise me up! He has given his all to me. And all I can do is open up my arms and say, "Father, allow me to do better by you." Oh, Allah! When I see the Minister—I need you to understand who I'm speaking of. I'm speaking of the Honorable Minister Louis Farrakhan who is our Messiah in our midst.

That might sound crazy as hell for some of you. That's understandable, but give me time to prove it. They said Jesus would speak to the masses, but Jesus 2,000 years ago didn't speak to more than 40 people at a time. In 1995, however, the Jesus in our midst had nearly 2 million people at the National Mall in Washington, D.C., there at the break of dawn, making prayer, waiting to hear from the Man of God. You can't tell me he ain't the Jesus in our midst! He's lined up with the Father! John 10:30 says, "*I and the Father are one.*"

John 14:31, "*But he comes so that the world may learn that I love the Father and do exactly what my Father has commanded me.*"

When you are willing to give yourself up, Jesus said we must die and be reborn again into Him.

John 5:19, "*Jesus gave them this answer: 'Very truly I tell you, the Son can do nothing by himself; he can do only what he sees his Father doing, because whatever the Father does the Son also does.'*"

Do you have children? My youngest daughter, Eiliyah, is 21 months old. She follows and does everything her older sister does. If we are speaking, she repeats the words that we are saying in like manner. If we are moving around, she gets up and moves around. If we are dancing, she is dancing, because we are a god to her because God made us an agent to the child. Aw, we about to get there?

John 10:15, *"Just as the Father knows me and I know the Father—and I lay down my life for the sheep."*

John 15:10, *"If you keep my commands, you will remain in my love, just as I have kept my Father's commands and remain in his love."*

There's something about being a father. To my brothers who are not in their children's lives, I'm pleading with you. Fix it! Do what you must to create that relationship. Be the bigger person. I get it. Things happen. But you have a child or children out there right now who are going through things that you have already experienced and that you can give the proper guidance to, the do's and the don'ts so they don't fall victim to the same mistakes and circumstances.

As parents, like I mentioned, we are god to our children, and rightfully so. God has made mother and father agents of Himself. He has made us the first examples of God to our children. If that is the case, when it says we are in the image and likeness of God, what does that make us? That makes us a god ourselves but with a little 'g'. We are not the Supreme Being. We are agents of the Supreme Being.

We're talking about family right now. If we don't know our roles, then that's a problem we have in our family.

I want to break something down for you, because we have what's called God structure.

Under God's structure, God comes first, then man, then woman, and lastly, children. Check this out. Check this out. If it goes God then man, that means God and man have a direct connection. The role of the man is to protect, secure, and make sure his family and his household is intact. He must have man first. Then from there, you have woman and she has a direct connection to God too. Let me break this down real quick.

God: All-Being, the Creator of the heavens and the earth.

Man: The head, the maintainer, provider, securer, leader of his family, driver, the future, the agent, and the help-meet to God.

The woman, who is the mother, right? The nurturer, the lover, the balance. She brings balance to the household. She brings balance to the man. She's the realist. As men, we like to go out in space at times. She's the reminder. "That sounds great baby, husband, king, however, what about these bills?" All Praise is Due to Allah.

What about our transportation? She makes sure, "I'll let you go a little to the right, a little to the left, but look, this is your boundaries." He sets the wide boundaries under the help-meet of God. But she sets the internal boundaries for the family structure, so she's the realist. She's loyal. She's the giver. She's the giver of self, spirit, emotion, life. She's the cultivator. She cultivates not just the children, but the structure of the household, to make sure everything goes smooth. As the man, when you walk up in that kitchen, she's like, "What are you doing in my kitchen? What are you messing with? You're not putting anything out of order of the structure that I've been working on." That's why sisters laughing. They know it's the truth.

She's patient. She has to be, right?

She's patient as she's watching this new baby learn how to maintain, provide and lead. She's like Brother Jabril and the Minister, and the Minister addressed that she's patient with the man, because she sees the true value. She sees his future. She understands where he needs to go, so she's patient as he makes his mistakes. And she's his help-meet, because she's also an agent to the children. The agent to him. She holds him accountable. "My dear husband, you seem to be a little off your prayers this week. How do you say that you have a direct connection to God and right now you're not leading us to prayer?"

My dear sister, Minister Aishah, talked about when you get up in the morning to make prayer and you make sure the house is ready for prayer. "Well, brother, you're not leading the house for prayer, so you're not giving me a reason to make the house ready for prayer." And they say a family that prays together stays together, and a family that prays together is successful together. Then you bring the children, who are the ones to be developed. Those are the ones who get cultivated. They're the ones you're fighting and sacrificing your whole life for, so that they will carry your torch that came directly from God and be able to take it to the next level. Then the cycle continues. That's why when you look at our children now, they're so advanced. They have yet to be tampered with. So that connection to God is so tight that they're able to do things that surprise you, because you cannot do it yourself. So if the children force us to stay on our dean, they force us to elevate ourselves so that we prepare to do right by them.

Allah-u-Akbar! All Praise is Due to Allah!

One of the hadiths of Prophet Muhammad (Peace Be Upon Him). It says, "A man came to the Prophet and said, 'O Messenger, who from among mankind warrants the best companionship from me?' He replied, 'Your mother.'"

I just got finished breaking down God's structure. So you're not gonna skip your mother and go right to your father. That breaks protocol.

The man asked, "Then who?" The Prophet replied again, "Your mother." The man asked, "Then who?" And the Prophet replied again, "Your mother!"

Show her respect. Honor her, because she's the one who spends direct time with you and who cultivated you. While the father is away from the house, who's the one home ensuring that you did everything you needed to? Okay.

Then the man asks again, "Then who?" And here goes the reply. "Then your father." You make sure she gets three to one. She gets three to one. So brothers, don't get all bitter and stuff because mom gets more love. If we as men, as fathers, are doing what we're supposed to do, the mother has no problem taking what the child's giving her and exalting the child to the father. "Oh, son, daughter, well, we wouldn't be able to do this if dad wasn't at work, making sure the lights are on. Son, daughter, we wouldn't be able to do this if dad didn't make sure we had groceries in the refrigerator." A loyal woman does not want to be the alpha of the household. It is not in her nature. She wants a man who takes control and gets things done.

So as the father is out striving to the best of his abilities to be the head, the maintainer, the provider, the security, the leader, the driver, the future, the agent, and the help-meet to God, it is the mother the child spends the most time with. When the mother is connected to God and sees, feels, loves, and desires the God she sees in the father, the mother will instill the same love for the father that she sees, feels, love and desires into the children. Our enemy has broken that from us. They have pulled us out of the household.

As Muslims, that is why we love Mother Khadijah Farrakhan so much, one of the Mothers of the Faithful. She has sacrificed her husband, the Honorable Minister Louis Farrakhan, for the children of the world. She has devoted her energy to help keep us close to our spiritual father. So we honor Mother Khadijah.

Through the grace of Allah, I have been parenting for just over six years, but I'm learning something new every day. It's not easy being a parent. I remember when I was a child, I couldn't wait to turn 18 to move out. "Oh, I can't wait. I can't. I can't stand these rules. Wait 'til I turn 18!" And I had a car. Man, I remember my mother and I would get into an argument. She would kick me out and say go stay with your father. I'd be in the room packing. She'd be like, "I bought that. That stays. That stays. You can take your draws with you. And you better have gas in your car, because I ain't giving you no money to get there!" (Laughs)

And if I didn't get that one, I would get, "Where you think you're going?" "You told me to move out." I didn't understand those rules then. Now that I'm an adult, I wish I could be a child again. We can't go backwards? All these bills, paying the mortgage, car notes, electricity, daycare, private school, tutoring. karate, basketball, etc. It gets expensive! And you can't say no to them. You gotta find a way to talk about it. "You didn't take care of that. Yeah, go do that first. I'll think about it. We'll see." You're trying to buy time. You know how it is to have your daughter come up to you, she got the nice little big eyes. She got that lil face. "Daddy." Man, and you gotta say no, but you know you can't say no to her. Like "ahhh, well princess, um let me see what we can do. Go ask your mama. She'll give you a better answer." Because you know the relationship between a mother and a daughter is different than the relationship with a father and a daughter. No, I said you couldn't do it. Thank you.

All Praise is Due to Allah.

But it is a challenge. It is a challenge. I want to tell you a story. The other day, I had a long day at work. I was tired. I didn't even eat. I just wanted to come home and go to sleep. I mean, I was exhausted, and by the time I got home, it's past the children's bedtime. So sometimes I'll catch them and you know the oldest, she'll try to the best of her ability to stay awake. She wants to see a father. That's such a beautiful feeling to walk in the house and your children embrace you. But this particular night, I didn't want to be bothered. I just wanted to relax. I'm tired, because I'm out on this plantation and they draining all my energy. Let's be honest. They take all your energy so you don't have no energy for your family. Now watch this.

"Daddy will you read his bedtime story?" I told you how hard it is, but my mind was made. "Nope." I ain't reading none of this. "Baby girl, it's past your bedtime." "But daddy, can you please read me this bedtime story?" "Baby girl you know you gotta go to school in the morning. You coming with all excuses in the world." So then you're like, alright. Maybe it's one of those small books. "What you want me to read you?" "The Holy Qur'an." Man! I jumped out that bed so fast. I'm serious. I jumped out that bed excited. That was a whole new burst, right. I thought I was tired. I had a whole new burst of energy. "What chapter you want me to read?" All Praise is Due to Allah.

Then I started feeling bad that I wasn't trying to read a bedtime story. She just wanted quality time with her father. So I started feeling bad about it. I got there. I'm all excited. Now I'm reading the Holy Qur'an. I'm looking at my daughter, like man. You want to read this book? You could have said any other book, but you want me to read this book? But what do you want me to read? "It don't matter daddy. Just start reading to me."

For my Christian family, that's the feeling you get when your child asks you to read the Bible to them, and you want them to be God-fearing, and it's a reflection and reminder that you're doing something right in all of the chaos you're dealing with. So that was a beautiful feeling; oh, beautiful feeling. And what it reminded me of was Proverbs 22:6, which says, "*Start children off on the way they should go, and even when they are old they will not turn from it.*"

When you give birth to a boy you give birth to an individual. When you give birth to a girl, you give birth to a nation. She gave me a reminder of the work I have to put in to help lift up this Nation. Wow. All Praise is Due to Allah.

It's hard, trying to keep balance in this. I'm still on family. I just want you to know. Because what I'm speaking on is something that's going on in every one of our lives. We're all dealing with this. At some point, if you haven't dealt with it, yet, you will have a rude awakening. There's no real preparation for it. It can be hard to bring balance with so much going on in this world and there's so much pulling at you. And I deal with that everyday, trying to bring balance between work, mosque life, Nation life, the 10,000 Fearless, other business endeavors and wife time.

The Minister taught us about when you come home. The wife has been at home with the children all day. She don't want to have children conversation. She wants to speak to you. Well, at my job I have to talk all day. When I get home, I'm quiet; quieter than a mouse. I don't want to talk, queen. "Really? Come on. Because you gave all these people all this time, but you can't give your family an hour, two hours, 30 minutes?"

I brought up balance for a reason, because I had a dream the other day, and it scared the hell out of me. I literally jumped out the bed screaming. This is how it went. I'm in the bed, dreaming. That's what you do, right? We're at the house, and we're having a party. We're just having a nice gathering, playing games and having fun. I'm like All Praise Belongs To Allah, because we don't get a chance to do that as often, so I'm enjoying it. And some believers got lost. I can't find the house, so I grab both of my daughters, and I get in the car to go meet them. And for some odd reason, as we're driving away, I don't see my baby in the car. I'm talking about the youngest, and I said she's only 21 months. I'm yelling out "Eiliyah! Eiliyah!" We double back, and I pull up to the main crossroads where I met them at, and she's running down the street, on the sidewalk just having a good 'ol time like children do.

I'm trying to figure out how she got out the car in the first place. I'm puzzled at the time. So I'm pulling out, but I see two wolves across the street, and I can see it in their eyes like, I'm 'bout to go grab that right there. So I'm trying to figure out, I'm in this car. You know cars don't move as quickly as wolves do in maneuvering. So I'm trying to bust out to get to her. They sprint across the street, and they pick her up and run back across the street. I'm jumping on the sidewalk, driving, chasing after them, trying to get my child back, and all I yell out is "Noooooooo." I jump out the bed at the time. So that's been on my mind for days.

I call one of my brother, brother Abel Muhammad, and I asked him for some guidance in symbolism. I started reading up on the wolf. And when you look at the wolf, there's two sides of the wolf. You have the vicious side and then you have the protective side. So then I had to start going back and reflecting on that dream. I'm thinking and I'm looking at them while they're running off with my daughter. Now, if they wanted to harm her, they could have taken advantage of her when they grabbed her right there. But they're carrying her away like you would carry your own child away, if you were an animal.

So he sent me a 'Tale of two wolves':

An old Cherokee told his grandson, my son, there is a battle between two wolves inside us all. One is evil. It is anger, jealousy, greed, resentment, inferiority, lies and ego. The other is good. It is joy, peace, love, hope, humility, kindness, empathy and truth. The boy asked his grandfather, "Grandfather, which wolf wins?" The grandfather replied, "The one you feed."

That made me reflect back on balance. You may think in your personal life, your individual life, there's balance there, but have you created balance for your family? You could have balance for self, but I didn't give you the other part of it.

The structure is God, man, family, then nation. So after you create balance for yourself, you must create balance for your family, because if there's no balance, then there's chaos. Man is a reflection of his wife and children. You can tell how much balance a man has by looking at the upkeep of his children. You can tell how much devotion is given to his family by the way his family operates. My brother gave me an accolade about my family. My response was, I have to ask my wife that, because she is my tester for my exam, internally. She lets me know where I'm doing good at and what areas of opportunity I have. What reflection are we giving the world when they look at us?

I mentioned a little earlier, we have been breaking away from that structure. Satan has separated us from our own family, as he did back in slavery, by giving us more hours, by cutting our pay, by forcing us to put more energy into what they want of us. We're chasing after something that we consider valuable, but Allah says simplicity means much more.

He has conquered us mentally, physically, spiritually, and morally. He has completely removed us from our homes and has taken charge, and he's feeding our own children, through the television, through computers and through social media. I love television and all that as well, but this is what he's doing to us. It's one thing to be at home and your child's watching something, and then they have a question and you're able to address it. But he's removing us from the home. So when they're watching this, they don't have anyone to answer it. Now they're processing it in their own mind, and they're coming up with their own conclusion. Or when they get to school, they bring it up with their classmates, and their classmates are giving them whatever their parents may have told him. That doesn't mean it's correct. But now, it has been deep-rooted into that child.

They fed us too. They fed us too, as parents. They fed us through this presidential election. We were so consumed in this election. Hillary or Donald Trump. Who do I want? The first woman president? Oh, he knows business but files bankruptcy every three years or so. Believe it or not, bankruptcy is a smart business move when you don't want them to have access to your assets. But we were so disappointed. People were so disappointed that she didn't win. People were so angry that Donald Trump won that they were going to Hillary Clinton like "We lost too 'massa." That's how we treated it. "We failed you 'massa." And she made us feel like we did fail her. People were so disappointed that I have brothers and sisters I'm close to on social media still posting the stats. Dude! It ain't gonna change. Yes, she got more votes, but she didn't play the game. He manipulated the game, right? He was selected before he was elected. Right? So it didn't matter. We were so disappointed that we allowed our own emotions to get involved. We went out shopping again over Black Friday weekend. It's interesting that we were boycotting before the election, and then after the election, all of the Caucasians were boycotting. We gave up on boycotting. "I'm done. No more protesting. I'm finished with this. I'm going shopping this weekend." There were about 3 million more shoppers this year for Black Friday weekend than last year. We are emotional spenders. You ever get mad, or you had a bad day and go buy you some ice cream, or you get some french fries? I'm ordering pizza tonight. Where those brownies and cookies? We're emotional, and that's a bad habit. It's a really, really bad habit.

We packed those stores. They didn't show the White areas. They showed us. They remember what we did last year, so they were trying to prove a point. They weren't serious about this. But there were a few of us that were steadfast and didn't give up the money, and because of those numbers, even though there were more numbers that came, our spending was still lower this year than it was last year.

I want to break something down for you guys. You know what I love about the Asian and Jewish culture? They do something called group economics. Ever heard of group economics? Well, the meaning of group is "a number of persons or things arranged or considered together as being related in some way." Right now, we're grouped in some way. Economics: "The science that deals with the production, distribution, and consumption of goods and services or the material welfare of human kind."

A dollar circulates in the Asian community for a whole month. Crazy, right? A whole month, 30-31 days. In the Jewish community, it circulates for approximately 20 days. The White community, 17 days. How long does the dollar circulate in the Black community? Six hours. "I got paid! Here you go." Six hours. Look at that gap. And then we wonder why we're not successful. African-American buying power is at $1.1 trillion, and yet only two cents of every dollar an African-American spends in this country goes to a Black-owned business. Two cents for every dollar!

We need to rebuild our community. Did you know that Broadway (Phoenix, Arizona) used to have the nickname West Harlem? It was the only place in the west that resembled how Harlem was. Yeah, surprising, right? When you drive home today, go down Broadway. Look at the abandoned buildings, the one stories, the empty lots. But when you look at it, you could tell there was something here once upon a time, but it's not like it once was. There were a lot of rich and wealthy Blacks here in Phoenix. You know, we used to pretty much run from 7th St. to 32nd Street. Baseline all the way to Van Buren was all us. If you go on Washington, heading towards downtown, there's a historical house right there. That was the house that was used as a hotel for us, because we couldn't stay in the White hotels back then. That's where Jackie Robinson stayed when he came to visit. That's where

Muhammad Ali came to stay, even though at that time, he could stay in any hotel he wanted. He chose to stay in that hotel.

There's so much history here in Phoenix. They don't want us to know that though. If you know your history, it's best suited so now you can prepare for your future. See right now we're like wandering the wilderness of Phoenix, Arizona, because we don't know our own history. And we're wondering why we're not getting the best results, but we're doing the same thing over and over and over and committing insanity. I know that our community is suffering, because there are vultures here taking all our money. We can't build our community, our nation, if we are not building our families. We need our family-owned businesses, our own group businesses.

Have you ever seen the series Queen Sugar? It's on the OWN network, Oprah Winfrey's network. I got a chance to watch it. My mother pretty much forced me to watch it, but it's really good. I want to give an example from it. They're out in Louisiana. The father has over 800 acres of land. That family used to be slaves to the White family around them. The family around them, the two families around them had a hard time, and they sold some of their acres. So they bought 800 acres. They want their acres back, but it sits right in the middle of the rest of their land that the former slave masters own. They did everything they could to try to get it back. They lynched family members, all the way to the point now that when the father passes away, the children don't know this yet. They're debating on what they're going to do with the land. "Let's sell it." We're so quick to give up something, because we don't know the history of it. So when they finally got a chance to find out, why do they want this so much? And the aunt comes out and tells them the history of their family and that family, and that strengthened their interest. You're not getting this from us.

We have friends and family who have things of value, but we have yet to ask: Why do you have that, daddy's clock right there? Well, we got that because of this, this, this and that. Please don't get rid of it when I make my transition. Why don't you have this right here?

We don't ask questions anymore. We assume you got this old stuff. But I bet if we took it to a pawn shop and we took it to someone who actually knew the value of it, they'll try and buy it from us at a low so they can sell it at a high. We don't know the value of it.

That made me think about The Birmingham Boycott that went on for about 380 days. I want to show you something. I'm gonna do something that's called the $100 test. What is this? Picture one hundred dollars, right? It's $100. It's a Benjamin. It's real. The hundred dollar bill represents any dollar amount of $100 or more. These are the rules. Each and every one of you represent a business, a group business or a family business. I want you to think right now of a business you've always wanted, a business that is needed in our community. Because this is either going to be considered an investment in the business or someone's paying you for goods, services, or making a purchase from your business. So this is what I want you to do. Every time somebody touches this one hundred dollar bill, it represents their business. We're going to circulate this hundred dollar bill around this whole room.

There are two things I want you to do before you hand it off to the next person. I want you to name off the number you're at, and I want you to name off your business. I want you to say it out loud. Engineering, recycling, health food store, clinical labs, coffee shop. Follow the money. 36 businesses.

Every time it touched somebody, that represented a day. So we just circulated $100 or $100,000 or $500,000 across our community for 36 days. That has put us over one month economic circulation. Look at what happened. We started building up our own family livelihood. We started our own businesses, and we invested in and reinvested in our own businesses. We invested in our community, which means we are building up our community, which also means crime has dropped. Lives have been saved and families and friendships have been developed. We are able to hear from one another on what businesses we desire to have which gives us an opportunity to pull our resources. There is no need to put our money in the hands of everyone else when you look at how we put the money back in our own pockets.

We talk about boycotting. We just created what's called a lifestyle change. When you put the money back into yourself, you don't have to think about boycotting. Boycotting is a reaction. We're being proactive, now. I don't have to say do I want Tide or the True Laundry. I enjoy True Laundry. It's just a plus that they're Black owned. I don't have to say Charmin over Freedom Paper. It's just a plus that they're Black owned. They're our community. We trusted one another. All Praise is Due to Allah.

This is one of the most important things I want you to get out of this: Be honest. In most businesses, we won't start them because we don't trust each other, because we're not honest. You were given an opportunity. It might have been a fairytale, but it's not. You were given an opportunity for a few minutes to imagine that business you want, which helps in the livelihood of your family, which means we're building up the family, which is the community, which means we are building up our own Nation.

Galatians 3:13 says: "*Bear with each other and forgive one another. If any of you had a grievance, forgive as the Lord forgave you.*"

We don't trust each other, because we had a bad experience with one another; or someone said something about someone and we took it on face value. When I reflect on that, it takes me to the Supreme Wisdom Lost-Found Muslim Lesson Number One, Question and Answer Number One. It says, "Why isn't the devil settled on the best part of the planet Earth? Because the earth belongs to the Original Black Man. And knowing that the devil was wicked, and there would not be any peace (we need peace) among them, he put him out in the worst part of the earth, and kept the best part preserved for himself ever since he made it."

Let me explain what that means. We're not perfect. There's no perfect family. We have issues and problems. We're dysfunctional. But if we're willing to settle on the best part of our mindset, Planet Earth, we can overcome those difficult times. We have family members that we may not get along with because of their lifestyle. They're alcoholic, they're addicted, they're drug dealers, they're homeless, they're stealers and they're liars. But we must go down to their level so that we can settle on their best part! That's the only way we can come and help Almighty God Allah raise his people up.

Let me give you another analogy. Let's go back to the good days when big momma used to cook on family Sundays, and you had that sister, cousin, or aunt who couldn't cook and you really didn't want her in the kitchen. And you didn't let her cook the fried chicken. You didn't let her cook the macaroni and cheese, because you know that was gonna be the main entree. What did you do? "Girl, go peel those potatoes. Can you go get some paper towels?" You sent her away from that. But what you did was you found where she could still be useful, so you settled on the best part of her. "You know what, you do a great job doing this. I think you will give us great value if you did this instead of trying to make that fried chicken. You make the macaroni salad. You do the potato salad. I just need to observe it before you deliver it to the family."

But we must settle on the best part. People make decisions based off of their circumstances and influences. I mentioned earlier how they have taken us out of the household. So we're going to make decisions off of our influences, or what we see is the best fitting, because we may not know any better. We have to have patience with each other. We must go down to the level to that person and help elevate them. That elevation also helps to build our family.

We have $1.1 trillion in spending power. You said you're not happy with the way this presidential election went, or you're not happy with how the government system works. Shut it down! Shut it down! We don't need guns. We need unity.

There was a situation in one of the hadiths of Prophet Muhammad (Peace Be Upon Him). That's right, I said a situation. A man came and stood urinating in the mosque. The Companions of the Messenger of Allah said, "Stop it. Stop it!" But the Messenger of Allah said, "Do not interrupt him. Leave him alone." So they left him until he had finished urinating. Then the Messenger of Allah called him and said to him, "In these mosques, we do not have the right to do anything like urinating or defecating. They are only for the remembrance of Allah, praying and reading Qur'an," or words to that effect. Then he commanded a man who was there to bring a bucket of water and throw it on the urine, and he did so.

Stop judging. There's a slogan, 'What Would Jesus Do?' You just got a scenario of it.

Page 47 of "*Closing the Gap*," (I love this part right here) says, "For Allah God so loved the world that he gave his only begotten son. He gave. He sacrificed him, and the son was willing to be sacrificed. I have no life of my own. My life is for the redemption of a people. And that is pretty hard, however, that is the necessary requirement to affect resurrection, redemption, restoration and reconciliation of the soul that is loss, including, when a person is like that he has no sin. He has shortcomings for sure, and he may commit sin, but by his long-suffering and continuing to pull on the good nature of Allah God in the people to make them better and better and better, Allah God just wipes away the sin he has and throws it into the sea of forgetfulness and covers his sin because of the work that he does of redemption. This is why Jesus is looked at as absolutely perfect and sinless."

We get the truth. We get guidance. We get scriptures. We get connections to Almighty God Allah that we find ourselves exalting ourselves amongst our own family, where we find ourselves forgetting that we were once in the same shoes as our family. We forget to extend our hand out as mercy and want to help lift and build up our family. In the church, we're taught that Jesus was crucified and sacrificed for our sins. However, we mistreat each other.

In the Book of John 8:1-12, it says:

> *"Jesus went to the Mount of Olives. At dawn he appeared again in the temple courts, where all the people gathered around him, and he sat down to teach them. The teachers of the law and the*

Pharisees brought in a woman caught in adultery. They made her stand before the group and said to Jesus, 'Teacher, this woman was caught in the act of adultery. In the Law Moses commanded us to stone such women. Now what do you say?' They were using this question as a trap, in order to have a basis for accusing him. But Jesus bent down and started to write on the ground with his finger. When they kept on questioning him, he straightened up and said to them, 'Let any one of you who is without sin be the first to throw a stone at her.' Again he stooped down and wrote on the ground. At this, those who heard began to go away one at a time, the older ones first, until only Jesus was left, with the woman still standing there. Jesus straightened up and asked her, 'Woman, where are they? Has no one condemned you?' 'No one, sir,' she said. 'Then neither do I condemn you,' Jesus declared. 'Go now and leave your life of sin.'" When Jesus spoke again to the people, he said, 'I am the light of the world. Whoever follows me will never walk in darkness, but will have the light of life.'"

We have to find ourselves being like our father.

Why did I bring that up? Because of our betrayal to Jesus, our betrayal to the Christ, is the reason why we are not successful as a people. Our disunity is a betrayal to Jesus. Our disunity is a betrayal to the Christ. Our arrogance, our ego, our pettiness, our disagreements, our fighting one another over who is closer to him, creates a betrayal to the Christ. We are like children fighting over who's closest to the Father. Minister Farrakhan said we have to clean up our act. We have to make a serious change. We have our own foot in our own way of progress. It is not religion that keeps us close to oneness with God. It's works of being up right and righteous, wanting for your brother, what you want for yourself; wanting for the community what you want for your family.

I am hoping that this year—this came from the Minister—I'm hoping that in this year of the family, we will go into our families and reconcile differences.

I love you, and I pray that my actions continue to show you that I love you. At the end of the year many people put together New Year's resolutions. Let's make these resolutions real. Let's make real sacrifices this year. Let's build our relationship with Almighty God Allah. It's time to grow into the mind of God. Let's build our families. Let's build our businesses. Let's build our communities. Let's continue this boycott. Let's change it from a boycott to a lifestyle change. If we change the way we think, we will change the way we build, which means we change the way we build our families. Can we inspire our city? Yes, we can. So let's get up. Let's get to work, because John 9:4 says, *"As long as it is day, we must do the works of him who sent me."* He's talking to you and I, because night is coming when no one can work. The best gift you can give—coming from the Minister—is you and your love for your family and friends. Let's get up. Let's get to work.

3

Do We Take the Teachings of The Most Honorable Elijah Muhammad as a Joke?

"The Teachings of The Most Honorable Elijah Muhammad is the greatest message that you could receive, because in it is a profound knowledge of Allah and a profound knowledge of self. You can only love yourself based upon what you know of yourself."

The Honorable Minister Louis Farrakhan

The Honorable Elijah Muhammad teaches us that we will receive a minimum of two severe trials per year. Two minimum hard trials, severe trials! And the Honorable Minister Louis Farrakhan touches on that. He breaks down the word "severe." To be severe means to be unexpected. I have gone through an unexpected trial.

My grandmother has been on life support for nearly two weeks. My family has had to travel back to the New Jersey to check up on her. As I traveled, it's interesting when you're away because you don't get all of the information. But now that I have experienced it, I have a comprehensive knowledge.

We're learning that person who has harmed my grandmother is on my grandfather's side. This coward! This coward has a bloodline to our family, but blood does not make you family. He was staying with my grandmother at one point. She took him in, but she had to put him out because he was stealing from her. But my grandmother, having such a big heart and being a God-fearing woman, wanted to heal him as Jesus would heal us. So she would take him in and feed him. But the brother, who was on drugs, would run off with her pocketbook and her purse. Being on drugs doesn't give you an excuse.

We have been dealing with a lot. This has been a lot of pain. Through this process, we learned that one of my uncles who is an imam wanted to put hands on this brother, but my grandmother said, "No, don't do that. He's family! Strike one!" Then, my other uncle who is either with the Newark Police Department or is a former police officer wanted to have him arrested, but my grandmother said, "Don't do that. He's family! Strike two!"

How many strikes do we need before we're out?

One day, he found his way into my grandmother's home and beat her so bad that she didn't go to church that Tuesday evening. And my grandmother doesn't miss church.

I love my grandmother. When I would go to New Jersey, I would try to find a way to go to everybody else's house, because we attended Sunday school, morning service and evening service. Don't let there be a conference that weekend because we were at Friday service, Saturday service, and Sunday service again. So we found ourselves in church all day long!

So the first sign that came up was, Mother King did not come to service Tuesday night. That's not normal for her. Then, my cousin comes home Wednesday after work, and he notices that my grandmother did not pick her mail up. He stays on the next level, so he's the one who found her unconscious on the floor in her home. He found her lying there for nearly 30 hours. That's painful! This woman has put in 85 years of her life and if you would see her right now before this circumstance. During Memorial Day weekend, she was at my uncle's house. There's a block party around the corner, and she found her way at that block party in heels and her church clothing dancing and turning up. This woman has been enjoying life that Allah has blessed her with.

So it's a lot of pain right now that I'm going through, and I'm trying to hold myself together. But Allah has put something on me. My life and my death are all for Allah right now. This is a time you will find yourself wanting to doubt God, but you can't doubt Him in this hour. Allah will put pressure on us mentally and spiritually to see how strong we are and how much Will we have. Will I turn my back? Will I turn back on my heels in this hour? Will I give up on Almighty God Allah who acts on His permissive will? Or will I sit back and learn and study while He's sending our family through this?

In one of lectures, I mentioned that I'm working on discipline right now. And I said Allah has to send me through a certain level of discipline to prepare me for my next level. Who would know it would be now? Humph! Whew!

This chapter, "*Do We Take The Teachings of The Most Honorable Muhammad as a Joke?*" Let me tell you how that came to me.

My grandmother's situation isn't the first time I was in New Jersey dealing with a family issue. A few years ago, my beloved cousin was murdered. My mother, my sister and I traveled to send him off. I saw my aunt and my little cousin at the funeral home, and I saw how they were being handled, so I told my sister and my mother, "Y'all go secure them and make sure they're taken care of."

I'm calling my cousin and my uncle like where y'all at? And this is an uncle who came into the Nation prior to '75 and who would go a different after the departure of The Most Honorable Elijah Muhammad. But there's a difference between Imam Warith Dean's teachings and the Teachings of The Honorable Elijah Muhammad given to us by The Honorable Minister Louis Farrakhan. So he would show up not knowing that what we have been given to us has become second nature, if we truly embody it.

As we were walking from the funeral home to the next place, which is about a block away, I placed one of my cousins in front of my uncle and one behind him. I took the outside, and if you ever play basketball, they say to use the baseline as a defense. So I used the inside, which would be the fences, and we created a diamond around my uncle. My little cousins didn't even have an idea of what was happening. And as we're walking with my uncle, he looks up at one of his sons, who's on security but doesn't even know he's on security. But I gave them a warning that if anything happens, I will hurt you two. Then my uncle looked behind himself and he saw his other son. And you can see that look in his eyes of coming up in the Nation, like, hold on, I know what this looks like.

Then he looked at me and I gave him a nod and said I got you. We wound up securing him as we went on to the Janazah (Funeral) services. And as these things start happening, I'm looking like man, look at how Almighty God Allah will just put it in you to take charge of your post and all temple property in view.

My aunt is shooting me text messages, saying the Nation has taught you well. My uncle said, "Thank you. I have seen how you took charge of your post." I didn't have to think about it. It's in my make-up. That was one incident.

Let's return back to when we were traveling to New Jersey to care for my grandmother, who is, thank Allah, still alive right now, even though they have taken all of her tubes out and are trying to send her to a hospice. But I tell you, Almighty God, Allah has His hands on this woman! Because they said she wouldn't make six hours after they took the tubes out and we are now past 24 hours. Allah-u-Akbar!

I got to New Jersey at 6 a.m. and caught a Lyft straight to the hospital. When I arrived, I saw how lax and how confused my family seemed to be with the circumstances. While at the hospital, I took on a shift, meaning I was bedside with my grandmother for nearly 30 to 36 hours. We did not want to leave her alone.

After my shift was up, my older sister came in and took over. Then, my mother would come and take on a shift. And it's interesting because majority of my family is in New Jersey. But once we showed up, everyone else decided to go back home.

This shows the makeup of what the Teachings of The Most Honorable Elijah Muhammad will give you, that you will put away your pain and your suffering to take care of a people who are in more need of you. So as these situations were happening, the one thing that kept coming to me was man, why do I just take charge of my post?

Have I taken the Teachings or have we taken the Teachings for a joke?

I pray to Allah that this chapter will ring in your ears. I pray that It will touch the part of our hearts that will get you back on the straight path that we have deviated from. As I was working on this chapter, there were many people who sent me messages about how controversial it would be. I've been hearing many people saying this is a very interesting subject. Well, I pray to Almighty God Allah that He blesses me to reach and exceed your expectations.

Now, I want to clarify a few things before we really get into this chapter. There will be times when I mention the Most Honorable Elijah Muhammad, and there will be times when I mention the Honorable Minister Louis Farrakhan. But I want you to know, when I'm using these names, they can be interchangeable at any given time. During the reading, you may see that I may make mention of the Messenger, but you can see that work through the Minister, and I may make mention of the Minister, but you can trace that work back to the Messenger.

Let's get started.

We've been given everything we need to fulfill our destiny. We've been given a blueprint. I'm not talking about the KRS-One album called "The Blueprint," and I'm not talking about the Jay-Z album called "The Blueprint." What I'm talking about is a blueprint given to us by the Most Honorable Elijah Muhammad. If we go back and look at what he's given us, we will see that we have more than just a foundation. We have been given everything we need to fulfill what Allah has blessed us to have.

The Honorable Elijah Muhammad taught us night and day for 44 years. Now that number 44 is found in Jay-Z's album, *444*, but that's another subject I'm going to address somewhere down the line if it is the will of Allah. But after 400 years of chattel slavery and Willie Lynch Syndrome, Allah will raise one up, right? That one is the Most Honorable Elijah Muhammad. He would be the head of all civilization for 44 years. That itself gives you your four, four, and four. But we're going get on that subject another time. Let's talk about this blueprint for a moment. You want to know about this blueprint? Let's talk about this blueprint.

When you go into the Teachings of the Most Honorable Elijah Muhammad, he gave us something called the Student Enrollment and the Actual Facts. That is the first base of our foundation. We can't even join on to the Nation of Islam until we understand that first. One of the first questions we are asked is, "Who is the Original Man?" That itself breaks up any misunderstanding of who we are. Then, he gave us lectures such as "*The True History of Jesus*" that would help us have a better understanding of who this Jesus figure is, who we've been worshipping and thinking of and praying to, and who we expect to come 2,000 years later.

He also gave us a book called "*Message to the Blackman*," with a chapter titled, "Who is That Mystery God?" He's been breaking down barriers to lay down a blueprint for us. It's like a simple mathematical equation, but we do not want to put the pieces together one at a time. Then, after he gave us "Who is That Mystery God?" in "*Message to the Blackman*," he would take us on to "The Making of a Devil."

So once we understand who God is and who we are, then we can see why God would produce out of us a devil so that we could purify ourselves. Then he says, "You know what? That's not enough." Because we got a lot going on in this country.

So he said, "How about I give you something called, '*The Fall of America?*"

"*The Fall of America*," and if we look at America's state right now, you can see it falling. And then in that, he had a subject titled, "Decline of the Dollar."

This is a book written in the 70s. *In the 70s.* He's already given us a blueprint, but we find ourselves seeking knowledge elsewhere.

Then he says, "You know what? After I give you what you need to understand, we need to pull our dollars and resources together." Then he comes out with something called the 'Three-Year Economic Program.' The program calls for Black people to pool their resources by contributing $10 a month to help fight against poverty, want, unemployment, housing, hunger and nakedness of the 30 to 40 million Black people in America.

Allah is only going to give you so much time with someone.

Then, every single week we have this beautiful paper called *The Final Call Newspaper*. In the back of *The Final Call* is something called the Muslim Program, where The Honorable Elijah Muhammad gives us What the Muslims Want and What the Muslims Believe.

Number eight of What the Muslims Want says, "We want the Government of the United States to exempt our people from ALL taxation as long as we are deprived of equal justice under the law of the land." I think we're still deprived of equal justice under the law of the land.

Then you go on to number 11 of What the Muslims Believe. It says, "We believe our women should be respected and protected as the women of other nationalities are respected and protected."

He knew that they weren't going to give this to us, but he needed to lay down that platform so that you and I would fulfill it, that you and I would step up and put the blueprint into effect. Then he would give to my beloved registered members of the Nation of Islam that beautiful book called *The Supreme Wisdom* that you can't even get until you decide to accept your own and be yourself. And one of the great questions in there is, "Why did we run Yakub and his made devil from the root of civilization?"

He has been separating us so that we can have our own land, so that we can have our own beans, and so that we can have our own economics.

Then he was like, "You know what? I got some more for you. I got 44 years." I'm going to just keep giving it to you, praying that we will wake up and accept what he's given us.

Then the Messenger is like, "Well, y'all still don't believe God came in the person, so let me give you another book." So he gave us *"Our Saviour Has Arrived."* In that book, it says He Allah makes all things new.

Then he said, "I laid down this foundation for you, but you know what? You won't be able to live and be able to enjoy the Hereafter nor enjoy heaven on earth if you don't have the right dietary law." So he gave us two books, "*How To Eat to Live*" Books One and Two.

All these I'm speaking of are books by the Most Honorable Elijah Muhammad. You can order them at *store.finalcall.com* to have in your own collection or your own library, to read and to have an understanding of this foundation that he's given us.

In How to Eat to Live, he goes into the reason why he taught us not to eat pork, to eat at the right time and not to overeat. He also taught what's prescribed to us and what's not prescribed and the reason why we fast. Fasting is becoming a popular thing, now, which is so interesting. They call it intermediate fasting But if you go back in the time that the Most Honorable Elijah Muhammad was among us, that wasn't popular to the world. We are now seeing manifestations of everything he taught us.

It's so interesting. I went and looked something up, and it talks about how when you fast, you actually increase brainpower. When you fast, you actually strengthen your immune system. Have you ever wonder why you look at members of the Nation of Islam and they all look like they're in their 20s and 30s? Fasting will give you a renewed life. I mean, it gives life back to you. Student Minister Abdul Iman Muhammad looks like he's in his late 30s and 40s when he's in his 60s. Have you looked at the Honorable Minister Louis Farrakhan in his 80s with energy like he's in his 20s? When you're not eating, you actually allow your body to renew itself. And this is what the Most Honorable Elijah Muhammad gave us. His only conditions is for us to believe in Oh Mighty God Allah, his Messenger (The Most Honorable Elijah Muhammad), and to be our righteous self.

All we have to do is follow the instructions that he gave us. The best messenger and the best salesman that we have is *The Final Call*, which follows in the spirit of *The Muhammad Speaks Newspaper*. We don't have to sell or teach. All you have to do is hand the paper to the right person. Spend time with them. Cultivate the words with them. Show them how Allah has blessed us to transform our lives.

But he's like, "That's not enough. Y'all need more. I gave you a lot, but Imma give you more." So he gave us a whole series called *The Theology of Time*, and if you look at The Honorable Minister Louis Farrakhan, his lecture series *The Time and What Must Be Done* comes from the mind of the Most Honorable Elijah Muhammad in *The Theology of Time*.

But that still wasn't enough. Well, with all that being said, where's the fruit at? Where's the fruit that was produce from that great tree? Did we forget about the great Malcolm X?

The great Malcolm X, who you would not know of if it were not for the Most Honorable Elijah Muhammad. The enemy wants you to know of the student but they never want you to know of the teacher. How about the great Muhammad Ali? Before he met the Teachings of the Most Honorable Elijah Muhammad, he was just little 'ol Cassius

Clay, but through the Teachings of the Most Honorable Elijah Muhammad, he became Muhammad Ali. He was no longer just an icon, but he was a world leader who would boldly claim that he would knock out his opponent and the round; who you saw in a corner making a Dua. With the guidance of The Honorable Elijah Muhammad Islam would be introduced not just to the U.S. but to the world on a large scale, because you would hear Muhammad so often.

Then the great Warith Deen Mohammed, who is the Son of the Most Honorable Elijah Muhammad. Many may have a problem with him, but I tell you, the Minister teaches us that he had his own assignment. His assignment was to take a few of us and take us into the understanding of the Orthodox Islam, which is really an understanding of how to get the Arabic part, to get that essence of Islam, which would be how to speak the language and how to connect on a universal level. But the Minister also said brothers and sisters, why don't you take what you got from there and bring it back home? You will be the ones to teach the Nation how to speak Arabic and how to pray in Arabic.

Then you have the great Honorable Minister Louis Farrakhan, who is such a humble man. He's so humble that I would have to retract calling him 'great,' if he were to read this. So you can't even call him great because he's not going to call himself great. He's going to say the Leader's great. He's going to say Allah is great. He's the one who's carrying us to the other side, and he's so humble that he doesn't even say, "Look at what I have done," but he says, "Look at what Allah has done for us."

And I can't forget the Muslim accomplishments. Prior to '75, if you go to, Saviours' Day 1974 when the Secretary got up and gave the reports of the Muslim accomplishments. This was an example of what we could have in our time if we will followed the blueprint of The Most Honorable Elijah Muhammad. During that time, the Muslims had executive jets. They had bakeries and grocery stores and cleaners. They had farmland. They had trucks coming in from Peru, bringing in masses of fish. They had manufacturing companies and apartment complexes.

I want you to understand, I'm not trying to beat up on any one of us. This chapter is a reminder for myself. But with all that being said, the Honorable Elijah Muhammad knew, if I gave you a blueprint, if I gave you everything you needed that you believed you needed, I have to be able to lay the barriers for how you can function within them. So he gave us the Restrictive Laws of Islam. And number 12 says do not commit acts of violence on ourselves or others.

And you know, I cannot forget about you and I: the pimps, the hustlers, the dope fiends, the prostitutes, the liars, the convicts, and even the highly educated ones. Almighty God Allah will use the Teachings of The Most Honorable Elijah Muhammad to raise you and I up. To my registered Muslims, ask yourself this question: Where would you be at right now if it were not for the Teachings of the Most Honorable Elijah Muhammad?

Let that soak for a moment. Sometimes we take what we have for granted.

You are probably asking right now, "So Brother Hannibal, with such a great blueprint and such a great foundation, why haven't we prospered as Black people?" I know that's a question everyone has, but I thank Almighty God Allah I don't have to answer it myself. He gave us that answer in the Holy Qur'an, Surah 45 Ayat 17:

> *"And We gave them clear arguments in the Affair. So they differed not until knowledge had come to them, out of envy among themselves. Surely thy Lord will judge between them on the day of Resurrection concerning that wherein they differed."*

When we didn't know any better, before we thought we knew everything, we were more submissive to Almighty God Allah.

You remember the first time you heard something that you never heard before from someone you admired or respected? You would be at the foot of their bed or the hem of their garment soaking in what they told you. You didn't have anything to say. If you had a pen and pad, you would take all the notes you could take to learn more. If you had a cell phone, you would take notes on your phone, learning more and more and more. But once we started getting the knowledge, we started thinking we knew more than the teacher.

Then we start challenging the teacher on what he or she knows. Next thing you know, we start differing from the teacher and from everyone around us. We became the most scholarly people, but for some reason, we can't produce anything.

We've been redeemed. Thank Allah for waking us up from our mental and spiritual death.

"I've been in the Nation this many years." Well, how much fruit can you bear? How many can you say you introduced to the Teachings of the Most Honorable Elijah Muhammad? This question is for myself, too. I want you to know that.

I know the Honorable Minister Louis Farrakhan was at the Big3 game. Do you think he's just sitting with Taraji P. Henson not fishing? Do you think he's just sitting with Ice Cube not fishing? He's still doing his work. Even if they don't join onto the Nation in the way you desire, he's planting the right seed that will not only change their life, but their work will start to change the life of the masses. All Praise is Due to Allah.

We think we know so much that we think we can out-teach and even out-smart our own teacher. We have become smart asses. That's what we have become. We have. We are so smart, we are so scholarly, that we think we can teach our own teacher. Yes, we do, and that's the reason why we take the Teachings of the Most Honorable Elijah Muhammad as a joke. What happened to that humility we had? Who do we think we are?

I know once you start thinking you're an adult in the home of your parents, at some point in time, you gotta get out the house. When you don't want to abide by the rules set by your parents, you got to get out that house. For some reason since we think we're so much smarter than our teacher, we are actually preparing ourselves to receive a heavy chastisement and the wrath of Allah.

I know who we are, and I'm in this boat, too. It reminds of the book of Matthew Chapter 25:14-30.

> [14] *For the kingdom of heaven is as a man travelling into a far country, who called his own servants and delivered unto them his goods.*
>
> [15] *And unto one he gave five talents, to another two, and to another one, to every man according to his several ability, and straightway took his journey.*
>
> [16] *Then he that had received the five talents went and traded with the same, and made them another five talents.*
>
> [17] *And likewise he that had received two, he also gained another two.*
>
> [18] *But he that had received one went and dug in the earth and hid his lord's money.*
>
> [19] *After a long time the lord of those servants came and reckoned with them.*
>
> [20] *And so he that had received five talents came and brought the other five talents, saying, 'Lord, thou deliveredst unto me five talents. Behold, I have gained beside them five talents more.'*
>
> [21] *His lord said unto him, 'Well done, thou good and faithful servant. Thou hast been faithful over a few things; I will make thee ruler over many things. Enter thou into the joy of thy lord.'*

²² He also that had received two talents came and said, 'Lord, thou deliveredst unto me two talents; behold, I have gained two other talents beside them.'

²³ His lord said unto him, 'Well done, good and faithful servant. Thou hast been faithful over a few things; I will make thee ruler over many things. Enter thou into the joy of thy lord.'

²⁴ Then he which had received the one talent came and said, 'Lord, I knew thee, that thou art an hard man, reaping where thou hast not sown, and gathering where thou hast not strewed.

²⁵ And I was afraid, and went and hid thy talent in the earth. Lo, there thou hast what is thine.'

²⁶ His lord answered and said unto him, 'Thou wicked and slothful servant, thou knewest that I reap where I sowed not, and gather where I have not strawed.

²⁷ Thou ought therefore to have placed my money with the exchangers, and then at my coming I should have received mine own with interest.

²⁸ Take therefore the talent from him, and give it unto him that hath ten talents.

²⁹ For unto every one that hath shall be given, and he shall have abundance; but from him that hath not, shall be taken away even that which he hath.

³⁰ And cast ye the unprofitable servant into outer darkness: there shall be weeping and gnashing of teeth.

Almighty God Allah gave one man five gifts, another man two gifts and a third man one gift. We're like that last man, and it says in verse 18, but the man who had received one talent went off, dug a hole in the ground and hid his master's money. We've taken the Teachings of The Most Honorable Elijah Muhammad, went and dug a hole and buried what Allah has given us. When the master comes back, he will see the one he gave five talents of gold to had doubled his work, and he will be so pleased that he will give him more gold. Next, the master will see the one he gave two bags of gold to had also doubled his work, and he will give him more gold. He will say, "Oh, you good and faithful servant." But then the man who had received one bag of gold came up. The man said, "I knew. I knew." And this is how we've been acting.

Here comes that knowledge right there. Here comes the scholar part. "I knew you were coming. So, you know, I know what you must be thinking, dear teacher, Master, I know what you are thinking. I know that you are a hard man, harvesting where you have not sown and gathering where you have not scattered seed, so I was afraid and went out and hid your gold in the ground."

"Here is what belongs to you. Here you go. Here's the knowledge you have given me. Thank you for waking me up. Here you go." But then the master replied, "You wicked, lazy servant which you have become. So you knew that I harvested where I have not sown or gathered where I have not scattered seed? Oh, see, you know me so well now. Hmm. Well then you should have put my money on deposit with the bankers so that when I return, I would have received it back with interest. So take the bag of gold from him. Give it to the one who has 10 talents."

The ones who have 10 talents could be our people in the community who are actually working this mission who have not met the Teacher, who have not met the Most Honorable Elijah Muhammad and who have not met the Honorable Minister Louis Farrakhan. But the works of these men have already been instilled in them, and they're working in the community themselves. They're doubling and tripling their works on God's green earth, and Allah is going to give them the blessings. But we say we are the ones who are supposed to be with this, and we want to bury our gifts and talents.

For whoever has will be given more, and they will have an abundance. Whoever does not have, even what they have will be taken from them. And throw that worthless servant into the outer darkness, where there will be weeping and gnashing of teeth. That's what we act like right now. We have taken the Teachings of the Most Honorable Elijah Muhammad as a joke! We become scholars. We can teach and are experts of everything. But I ask you again, where are our results? If we can't even compete on the level of the Honorable Minister Louis Farrakhan, who's been on this earth for over 80 years, who's been absent of his father for 40 years, who's been doing this for over 60 years, who do we say we are? He actually posed a question to us one day, and he said if he returned to Allah and Allah asked him, "Brother, did you give all that you could give?" his answer would be no!

I want that to sink in for a moment.

In the Supreme Wisdom under the Original Rules of Instructions to the Laborers, point number 13 says big fields are awaiting for the wide awake man to work out. Big fields for the wide awake. We're scholarly, so we must be wide awake. But we have not taken advantage of that big field. Hmmm.

How much of that field are we working out of? I'm telling you, I'm speaking to myself right now. Allah blessed the Most Honorable Elijah Muhammad with much success, so why don't we follow the blueprint? We don't have to recreate the wheel. It was given to us. All we have to do is follow what he's given us. All you have to do is make modifications according to your circumstance or your situation. It says the harvest is ripe but the laborer is few. Look around you.

The harvest is ripe, but look at the labor. Look at the labor. Hmmm. I get it. We must be afraid of our people. That's what it is. We've become way too bougie. We've become way too scholarly, now.

We forgot when someone met us at our door. Somebody caught us at the grocery store. Somebody saw us at the traffic light. We forgot how we were introduced to the Teachings of the Most Honorable Elijah Muhammad, because we don't go out to the grocery store no more with the papers. We don't go knock on the doors and sit in as the Mahdi did. "I have silks for you." We're just like the elders from Children of Israel. We're so afraid. We think there are giants out there. We're so afraid of our people, we think they are giants out there. But we don't even have to speak. All we have do is introduce them to what Allah has given us. We don't even have to be the most studious, but if we can show how Allah has transformed your and my life, that itself would change their lives. That itself would show how Allah is a healer of people. That itself would show how Allah is the healer of all humanity.

When we go into the Supreme Wisdom again, under the Original Rules of Instructions to the Laborers, point number two, the student could practice his or her labor while under study if they were sincere. We want to study, study, study, study. "Oh, I gotta do some more studying. Let me continue to study." At some point in time, we have to apply what we're studying. If you go back to Kanye West's album *College Dropout*, he was talking about the guy who had all the degrees. I got this degree and that degree and that degree. Man, how much money you making. Aw, it doesn't matter about money. I got more degrees coming. Then we die broke, but we're the most scholarly people out there. Allah promised us good homes and friendships in all walks of life, but we're broke. He promised us money, but we're broke. That means it ain't Allah. That's on us. That's on us. That's because we've taken these Teachings as a joke. Oh Allah.

What people love about you is when you apply what you study. When I went to the point where I was able to apply the Teachings and see what Allah has given us, well, when you study and you apply, that's where you get the yin and the yang. That's where it complements each other. It balances you out, because as you study it and you go apply it, you see, "Okay, I must not understand what I was studying right there. Let me go back and revisit that." Or as you're actually working, you'll see, "Man, I might need to go back and study some more." We can high-five all the way to the sun, which is 93 million miles away. We can sit out there for a while and teach, teach, teach, but then for some reason we forget about what's happening on Earth.

Oh, Allah!

Allah has been showing us all through the books of the Most Honorable Elijah Muhammad and the Honorable Minister Louis Farrakhan how He wants to bless us with the blueprint of the Most Honorable Elijah Muhammad. Don't take my word for it. Let's go to Deuteronomy 28 - Blessings for Obedience:

> *If you fully obey the Lord your God and carefully follow all his commands I give you today, the Lord your God will set you high above the nations on earth.*
>
> *All these blessings will come on you and accompany you if you obey the Lord your God.*
>
> *You will be blessed in the cities and blessed the country.*
>
> *The fruit of your womb will be blessed and the crops of your land and the young of your livestock—the calves of your herds and the lambs of your flock.*
>
> *Your basket and your kneading trough will be blessed.*
>
> *You will be blessed when you come in and blessed when you go out.*
>
> *The Lord will grant that the enemies who rise up against you will be defeated before you. They will come at you from one direction but flee from you in seven.*
>
> *The Lord will send a blessing on all your barns and on everything you put your hands to. The Lord your God will bless you in the land he is giving you.*

> *The Lord will establish you as his holy people, as he promised you on oath, if you keep the commands of the Lord your God and walk in obedience to him.*
>
> *Then all the peoples on earth will see that you are called by the name of the Lord, and they will fear you.*
>
> *The Lord will grant you abundant prosperity—in the fruit of your womb, the young of your livestock and the crops of your ground—in the land he swore to your ancestors to give you.*

You can tell we have not gotten that blessing right?

We haven't gotten that blessing because we've taken the Teachings of the Most Honorable Elijah Muhammad as a joke. Let me show you what we're about to get. It's called the "Curse for Disobedience." I'm only giving you a few verses, though, because there are a lot of them. Starting with verse 15:

> *However, if you do not obey the Lord your God and do not carefully follow all his commands and decrees I am giving to you today, all these curses will come on you and overtake you.*
>
> *You will be cursed in the city and cursed in the country.* (We're cursed in our own city right now. Think about it.)
>
> *Your basket and your kneading trough will be cursed.*
>
> *The fruit of your womb will be cursed, and the crops of your land, and the calves of your herds and the lambs of your flocks.*
>
> *You will be cursed when you come in and cursed if you go out.*
>
> *The Lord will send you curses, confusion and rebuke in everything you put your hand to, until you are destroyed and*

come to sudden ruin because of the evil you have done in forsaking him.

The Lord will plague you with diseases until he has destroyed you from and from the land you are entering to possess.

The Lord will strike you with wasting diseases, with fever and inflammation, with scorching heat and drought, with blight and mildew, which will plague you until you perish.

The sky over your head will be bronze, the ground beneath you iron.

The Lord will turn the rain of your country into dust and powder; it will come down from the skies until you are destroyed.

If we're not willing to do it, Allah will find a new people. Allah will find a new people.

The Honorable Elijah Muhammad has given us everything we need. And if you look at this, many of us are dealing with these curses right now in our own lives. So I ask you this question: Why are we dealing with these curses? Because we have not been obedient to what Allah has blessed us with.

We can avoid all of the destruction Allah has for us if we put our egos aside. In John 3:3, Jesus told Nicodemus, "Truly, truly I say to you, unless one is born again he cannot see the kingdom of God." We died so we could be reborn to walk with Christ, but for some reason we started thinking we were above Christ.

So I say to you, we must die again that we may be born and see the kingdom of God. In our prayers, we say, "Surely my prayer and my sacrifices, my life and my death are all for Allah, the Lord of the worlds."

Surely my prayer, my sacrifices, my life and my death are all for Allah, the Lord of the worlds. Do we believe that? Do we really, really, really believe that? Did we forget that when we were in the wombs of our mothers before she even knew that she was pregnant with us, Allah gave us that? Allah gave us a body where our spirit could function within so that we would be of service to Him.

We ask for many things, but we do no work to achieve what Allah has given us. Prayer counts for nothing unless carried into practice. Well, let's remove prayer for a moment. And I want to replace the word prayer with belief. So belief counts for nothing unless it's carried into practice. We can say we believe all day. "Oh, I believe. I believe." But do our results show that we truly believe? Do we really believe the Most Honorable Elijah Muhammad met God in person? Do we really believe that? Because if we say we believe it, our results will show it.

Do we really believe he is still physically alive? We have been very disrespectful to our teacher. He stepped out of the room and left his lead student in charge. And we've acted like monkeys. We've jumped around, throwing spitballs in the room, played loud music, got in fights and arguments, broke and damaged property. When we disrespect The Honorable Minister Louis Farrakhan we disrespect The Honorable Elijah Muhammad. If we believe Jesus died for our sins, and he will come for us 2000 years later, we believe that right? But we don't believe a Georgia born black man can meet God, heal people resurrect people for 44 years, and escape a death plot. We believe a man who was killed 2000 years ago, would come back up and raise us up. We misunderstand the Teachings of The Most Honorable Elijah Muhammad and the scriptures.

Our actions represent our belief, and we can no longer just believe. We must now know this is true.

The Most Honorable Elijah Muhammad's time among us reminds me of the story of Job. Job was a beautiful man. He's an honest and respected man. He always refused the devil. Job had sons and daughters. He owned 7,000 sheep, 3,000 camels, 1000 oxen and five female donkeys. He was considered the richest man in the east. That reminds me of The Honorable Elijah Muhammad, but we'll say the richest man in the west.

Satan came to God and said, "Well, you're protecting him. You're protecting him." So God told Satan to do as he pleases with Job. Satan could take anything he wanted to take away from him except for his life. You can do anything you want to do with the Nation and the people. Do not touch the Most Honorable Elijah Muhammad.

So Satan caused famine. He destroyed Job's cattle, his animals and his family. Satan sought to destroy the Nation of Islam. He caused the Nation of Islam to fall into such a slumber that it seemed as if it were dead. And after all that happened, Job did not curse God. The Most Honorable Elijah Muhammad did not curse God, because he saw that God knew what was best for him. So after 44 years of building up a Nation that Satan would come and destroy, God would allow the Most Honorable Elijah Muhammad to rebuild that nation.

And he would rebuild it through the mercy of Allah, through His extended mercy, by taking that lead student and putting him in that seat to now be the teacher in absence of the father. Allah always sends us signs and warnings. After the Children of Israel's deviation from Moses, He sent Aaron. As you see Job rebuilding, Allah blessed him with a new family, with new crops, with new land and with new riches just as we now see the Honorable Minister Louis Farrakhan, Al-Furquan, The Discrimination, being blessed.

He would be that judgment, that criterion, when Jesus comes with a sword dripping with blood. That sword is not an actual physical weapon, but that sword is the tongue, which is a double-edged sword. It can be of peace or it can be of judgment. It could be a blessing or it could be of harm. I'm speaking of the Honorable Minister Louis

Farrakhan. He would have the will and the love to rebuild his father's work. How do you and I say we love the Honorable Elijah Muhammad when we do not know him? Our love of the Honorable Minister Louis Farrakhan will cause us to love The Honorable Elijah Muhammad.

And that's the reason why the Messenger would have to instill in the Minister everything he would need, so that he could, in turn, instill in us and cause us to stop being disrespectful to the Messenger of Allah. That's why the Honorable Elijah Muhammad would tell us to listen to Minister Farrakhan, to look at him, to go where he tells us to go and to stay away from where he tells us to stay away from. The Honorable Minister Louis Farrakhan knew that the Honorable Elijah Muhammad would want us to be raised up to a point that Allah would give him mercy. Allah would give him 40 more years among us. For all the flaws, sins and shortcomings that we have committed, Allah would still give us mercy.

The fact that you can read these words tells you that Allah has given us mercy right now. Because when the Honorable Minister Louis Farrakhan departs from us, that's when the chastisement will truly come, and we will reap what we have sown. The disrespect that we've had, we will reap from it.

The love that the Honorable Minister Louis Farrakhan has for his people, he teaches us how to study. He teaches us how to pray again, in the rebuilding of this Nation. If you listen to the Honorable Minister Louis Farrakhan during an interview with Brother Munir, he said to us that the Most Honorable Elijah Muhammad did not write a will. Job did not write a will. But he would write a will into the heart and the mind of the Minister.

When you study the vision-like experience of the Minister going up to the Wheel, that's Allah writing the scroll. The scroll is the will of Allah being placed in our Minister. That's the reason why our dear Minister doesn't have to study anymore. He doesn't even have to study anymore. He produced the Study Guides from the scrolls Allah gave him, so that as we're rebuilding ourselves, we don't have to point fingers at anyone. We go grab the Study Guides and work on our self-improvement! And if you have a hard time learning how to work on your self-improvement, I tell you to go out on Fridays to your nearest Muhammad Mosque or Muhammad Study Group, because that's always the study, self-improvement. The problem is that we've become so ungrateful that we sit and just listen to the Minister, nod our head at the Minister and enjoy listening to the Minister like he's a lovely song. Meanwhile, the Minister is constantly giving us warnings and signs and telling us what to do. He is striving to save our lives.

Even if he doesn't say, "You, Brother Hannibal. Get up and go do this," he said we as a people must make our communities a decent place to live. You and I must get up and produce economics for our people. That's an instruction. When we don't do it, we become disrespectful. And when we become disrespectful, we take the Teachings as a joke. The Minister becomes like a lovely song to us.

When you love a song that you heard, you will sit and listen to it and dance to it. It's like going to a concert. When you go to a concert, you're not going to learn. We treat the Minister like he's a concert. We go to listen, enjoy it, tap our feet, jam out, clap out and shout Allah-uAkbar.

We treat him like a concert. But if we do not change our ways, the wrath of Allah is right at our doorsteps. We pick and choose what we want to abide by from the blueprint of the Honorable Elijah Muhammad, and that's the problem!

"Well, you know, I like yams. I don't like green beans." If Almighty God Allah serves you a plate, I don't care if you don't like it; you eat that. If you're fasting and we're at a Janazah and the Minister tells us to eat the peppermint, you don't argue with him.

Disrespectful!

The Honorable Elijah Muhammad has instilled in the Minister the same blueprint. They say the Minister has deviated. The Minister is fulfilling. He is fulfilling prophecy. He is the master of prophets. The

Messenger said there will be one who will come behind me who will have to deal with one-third of the work. He told the Minister to take this and put it in your own fine language. He told the Minister to take us and connect us with the Islamic world. The Messenger gave us a wake-up message. We should be awake!

Our disrespect has caused a gap, and if you ever read the book *Closing the Gap*, that gap is expanding.

That gap is expanding, and because of the expansion of that gap, we create idle minds. From that idle mind, we find fault in one another, which produces pettiness, envy and jealousy. That then leads to hypocrisy. If we find ourselves busy in the work, we don't have time. We don't have the energy to focus on the drama of other people. If you had a long day at work, when you get home, you don't want to hear about drama from other people. But because we find ourselves backbiting, slandering and gossiping, that's how you know we're not busy in the work.

All Praise is Due to Allah.

September 2017 marked 40 years that the Honorable Minister Louis Farrakhan has been absent from his father in the rebuilding of the Nation. The Honorable Elijah Muhammad told him that there would be modern technology that would help The Honorable Minister Louis Farrakhan reach the masses. We haven't helped him reach the masses because of our idleness. So Allah gave him something called social media. Due to social media, the Minister has been able to touch every nook and cranny, because we won't go to every nook and cranny. Allah had to give him something to aid him. So we saw the picture of the Minister with Taraji P. Henson and how fast it spread, and we saw the Minister speak and bring up Ice Cube and how fast that video spread.

Our Minister is working. What are we doing?

The Honorable Minister Louis Farrakhan at almost 90 is still fishing. Still fishing. Still fishing. I wouldn't be surprised if Taraji showed up to the mosque that Sunday. I wouldn't be surprised if Cube showed up to the mosque that Sunday. Fishing. Then Jay-Z gave him the plug in 4:44. Why did he go to the NBA?

Black economics. We really truly have to stop taking the Teachings of the Most Honorable Elijah Muhammad as a joke.

If we stop taking the Teachings of the Most Honorable Elijah Muhammad as a joke, Allah will put their mind in ours, and we will be as one with Almighty God Allah.

All we have to do is get up and do the work. That's it. We ain't gotta be the most studious. We ain't gotta be the smartest, the most intelligent. All we have to do is humble ourselves and be willing.

Remember how we were when we first heard the Teachings? Remember how it was when someone gave us something we never heard before? It was like really? Hold on, hold on. Say that again. Did you know that? If we get ourselves back into that mindset, you will see, I guarantee. Allah is my witness! If we just change just a little on how we think and how we function, if we just come with a clear mind and say, "I'm not going to judge and I'm not gonna act like I know everything, but I'm gonna listen to what you have to say and Imma try it to the best of my abilities," I guarantee you will see Allah manifest in you. That's why the Minister can sit with children and listen to them and see how Allah's manifestation in them is coming out and then be able to use that to help us.

All we have to do is get to work and Allah will prepare the people in the climate for you and I. If we just wake up, make Fajr Prayer. Make whatever prayer that you make. Call on God in whatever name you call Him. Ask Him to soften the hearts of the people. Say, "Allah this is what I want to do today. It may not be fulfilled today, but I'm determined with the will to get it done." As long as Allah is backing you, watch how Allah will put the people right in front of you. You will walk right into the path and it will connect with you. You're like Allah-u-Akbar! I need that. Allah will not forsake you and me as long we do not forsake Him. So who are we waiting on? Who are we waiting on? Are we waiting for someone to tell us what to do? Allah gave you your assignment when you were born. Allah already put it in you before you came out of the womb. Allah allowed you to go through the pressure of coming out of the womb of your mother. So no matter what comes in front of you, you have the strength and power to overcome it.

Allah-u-Akbar! Are we waiting on the Minister? Are we really waiting for the Minister? I know in this time we are not waiting for the Minister. Okay, we weigh in on it.

Well, he's been telling us what to do. He gave us the blueprint. He gave us the 20th Anniversary of the Million Man March. There was a blueprint in that. He gave us 1995. There was a blueprint in that. He gave us the Divine Instruction! Divine Instructions! There's a blueprint in that. He gave us the local organizing committees as a blueprint. He gave us the 10,000 Fearless as a blueprint. He gave you the Nation of Islam as a blueprint! What are we waiting on?

He's been giving us the blueprint, so I know we're not waiting on him. I know. I'm not done yet. But I'm trying because if somebody comes to me and says I'm waiting on the Minister, I might slap you. I'm not gon' lie! The minute you wait on Him, I might slap you. I'm not gonna lie. Because that means we're not studying and we're not applying. All I'm asking you to do is apply it, even if that's all we do. Wherever you're at right now in your studies, just apply it.

Just apply it and watch Allah blesses you. For my Muslim family, we're waiting on the laborers, huh!? We wait on the laborers, huh? That's it! We're waiting on the laborers to tell us what to do. Hmm. Okay. The laborers have their role. They have their role. But in the scripture, it doesn't say the laborers. It says the believers. If we get to work, trust and believe we make it easier for the laborers.

The responsibility is to check-in. Let them know what you're doing. Stay in connection with the laborers and allow them to help guide you. That's why they're the laborers. We don't have to wait to do God's work.

1st Corinthians 3:16-17 says:

> *Don't you know that you yourselves are God's temple and that God's Spirit dwells in your midst? If anyone destroys God's temple, God will destroy that person.*

Are you paying attention?

> *If anyone destroys God's temple, God will destroy that person; for God's temple is sacred, and you together are that temple.*

How about Ephesians 2:19-22?

> *Consequently, you are no longer foreigners and strangers, but fellow citizens with God's people and also members of his household, built on the foundation of the apostles and prophets, with Christ Jesus himself as the chief cornerstone. In him the whole building is joined together and rises to become a holy temple in the Lord. And in him you too are being built together to become a dwelling in which God lives by his spirit.*

That must mean God has left us, because we are not producing from what God has given us. I remember Martin saying that on 'You So Crazy.' Does anybody know that one? 1st Peter 2:5:

> *You also, like living stones, are being built into a spiritual house to be a holy priesthood, offering spiritual sacrifices acceptable to God through Jesus Christ.*

What are we waiting on? Our sole purpose is to deliver our people to the Lamb of God. I want to make sure we understand that. That's the first work. If we don't have people, we can't do the extra work. So the first work is to deliver them to the Lamb of God. But I want to hit you with this one.

If we delivered everyone to the Lamb of God, there must be something else that must be done. Because once we get you all here, you're here. You're here. So, what's purpose number two? What's purpose number three? What's purpose number four? What's purpose number five? Well, we're taught that we must have schools. So that seems that might be one of the purposes. Now that we have a body coming in, we get the educators. That becomes a purpose. We're taught that we need to have hospitals. I know we're not still going into these St. Luke's, St. Mary's and the of the other Saints who's trying to kill us. What's that hospital in L.A. that nobody wants to go to? MLK Hospital? And they'll jump out the ambulance. "I'm good. I'll walk to another hospital." That's a sign.

What's the next purpose? Economics. We can bring everyone in here, but if we don't apply purpose, the other part of the blueprint, into work, why are you here? We need businesses, land, etcetera. So you can never say I don't have anything to do. You always have something to do. In the mosque, but in the Nation because the mosque is a component of the Nation. I want you to understand that real quick. If the mosque is a hospital, it's a hospital for the sick. We are all sick. We've all been sick. Well, who are we to get better, go out and do something but don't bring more sick people to the hospital? That means the hospital falls apart. We have to bring people who are sick into the hospital so that they can be a better benefit to the Teachings of the Most Honorable Elijah Muhammad. If we help bring people in, they become an asset to you and me, which means Allah will put them in the right place in the right climate that will help us fulfill our purpose and destiny.

Oh, Allah. Oh, Allah.

We have taken the Teachings of the Most Honorable Elijah Muhammad as a joke. But guess what? We can change that. If you opened your eyes today, we could change that. The question is, do you want to change it? You don't have to answer me. That's between you and Allah.

I'm trying to fix myself right now. He ain't finished with me yet. I have plenty of flaws. My guest count's way too low. My charity is way too low. My "converts" is way too low.

So I'm not speaking to you as someone who came straight down from heaven. I'm trying to get myself out of the sunken place. If this is your first time hearing about this, all you have to do is commit yourself. Just commit yourself. Commit yourself to wanting to make yourself better. And as you make yourself better, commit yourself to wanting to make others better. Instead of driving by someone who you see struggling, pull over. Check up on them. That person you see every day walking to the bus stop, check up on them. That elderly in your apartment complex or that neighbor, check up on them and watch how Allah will give you friendships from all walks of life.

If you already know of this program, all you and I have to do is what? Recommit ourselves and rededicate ourselves. Anything that has a "re-" to it, do it. Allah-u-Akbar.

The Honorable Minister Louis Farrakhan laid more than a foundation of 40 years absent of his father. We don't understand that, but I need to let you know he must go away. As long as he's among us, we're going to be disrespectful to the Teachings of the Most Honorable Elijah Muhammad. But we can change that. We can really change that. But we're forcing him to have to go away so that we can step up and become those apostles you read about in the scriptures. He will go to the Father to get another book. That other book will take us to another thousand years.

Let's give him all that we have before he goes. Let's show him, the Honorable Elijah Muhammad and Master Fard Muhammad that we don't see them as a joke. Are you willing to do that? Okay.

The Minister said on Twitter:

> *Never be afraid to step out on faith if you really want something. All of the talking is over.*

All of the talking is over. We have to get to work. All of the teachings is over. We've been given everything we need, everything. If you and I have any confusion or misunderstandings, all we have to do is go back. Just take a step back and look into our scriptures. Order DVDs or CDs. Listen to some YouTube videos of the Minister. Break up these books that lay out the blueprint of our foundation. And if we do that, we will hold firm to our Flag of Islam. The Minister also said our talent is our gold. Our talent is our oil. Our talent is what God has given us that others have exploited to their advantage.

Let's wake up. Let's get back our gold and our oil. There are big fields awaiting us.

4

Understanding Variables of Life

"Doubt halts the process of decision-making and decisive action. It undermines Faith. When Faith is undermined long enough it disappears."

The Honorable Minister Louis Farrakhan

We are on a continual journey. This journey that we are on is a journey of continued demand. What will you and I give? Sometimes it may be overwhelming, or we may be overcome by duty to the point that we say, "I can't do that. I don't have time. I don't have enough money in my pockets to give." But I tell you, that is not what God is asking for. He is asking and demanding us to perfect ourselves. The perfection of ourselves is the perfection of God Himself. Hidden deep, deep, deep in our—that ain't enough deepness, is it? Let's go deeper. Hidden deep, deep, deep, deep, deep, deep, deep deep in our DNA is the original man. And if we go to where the original man is, we find that the Original God Himself is there, and that Original God is the perfection of us, which we've been seeking. From the day we came out the wombs of our mothers, Allah has put us on a path to perfect us.

Genesis 1:27 says, *"God created mankind in his own image, in the image of God he created them; male and female he created them."* Then Ephesians 4:24 says, *"And to put on the new self."* Why would we need a new self unless there's something wrong with the old self, which in the likeness of God has been created in the righteousness and holiness of the truth.

Now this is part of our first variable of life. If we don't know our history, we don't know where we're going. So the question becomes, who are we? Whose are we? The Bible addresses who we are, but because we don't actually believe in the book, we fail to see our Godship.

We are the original man. Well, for my registered brothers and sisters, we had to go through a process, and part of that was Student Enrollment. The first question we had to learn to be able to even get on the other side was, "Who is the original man?" Well, who is the original man? *The original man is the Asiatic Black man, the maker, the owner, cream*—which rises to the top—*of the planet Earth.* Why would we have to rise unless we're at the bottom? *God of the universe.* So we are in His image and likeness. We are of God, who is the universe. We just have yet to tap into our own God universal powers. Let's think about that for a second.

The Honorable Minister Louis Farrakhan had an article in the Final Call Newspaper. One of the sections in the article was titled, "'Satan', 'The Devil': The natural enemy of The Original Man and God." It reads, "When God creates a creature, He gives it a *nature* that justifies hits existence when it behaves as The Creator created it to be. You don't justify your existence by being other than who you are; you justify being here by learning and being yourself. Every creature that God created, He gives it an aim and a purpose that's not written in a book. It's written in the *nature* of that creature."

So it is written in the nature of the Black man and woman to be God. If we're not acting like God or fulfilling our potential of God, that means we are doing other than self. That is why we must master self and the desires of self. There's something that we're facing that's preventing us from getting to that level.

When you are looking in the mirror, there are two things we're looking at. We are looking at God, and we're looking at an internal devil. When we look in the mirror, we have to apply what we read in James 4:7, which says, *"Submit yourselves, then, to God. Resist the devil and he will flee from you."* When we look in the mirror, we see two individuals, and who has power over us depends on how we start our day.

So we have to apply James 4:7. We have to submit ourselves then to God. We're looking in the mirror, I submit myself to you Allah, and I will resist the devil that's trying to take over me today. When you have that power, that will and that determination, you will see and feel the presence of your own internal enemy flee your body. All Praise is Due to Allah.

The challenge is when we look in the mirror, we're not recognizing there's two parts trying to take over for the day, so we are overcome by the devil within ourselves. That's why we're slouched over when we're walking. That's why we've become stagnant in our lives. That's why we find ourselves stuck. As we watch everything around us move on, we find ourselves stuck in the same place. We find ourselves unproductive, lazy and tired. We cannot master our external environment if we have yet to master our internal environment. Once we master internal, external becomes easy to handle. That's why we're so beat up by the world, because we have become weakened by the world's power over our own selves.

The decisions we make today will impact our lives 10 years from now. Many of us are still recovering from the decisions we made 10, 15, 20, 30, 40 years ago. Why do you think our marriages are not happy? Because there were decisions we made years ago that we're still reaping from. And we don't understand what's taking place, so we go into relationships with the same baggage. We want a house, but we have bad credit. Why do we have bad credit? Because we made a bad decision in the past and never corrected it. I want to start a business, but I have a felony. Well, most states won't allow you to start a business with a felony. So now I have to put a business in somebody else's name and have faith that they're going to operate the way I want them to. We want to travel the world. We want to at least get out of Arizona. We want to travel the world, but we can't get a passport because we're behind on our child support. These are realities.

And the interesting thing is, I'm never going to take away the child and put any blame on the child. But we were being foolish in our decisions, and we're unprepared for the relationship. Then, in our frustration and our disagreements, we say, "I ain't paying no child support. She's spending the money." "Well, now yo brother, we need you to fly with us with the Minister. We're going to Jamaica." "I ain't got no passport." We are being impacted by the decisions we are making, And we're not making the best of decisions. So the variables of our lives are impacting the future decisions we want to make.

Believe it or not, I don't have the best credit. I got better credit, now. But when I got married, my wife wanted the house. I looked at my credit. I recognized the bad decisions I made in college. I said, "Queen, give me two years. Allah is my witness, we will be moving into a home." She gave me my two years. I focused on my credit, and I saved some money. By Allah's will, we purchased our first home years ago. But that took me looking in that mirror and seeing I was not making the best decisions.

We want to start this job, but we can't get a driver's license because we have bad driving records, so we miss out on employment. Those decisions and incomplete work are called unfinished chapters of our lives. We're reading a book, but we don't finish the chapter, and we jump to the next chapter and we get confused in the next chapter. Why don't I understand? What's this formula? What's going on here? Well, we stopped at page three, and you jumped to page 45. That's a lot missed in that process.

Those are the things we desire to do, but when challenges come, we jump ship. We're quick to start something, but when a little bump comes our way, a little brush, we're quick to jump ship. As we're making moves, Allah is placing things in the atmosphere for purification and to have things ready for us when we get to certain checkpoints, but as Allah starts purifying us, we decide we don't like the purification process. That gets kind of hard and rough.

As Allah is purifying us, He's also putting something in the future for us to walk right into. Have you ever been struggling on something. "Oh Allah, how I'mma pay this bill?" Then next thing you know, right before it's due, somebody comes to you and says Allah told me to give this to you. Or somebody calls you and says, "I owed you some money. You came to my mind." That was us continuing through the purification process. But what happens? We get a little purification our way, a little trouble our way, and we jump ship. That becomes an additional unfinished chapter.

One of my favorite Surahs in the Holy Qur'an, Surah 13, The Thunder, verse 11, says, *"For him are (angels) guarding the consequences (of his deeds), before him and behind him, who guard him by Allah's command.* This is my favorite part of this verse. *Surely Allah changes not the condition of a people, until they change their own condition.*

Please don't get upset with me, but I'm going to add something to it. Surely Allah changes not the condition of a people until we change our attitude, until we change our will, until we change our determination, until we change our desire and until we're willing to go forward with what Allah put on our hearts. Because we'll say I want to change something, but if we don't get up out of the bed and start working on it, why would He change our condition if we haven't changed our hearts?

We have unfinished chapters in our lives. And the thing is, we must clear these chapters in order for us to move forward. The Minister introduced Dianetics to us years ago. We found we had engrams deeply rooted within ourselves. And we're making mistakes, causing problems, having issues, getting angry, having frustrations. And then as we started going through the process of Dianetics, things started coming up and we started rebuilding ourselves. You started finding out situations that you, as a child, witnessed of your parents but didn't recognize. And that situation was what caused the same type of attitude as an adult. But as we start reducing and clearing those engrams, we start freeing ourselves from the stress. Then, we start seeing ourselves able to move more freely, because we don't have that pressure, that stress, hanging on our bodies.

To my Muslim family, you might be upset after I ask this question, but I have to ask it. Do you remember when you first accepted Islam? Do you really, really remember when you first accepted Islam? When your energy was high. When we had drive, desire, dedication, work ethic, aspiration and determination. Do you remember those days? What happened? Now I don't want you to answer out loud, but I want you to think about it. What happened? We've allowed situations in our lives to determine and detour us off of the path that we seek to have.

To you the reader, do you remember the same energy, when you wanted to start a new business? When you want to go to school, start a career, when you wanted to start a family, relationships, build a community, etcetera. The next thing you know, you give up. What happened? Those are things we have to think about on a daily basis. I would love to have the same spirit I had when I accepted Islam. Imagine if we all had that same spirit right now. You would see Muhammads running all over Phoenix. People would say, "I saw Muhammad here, Muhammad there," but something has happened and we've allowed internal and external forces to keep us from what Allah has promised us.

Who do we blame? Nobody but ourselves. It's okay to acknowledge it. I'm gonna be honest with you. We've been defeated. Look in the mirror. It's okay though. We've been defeated. Think about those desires we once had. Think about where we are now as individuals and as a people. Doesn't that hurt? It's a reality check. As I always say, I'm never here to beat us up. But I have to remind us of where we are and where Allah wants us to go. That has to do with the decisions we have made and the unfinished chapters we have started. They are weighing heavy on us, and sometimes we do not even recognize them. It's like walking into a wall or finding a ceiling cap in our lives and we don't know how to get beyond. It must be cleared.

Have you noticed every time we want to do something or we get inspired, it's only a few moments later that we start to think about all of the challenges of doing what we were inspired to do? We think it's too hard. We think it's impossible. Well, let me tell you something, that's not you. That's not me. That's not us. That's the internal devil that we're facing every day. That's the internal enemy we're facing every day. We have given this little enemy too much power. That place we're at right now is where our inner demon wants us to be at. Every time we get inspired to do something, he reminds us of our place. That's why we're stagnant and we lack progress.

The Minister posed the question to us, "What will you give to see the day where there is no devil on the planet, where there is peace all over?" Until we purify and get that devil, that demon, out of us, he's gonna remain on our planet.

I want to try something. Take a deep breath. Inhale. Hold it. Exhale. Do it again, but this time when you inhale, inhale the power of Allah. Then when you exhale, exhale the demon out. You ready? 1...2...3...inhale...exhale. You feel a little better? Do it one more time. 1...2...3...inhale...exhale. It takes time because we're fighting someone we've given all our power to. It's not gonna be easy to get him out right now. He's like, oh you frontin'. We'll see how you feel when you pass McDonald's. We'll see how you feel when you say you're gonna eat at four o'clock. We'll see how you feel when you take that bow tie off in the car. It's not gonna be as easy as that, but it takes time, practice and dedication.

I want to read a prayer, and I want you to read this prayer out loud with me. It's the Refuge Prayer. I want you to take your hand and put it on your heart. Now we're not doing the National Anthem. You ain't got to take a stand. I just want you to put your hand on your heart, because I want you to feel the sincerity of your heartbeat as we read this prayer. Now, if you're not comfortable saying Allah, that's perfectly fine. You can say God in the place of Allah. You can read in silence or you can read out loud, but I want you to feel yourself when you actually read it.

"Oh Allah, I seek Thy refuge from anxiety and grief. And I seek Thy refuge from lack of strength and laziness. And I seek Thy refuge from cowardice and niggardliness. And I seek Thy refuge from being overpowered by debt and the oppression of men. Oh Allah, suffice Thou me with what is lawful to keep me away from what is prohibited. And with Thy grace, make me free of want of what is beside Thee."

Take your hand from your heart. Now put it back on your heart. How is your heartbeat? Is it calmer? That's the prayer we should say when we're looking in the mirror fighting, determining who has power for that day. If we say just this prayer alone, look at how Allah will take us into the day. All of the trials and tribulations that we're facing will be moved aside, and we will be given greater strength. Allah will make all of the shortcomings that are sitting on our shoulders easy to carry. All we have to do is seek refuge in the Originator of the heavens in earth. All Praise is Due to Allah.

The Honorable Minister Louis Farrakhan said on Twitter, "Regardless of the depth of darkness of a situation, light is always present in the darkness. But when you are hopeless and filled with despair over your circumstance, you cannot find the light."

When we're having a bad day, go to that mirror. Look yourself in the eyes. Read that prayer and watch how Allah will give you light in this dark hour. Oh Allah.

He also says that if you will come back to God and develop again a true faith in God, you would know that there is nothing that you desire of good that you cannot achieve.

We are facing variables in our lives right now, and every day we must fight that internal enemy. If we're fighting that internal enemy, there are three fears we must face to do it: the fear of failure, the fear of the unknown and the fear of success. Our inner weaknesses control us by these three fears.

The fear of failure. What if my goals and dreams don't work out? We're afraid to even go forward, because we're afraid that we're going to fail. What are people going to say about me if I don't do good?

One of the best lines in Jay-Z's 444 album is, "A loss is not a loss, but a loss is a lesson." When you play in a sport and you play for a team, it hurts to take an L. But when you went back to practice, you work harder to get that W. In life, we're going to take losses. We're going to go down to the bottom. But once we hit rock bottom, we don't dwell on the bottom, but we fight our way back up! Allah-u-Akbar!

The fear of the unknown. We may fear the unknown, but it's a poor success strategy. It is good to be prepared and in the right place mentally and physically to help face uncertainties. We go, "Wow, I'm stepping out on faith. I'm gonna quit my job. I'm stepping out on faith." Okay, All Praise is Due to Allah, but what's your success strategy? And then what happens? We fail, and we pick up two fears in the process. Now because we failed, we have the fear of the unknown. Now we have two out of three holding us down.

Everything we do as we develop and grow has an uncertainty factor to it. As a child coming out the womb of your mother, you see people talking, and you don't know how to talk yet. That's an uncertainty, but you start studying, "How are they moving their mouths? How are the sounds coming out?" And then next thing you know, you say, "Da-da." I know the women hate that part, because those are the first words you hear.

Then, you don't know how to walk, or crawl, but you see movement happening from older individuals, and you study how they're doing it. So you see a child trying to take steps with weak legs. The legs are weak, but the more movement and fighting and pushing forward the child does, the more strength the legs gain. The next you know, the child is walking. And as a parent, that's the biggest joy on your face. "Oh my God! Oh my God! My baby is walking!" You start recording and sending pictures.

We go through the same principles as adults, but when we can't walk, we give up. When we can't talk, we give up. When we don't want to fight we give up. Who are we fighting for? I asked the question earlier: Who are we and whose are we? If we're Almighty God Allah's, He's going to send us trials. You think it was easy to produce Himself out of triple darkness? You think it was easy to sit in the womb of your mother and have to wait for the day when you have your own life? She's at the door of death for you to have life. She survives so that we can move on. Our life has nothing but uncertainties in it. If we buckle every time an uncertain situation comes to us, we might as well stay in our room and find somebody to pay the bills until that uncertain time when they cut off the electricity.

Then we have what's called the fear of success. Really? People fear success? That sounds weird, right? But believe it or not, many of us fear success. We find that most people are more influenced than they realize by what others think. The idea that someone might criticize or reject them stops many people in their tracks. "Oh man, I got this great idea." "Aw, brother, it ain't gonna work." "Sister I think we should come together." "Aw, that ain't gon' work." We allow someone else's fear to overtake our desire. That shows a weakness in self. We're afraid of being on top of the world. Allah wants us to be on top of the world. He wants to give us His kingdom. We're afraid to have His kingdom, because we're afraid of what people might think of us. We're afraid to be confident in public, because we're afraid people might think where arrogant. We're afraid to speak our voices because we're afraid they might think we're argumentative. But Allah gave that to us.

Steel sharpens steel. So that person who might be fearful might see hope when they see you and I do it. They might be afraid to do something, but then they saw you and I do it. Let me give this little example. One of my brothers was talking to me the other day, and he was like, "Brother Hannibal, you remember when you sent me that picture of animation you were doing of the Minister when you was practicing?" I said, "Yes sir." He said, "Brother, I was a little upset." "Why were you upset?" "Because that's something I've been wanting to do for the last two years and I didn't know how to. Then I saw what you sent to me ... now I want to come to you and figure out what you are doing because I have ideas on how I want to fulfill it."

You and I never know who is watching us. We don't know. And the decisions we make don't just impact us individually. It impacts the collective. When we make a positive move, we give a young child hope. When we make a positive move, we give our elders hope. When we say "I'm done. I give up," we prove the wrong point.

The fear of success. In order to be successful, we must stop overwhelming ourselves with big goals. We're overwhelmed by big goals. It seems unrealistic. And sometimes it can be. I want to tackle the world. Alright, Brother, that's cool. How you gonna do it? What we must do is decide on what that big goal is and create small checkpoint goals to achieve it. If we set a big goal but we don't have an action plan in place, it's just a dream. Many of us are dreamers. We have to challenge each other by doing it. What do I mean by that?

We have an enemy we have given so much power to that makes us feel weaker than we are. If we challenge him, piece by piece, with small goals, we will find how weak the enemy really is. We don't have to attack with big goals. We attack with little goals. So if the purification process for self is I want to get to one meal a day or I want to get to one meal every other day, I don't just say I'm fasting tomorrow. Because if I fail at it, I'm upset with self. But if I'm eating five meals a day, I cut it to four. Then I say you know what, three days later I want to cut it to three. Then I cut it to two. Then I cut it to one. Next thing you know, you see a week later, two weeks later, you're down to one meal. It became easier, and the greatest part about it is, it builds confidence.

Many of us lack confidence. We all have insecurities, but we're beat up so much that it's hard for us to face them. So we take them piece-by-piece. For example, I found myself being a dreamer. I found myself saying I want to do this, I want to do that, and then months later, I realized I didn't do anything. Towards the end of last year, I said, I'm gonna challenge myself to complete something. I was trying to figure out what it was going to be. I was raising my Saviours' Day Gift last year, and I was utilizing a photo magazine. That was my first challenge.

I said, I'm going to start this process of gathering the pictures. I'm gonna start this process of trying to find the content. I'm gonna start this process of laying it out. And I had to start with one picture, then two pictures. Then as it started to build, I was like, oh, man, this is starting to look good. Now, once you acknowledge how good it looks, what does that bring to you? Confidence. So that insecurity I had of completing it started slowly going away. The next thing I know, I look up. We're towards the end of December. I got a photo magazine of the Honorable Minister Louis Farrakhan. Now, that's exciting to me, because I wanted to complete something. And from that photo magazine, it went from just a present to give to the Minister to being able to raise my Saviours' Day Gift of $1300 dollars by giving away free magazines. Allah-u-Akbar!

I wanted to travel abroad. I've traveled all through the United States, so the abroad part was the harder part. For most people who've never traveled before, never flown before, the first part is getting on the plane. Then once we see we landed safely, okay, it's not as bad as I thought it was. And then once we go to a further state where you're on a plane longer than 45 minutes going to LA, we decided to go to Chicago. Oh, this actually ain't that bad. Then the Minister goes to Atlanta. Oh, that's a little bit further. We start building momentum. Well, I felt I was at a ceiling cap on my flying. I wanted to learn more. I wanted to get a broader horizon. So I decided, let's go to Dubai. Now my wife and I, our goal is to travel international at least one time a year. That's me challenging myself to go further than the norm of Brother Hannibal.

I did the same thing with school. I found out I had an unfinished chapter: college. I started college, was doing good, ran into some circumstances, and then I dropped out. Then I started recognizing this year, I have a whole bunch of unfinished things. I need to go close these chapters off. So I decided to go back to school. Me personally, I'm upset with my grades. I ended with two B's and an A. For me, that's unacceptable, because I knew I could have gotten straight A's. But I also know I had circumstances and setbacks in the process, like my grandmother, but I pushed to try to get an A out of every class. That was my challenge. My goal is to get to a master's degree in engineering, but I can't get that if I don't finish the first checkpoint, which is a bachelor's. So I'm taking it step by step.

Let me give you another one. My wife would laugh and say you don't study enough. I'm like queen, I'm always studying. Then I found out that I wasn't reading enough. I might read, but I wasn't completing my books. So what I decided to do was grab a little small book like The Flag of Islam, The Meaning of FOI, The Constitution. Let me do one of these little 10, 12, 15 20 page books. Let me grab my little daughter's book. Let me try a children's book. It's funny, but the goal was completion. That's the goal at the end of the day, completion.

Once I finished then I'm like, alright. Cool. You building up momentum. Then you go from that to like a 40-page book. Then you find yourself in "Is It Possible," a 107-page book. Then you're at 300 pages, 500. Next thing you know, you're coming up on Ramadan and many of us struggle to finish our Holy Quran reading. But I had to build up the momentum and get the discipline to prepare myself for it.

These are small achievements. The enemy's like, aw brother, you don't have to do all that reading. You ain't got time for that. You busy. The excuses were kicking in, so I had to have a strategic approach. Let me start with something small to catch myself off guard. Let me keep a book in the car so I can just grab it. Let me put one in my backpack so when I get bored, I can go in my backpack and just pull something out. It challenged me to do better, and those small achievements allowed me to start beating back up on an internal devil that lives in me that I'm trying to conquer. So I have some questions for you. I gotta ask some questions.

Question number one: What drives you?

Number two: What motivates you?

Let's try number three. What inspires you? We have to think about what motivates us, what inspires us and what drives us.

But I want to flip those questions, now. And I want you to really think hard on these answers. What are you driving? And I'm not talking about a car. What are you driving? How much energy are you willing to put in the drive to success? What are you motivating? I mentioned there are people who are watching every move that you make who may not say nothing to you. But who are you motivating? And what are you inspiring? Until we can ask the simple questions, we will remain stuck and stagnant.

What do you do when you first wake up in the morning? If your answer is pray, that's good, because everyone doesn't do that. That's not everyone's routine. Everyone doesn't wake up and start reading in the morning or go through the scriptures or drink a glass of water to get the organs moving. Everyone doesn't have the same setup. Some people's routine is to wake up and look at their Facebook, Twitter or Instagram before they go make prayer, before they go get some water; right after the alarm goes off, "Who hit me up?" Waking up to social media or coming home and having a Netflix and chill type at night is not going to produce the results we're trying to achieve in life.

Now I'm not saying you can't check your social medias. I'm not saying not to have a Netflix and chill type of night. There's nothing wrong with that. I'm just saying it can become a distraction, if we say we have desired goals. Most successful people do not find themselves on social media all day, unless it's part of your work to be on social media because you're driving something. You're inspiring something. You're motivating something. Many of us go onto social media and we get caught up in a daze. It becomes an illusion.

We wake up. "I have this idea but hold on. I got 15 notifications. Let me check them out." And you go from your notifications to reading to watching videos to going down your timeline to sister said what to brother said who? Oh my God, look at this ratchedness. Look at this Worldstar. And next thing you know, three hours went down the drain.

There has been no progress on that desire we had to fulfill and change the variables of our unfinished chapters in life.

The question becomes, what are we doing more of? Are we trying to build ourselves up, or are we concerned with what everyone else is saying and doing? If I asked you a question about your life or aspirations and your response is mediocre but you know everything going on with Love & Hip Hop, Basketball Wives, Real Housewives of Atlanta, Insecure or a sports game, there's a problem here.

"Brother, How you doing?" "I'm alright." "What are your goals in life?" "Ehh." "You catch the game last night?" "Oh, bro! Did you see Steph Curry hit him with that three?"

It shows. It shows in our energy. We're putting our energy in the wrong places, and then we get upset when we don't have the results. I'm not saying not to watch this stuff. I'm not saying not to go on social media. Because you will watch whatever you desire to watch and do whatever you choose to do, but I want you to know this. There's only 24 hours in a day. And eight to 14 of those hours, we deal with work. That's including drive time and preparing to get to work. So we already lost more than half of the day giving it to someone else. By the time we get home, all we want to do is rest and have leisure time. When do we actually finish the chapters?

We're not going to close this 10, 20, 30 plus year gap we've made through our life if we're not trying to look in the mirror to face it.

I was in banking for nearly 10 years. And when I would talk to someone about a credit card, a loan, anything with credit, that was like a curse word. "No. No. No. I'm good. Don't talk to me about that." Whoa, bro good man, you alright? We straight? Don't swing on me. In that process, I found out that many people are afraid of their credit. When I say, "Alright, cool. When was last time we looked your credit score?" the response is, "I don't know." Then you don't know if you can buy a house. You don't know if you qualify for this.

The thing is, we're afraid to look at the decisions we've made, because if we look at them, we're brought back to reality. And once we come back to reality, we have to now face it. So either you will act like the person who rolls their window up when you try to say, "Final Call?" and the person who acts like they don't see you. Or you try to lock the door.

It's hard to face the reality, but as we work through the challenges of it, it becomes easier to face. Next thing you know, you've completed a chapter, which increases your strength and the confidence. But if we don't, then we're committing acts of insanity. Many of us are insane. Be honest with yourself. We're working and working trying to figure out what's going wrong but we continue to make the same mistakes. Yet, we're expecting over and over and over to have different results. That's insanity, because we won't step back and say, "Hold up. Every time I make this left here, it takes me to a dead end. Maybe I should go right next time. Maybe I should go straight next time. Well, actually, why is there a dead end here in the first place?" Now I'm in a daze focused on the dead end and forgot what my purpose was. I had an appointment I had to get to.

There's a beautiful book called Closing the Gap, Interviews of the Heart, Mind and Soul of the Honorable Minister Louis Farrakhan. It was written by Bro. Jabril Muhammad and is comprised of interviews between him and the Honorable Minister Louis Farrakhan. On page 409, the Honorable Minister Louis Farrakhan says, "Whenever a scientist desires to produce something, he has to look for the right material. There is no creative act that does not involve some form of material. Sometimes you try one piece of metal and it doesn't work. You try again. But you're always looking for the right material to produce the right results. That's not in the mind of the material. It is the mind of the creator, or the person that has an idea in mind, for the material. The material does not matter until the idea of the carrier wants to use the material for a purpose."

Mind over matter. As we set in our mind, "This is what I desire to do. This is what I'm going to do," the next thing we must create is what's called work ethic. We have to build up our work ethic. It's one thing to have this great, beautiful vision board that many of us will start making towards the end of the year. "This is what I want to achieve for 2018." We go find magazines. We start cutting stuff up. We put planes on it. But it means nothing if we don't have a plan of action to fulfill what's on the board. It means nothing if we do not plan out how we want to fulfill it. We're all students in the classroom of life, so we have to figure out, how am I going to stay studious to fulfill what the teacher has in front of me. Because he gives us the free will to function how we see fit.

In the Supreme Wisdom's Original Rules of Instructions to the Laborers Point No. 2, it says something simple like this: "The student could practice his or her labor while under study if they were sincere." There's no magic trick. It's nothing major to it. It's just being sincere, studying what works, studying the mistakes we have made in our lives, and then working on them. If you ever had a bad relationship or you were not in communication with your children, the first conversation is hard. It's challenging. You don't know the uncertainty of what's coming from it. But the more and more you two open up and get to work through the problems, you will see it becomes easier, and you will see that person who said they hate you. They will start welcoming you into their lives. It's a challenge, but the success or failure at results depends on how we take on the challenge.

There's a position awaiting us, but we must organize and qualify ourselves to fulfill the position. I want to introduce us to a time management organizational method. It's called SMART. The S represents specific/specify, the M represents measurable, the A represents attainable/achievable, the R represents realistic/relevant and the T represents timing. Now if you're doing a mathematical equation, sometimes you have to put it certain ways.

I like to work the S and T together first. So when you read it, it says, do you know exactly what you want to accomplish with all the details? Goals must be well-defined. They must be clear and simple. The M: Can you quantify your progress so you can track it? How will you know when you reach your goals? This is where we fall apart at. We fall apart at the M. We specify, "I want to do this," but how do we measure our results? This is where we fall apart in things we decide we want to do. The A, attainable. Is your goal a challenge but still possible to achieve? Goals must be achievable. The best goals require you to stretch a bit to achieve them, but they are not impossible to achieve. R, realistic. Is your goal realistic and within reach? Are you willing to commit to your goal? And in timing, does your goal have a deadline? Every goal has a deadline. Goals must have a clearly defined timeframe, including a starting date and a target date. If you don't have a time limit, then there is a no urgency. There's the problem. There is no urgency to start taking action towards achieving your goals.

Let's go through an example of someone wanting a bachelor's degree. It's November and the person has until May. The person is taking five classes and has 175 credits and needs 190 in order to graduate.

The S, the specific goal, is obtaining the degree. I want to go to the T next, before we measure. How much time should be committed to accomplishing that goal? There's about six months between November and May. So we specify a bachelor's degree. Six months. Now, let's see if it's measurable. The person needs 15 more credit hours. Now we're measuring it. Is that possible? Why is that possible? Because there's more than enough to at least go this year, right? Full-time is usually 12 credit hours. Each class is usually three credit hours. Five classes would be enough to graduate. So we specified. We got the timeframe. We saw that it's measurable. Is it achievable? Yes. Now the question becomes, is it realistic? Depends on the commitment to it, right? It also depends on if all five classes are passed.

These are things we have to look at when we're laying out our day-to-day life and our goals that we're trying to achieve. We even take the same method to go back to the same unfinished chapters of life. I made a mistake. What was the mistake? Doesn't matter how far back it was, I want to fix the mistake. How much time? Do I have to fix it? Can I measure? Is it possible? Is it attainable? And is it realistic with whoever or whatever I need to do to correct it? Does that make sense?

We have to put things in place, methods in place, that's going to make it easier for us to achieve our life goals. When the Minister comes to us and he tells us brothers, sisters, you can do it. It's not realistic. He's putting the inspiration in us to actually go find a way to achieve it. He says brother and sister, I want you to accomplish this. He didn't put a timeframe on it. It's on us to put the timeframe on it and move forward with it. He specified for us what he wanted. We set up the timeframe, and we see if it's attainable, if it's realistic in that timeframe. And can we measure our result? So halfway through the semester, if the person is not doing good in their grades, will they still graduate? They may have to take a step back and say, "Okay, hold up, this ain't working. I may have to drop this class before it hits me. Take these four finished and then I'll just wrap it up over the summer." It doesn't mean they can't finish the goal. They were just off on the measurement for the method. That simple.

Last but not least, we have to take action towards our goals. Results won't magically happen just because we say we want them and just because we ran them down. Even if we come up with fantastic smart methods, we still must put them into effect.

I have a question for you. Did you just learn something? Was it hard to learn? Was it boring? Was it fun? Was it easy to do? The reason why I asked was it fun is because learning is supposed to be fun, and if learning is not fun, you're not going to learn because you're bored of it before you get into it. In Closing the Gap, Brother Jabril asked the Minister a question about fun and the meaning of fun and the Minister went into how fun is learning something new. And he gave the example when you see children going on exploring and learning things about themselves and the world, they're having fun as children by themselves. They're having fun because they're learning new things about themselves, and they're accomplishing stuff. We as adults can have fun if we find things that are fun that we're learning to do. The first time we stepped foot into the Nation and we were going to Study Group, we had fun. Why? Because we were learning more about ourselves. Every single day, we should have fun learning more about ourselves. We may have challenges in that process, but it should be fun, because we learned something. And as we take what we learn, we duplicate it and we continue to move on with that progress.

We must set the large goals that we want to achieve. We said what you could considerably think of as a large goal. A person wants to graduate with their bachelor's. But we set in place smaller, achievable goals to get there. We identified what they would need in order to do that. I need five classes. That doesn't seem heavy, because they're further along. But if we went from the aspect of when they first started school, it would be the same method. How many classes will they need to graduate in four years?

What do I need to start my business? How much time do I need to do it? When do I need to reconcile my relationship with my children? What do I need to do to amend the relationship I have with my ex? There's a process that goes into that, which is the Eight Steps of Atonement, but we have to put methods into that.

One of the first variables of life that I spoke of is understanding who and whose you are. The second one I spoke of is identifying that devil within and mastering self. The third one is the everyday fight of mastering self and the environment we live in. The fourth one is to use the small achievements to conquer the large goals.

Allah is with us. We really made it out, if we think about it, because we're alive today. And there's many of us that did not make it through 2017. But Allah got us to here.

I'm telling you this: never give up. Never give up, no matter how hard it gets, no matter what challenges we run into in life. Take a step back. Revisit the method, the steps we're taking, but never give up.

I pray to Allah that our efforts and our progress individually and collectively will increase. And I also pray to Allah, that we go out stronger today than when we first opened this book. I want you always to remember that the Minister said this: It is a gift from Allah that comes when we submit ourselves to do His will and not our will. When we're at peace with Allah, who is the Sovereign Lord and Creator, then you can make peace with others. And my last quote is from the Honorable Elijah Muhammad: Brothers and sisters, work cheerfully, and fear not.

5

Respect For Life In The Spirit Of God's Word

"We cannot run from being tried. The Holy Qur'an teaches us that Allah is going to try us with something of fear, hunger, loss of property, loss of life and diminution of fruit, but give good news to those who are patient and steadfast under trial."

The Honorable Minister Louis Farrakhan

The chapter, "Respect for Life in the Spirit of God's Word" is a very important chapter to me. Pay close attention to what is revealed in this chapter.

Respect for Life: Respect for the existence of life granted to you and I; respect for the body that houses God.

The spirit of God: The spirit of God that heals the body and the life we are seeking to live.

Allah gave His only begotten Son. That Son is here in our midst, today. He is willing to give his life for our salvation. Are you and I willing to give ourselves to Almighty God Allah and to submit to His Will? Are we willing to respect the life Allah has given us and grow into the spirit of God? Are we willing to give up the ways of this world that God can fill us up with Him?

I'm not empty. I'm so thankful right now. I'm not even grieving. I don't want to say it's crazy, because it's not. But I'm not grieving. I'm not gonna say I haven't grieved, but it was so short.

There's so much that has happened over that weekend span, and there's a lot that you're gonna get in the Janazah, but I want to communicate with you for a moment.

I have a newfound respect for the phrase "rest in peace." As my family and I looked at our father, and trust me I'm staying on the subject, as we looked at him, he was so peaceful.

I can bear witness as a parent; we've all been through this situation, where you're laying down in the bed. You're comfortable, and your spouse or your children, they're getting ready to go somewhere, and they ask you, "Do you want to come?" And you're like, "Nah. Nah. Nah. Y'all got that. Imma go 'head and lay down here for a moment."

That was the spirit in that room. My sister and I spoke on that, because it was very interesting when you do a comparison from mother to father. Allah has been putting it on us over these last couple of years. There was a certain fight. There was a certain fight you could see in my mother, but in my father, not that there wasn't a fight. It was more of, "I've watched you all handle all obstacles that came your way and look at how Allah made you successors. I have confidence in you that you can fulfill anything else!" That was the spirit that was happening that weekend.

I'm thankful to Allah for my father. Brother Rahman made a statement that a gladiator fights, but he fights for a prize, while a warrior, he fights for a cause. Well, my father has the name of a warrior! So, when I look at the respect for life that Allah has given us, we have work to do, family! To be able to see your father on those last hours and days, and to be able to read off and to recite off to him the "I Am a Soldier" speech from Brother Rahman, to be able to give him words of encouragement, to be able to talk to your father and repent for any wrongs you may have done by him and to ask Allah that He will open up your breast that you can carry on the remaining of his burden, give me his mission, give me his assignment, I tell you family, my father's not dead! When you see me, you see my father!

Allah-u-Akbar! I'm not empty. What I see right now, oh, my God! It's like a child watching their parents play cards, and you come and sneak up under their arm, and they're showing you their deck. They're showing you their hand, and they're telling you, watch this right here. I can feel Allah covering me.

On September 23, I contacted my brother, Hilario, and I asked him a question. Brother, why haven't you sent the update to the Believers? We wanted to make sure you had actual facts because that's not what was happening that day. We were receiving phone calls and text messages saying, "Sorry for your loss," but my father was still alive.

My brother told me, "Brother, the internet is down. There's a tornado warning in Phoenix!" Now, for all of my lifetime, I've never heard of a tornado warning in Arizona. I'm telling you the Minister said to watch the weather! We got unusual weather coming through the city right now, as Allah, I tell you, He is cleansing the city right now. There is sooo much that's about to happen.

Respect for life, in the spirit of God's word. We are in an hour where unity in the house is more important than anything.

The Minister said in Grand Rapids this week: "I have come tonight to let you know the end has come!"

I'm telling you, I'm in the ring. I'm not trying to box with God, but God's about to whip me, right now. Because He's been throwing 'em, and they ain't been jabs. They feel like uppercuts with Mike Tyson in this piece. But He's purifying us for something that's grand. I can't tell you what it is, but I can feel it in my body! God is so present today! Brothers and Sisters, He has been so patient and merciful with us.

We are starting to reap the beginning of the chastisement if we do not pay attention. The Minister mentioned as the storms were going through the Bahamas, he made a prayer to Allah. He didn't ask why, but he was asking for mercy on them. And Allah slowed it down for a moment, like, "Huh!? Brother! Have I not been merciful all this time!? Have I not been patient all this time!? Have I not given you 40 years beyond your Father as of this time!?"

I will remove you in a few, and the chastisement will be heavy and severe if we do not clean up! Look at the weather!

The Minister said this is the day of the manifestation of losses. We have to pay today for every offense we do for the knowledge that has come to us! The Chastisement of God has already begun.

He said God wants to save us, but we don't want to be saved. We glorify this world! We could say we don't, but I can guarantee by the end of the day, there's going to be something we're going to be doing that we should not be doing. You are probably doing something right now. This world is nothing but an illusion. This world is nothing but the matrix. I know we see the woman in the red dress. Yeah. I know you don't want to hear that. I know we love the taste of that fake steak out there. Now, let's bring that to right now terms. Fake steak. GMO. I'll let that sit for a moment.

We're being fed fake food now. What were they talking about? What was Allah showing them in that movie "The Matrix"?

The Minister said each of us has a devil walking with us day and night! He says, Satan came in with God, at the beginning. We thought he came later on. What is he showing us? He said the devil came in the origin of God. That's why he (devil) comes after truth. He (devil) knows that truth supersedes everything, so he waits 'til after you get the truth. Then he comes and sprinkles a little bit of falsehood with it. He (devil) is that whisper in your ear, looking for an opportunity. He (devil) is a snake enticing us. If you really think about it, every time we get motivated, inspired and we're determined to do something better with our lives, there's always a voice that says, "Don't do that. You can't do that. Don't waste your time. They ain't gon' buy it. Nobody's gonna care! They don't love you."

All the different things we hear, that is the devil in us trying to keep us from perfection! Because of us answering that phone call, we have merged God and Satan together, where now, we get confused about who's the one calling upon us; causing confusion of what is right and what is wrong.

We have become, look at today. We're in time where we have become very sensitive to wrong, but disrespectful to what is right. We must separate Satan from God by killing off the whisper, as it's looking for a way out of us. When we hear that voice, we tell it to sit down. Shut up, and move to the back! And we lock it up! We move out on the faith that we initially had when we got up off that prayer rug, and we stay determined to move forward, no matter what obstacles come our way, because we know Allah would not give us anything we could not bear!

Allah-u-Akbar!

The Minister said, "This is the time of the Visitation, Visitation of the Son of Man." Well, I tell you believers, family, we cannot love Jesus and not be pregnant with the spirit of God. Imma say that again. We cannot love Jesus and not be pregnant with the spirit of God! If we say we love Jesus but God ain't speaking out of us, we loving somebody else.

The Minister said, "If you really get acquainted with Jesus, He really loves us, and wants to heal us from being affected from the living amongst strange people, who have affected us with their freakish ways."

He said, "You're ducking and dodging God." We out here playing dodge ball, trying to avoid the trials God is trying to give us, while He has you and I figured out!

We owe Allah our life. He is the One Who gave us life, but we dodge. We duck. We see Him. We turn around and take off running. We hide behind the sycamore tree, trying to avoid what it is Allah wants us to become; afraid to get in the gym and hit those spiritual weights that will allow us to grow into oneness with God!

We are trying to avoid it, when we have to walk through the fire! We have to get up! We have to be willing to take on that challenge, because if we don't, my brother used to pose a question: How will you be remembered when you're gone?

Oh Allah! Almighty God Allah is extending out His Hand, awaiting you and I's return home. He has so much mercy and grace for us that He allows us to continue on in this world, making mistakes with the free will, and He'll just give us a little nudge to bring us back.

It's like if you ever went bowling before, I'm pretty good at it. But if you have children, they might put the bumpers up. And as you roll the ball, it bounces off the bumpers, going back and forth 'til it hits the pins. Well, Allah gives us the free will, but He also has barriers that we must stay within. As we get closer to those barriers, He knocks us back towards the center. It's up to us to balance back out our lives so that we can get back on that straight path.

Oh, Allah! It is time that we get ourselves right with God. The calamities will increase. I'm serious. They will increase. We are at the beginning of the chastisement.

There will be so many calamities, that you and I will become numb to death. We will become numb because we won't have time to grieve. It will be like rapid-fire as it happens. If you ever rode on a roller coaster, it takes time to get to that top, and you hear and feel it jerk, jerk, jerk, jerk, but as it comes over, it speeds up.

"The respect for life in the spirit of God's words." This is only a body. This has a timeline to it. We are being given a great opportunity for a little piece of time, a little piece of God's time. That's not a lot. And then after that little bit of time is over, we go back into an infinite of time, until Allah decides He wants to use us again.

To my beloved families of the mosque and of the church, we're getting old. I know I'm only 35. Imma count myself in this. I know you don't want to hear that, but we're getting old, physically. We're becoming toothless. You ain't gotta show me that you got all your teeth, though. We're losing hair and going bald, but I have a question for you. Where are the young people?

Where are the young people? They don't come to the mosque or the church. There's a disconnect. We have to reconnect that.

There's a disconnect between the young and the old. It's not new. We dealt with it through slavery, but the Devil was still in us controlling that part that's keeping us disconnected from the old and the new.

The Minister said to us one time, paraphrasing, young people bring a new spirit. Can't you feel the spirit of the youth when you encounter them? Even in a more, empty environment, they're still teaching what Allah placed on their hearts. The Minister also said, young people bring new life. Young people are the transfusion of new blood.

I love my brother Wahid. Brother Abdul Wahid would say, I just want to be around the young people. They keep me young. A lot of the disconnect is, I want to let you know I'm an authority figure, or I'm a parent, and I want you to know you're a child. As a child, I want to let you know you don't know anything, and children haven't experienced anything yet.

Ahh. I must have pissed some people off just now. It's alright. It's alright. But we have to reconnect that relationship between adult and child, between seasoned and youth. We have to be OGs to them, and I ain't talking about original gangstas. We gotta be some original Gods for these young men and women, showing them the proper way, with the understanding that they got us in them. What do I mean by that? If you are a stubborn child when you were growing up, guess what? Your children are stubborn, too.

If you had to bump your head when you were growing up, guess what? Your children gotta bump their heads, too. I watch it with my daughters. But it's one of those things that if you know they're going to bump their head, can we soften it up with some cushion? You have to go on and live your life, but allow me to guide it from afar. My hand is still in the mix, there, but you just don't know it. And when it comprehends from that child as I did, you will pick up the phone and say, "Mom! Dad! I get it! I understand. Thank you! I thought you just didn't like me. I thought you were just upset and didn't want me to have fun, but now I get it!"

I remember my brother Ronald telling me one day, you don't realize how good you got it. And I'm complaining, because his curfew was like 2-3 o'clock and mine was 1! I'm like brother what you mean I don't get it? I'm trying to stay out late with you all. But I had to come into an understanding. It took years later. My family was still bearing the burden of the loss of my older brother. And once that clicked, I understood why they were overprotective of me! "I ain't losing another son." I couldn't get my mother to stop calling me on the way to L.A. "Mom! I'm on the way. Leave me alone!" She was concerned. It kicked in. I spoke to a brother that spoke so highly of my father. My father never met him in person. But when I was in Houston, my father called him, because I had a situation that took place. And he said I haven't been able to get in contact with the officials. No one has been able to help me, but my son is in your city, brother. Can I count on you to check in on him, or do I have to come myself? A soldier!

It's in a parent's being. It's in you to protect your child, but we have to teach the child why they're being protected and what they're being protected from. We have to teach them. We have to teach the child how to maneuver through the traps of the world. We can't keep them locked up in the homes, because when they finally come to the world, the world becomes overly enticing to them, and then we lose them because it doesn't seem as bad as parents said it was. Oh Allah!

A nation cannot rise without the plans of young people being at the forefront. A nation cannot rise without young people being around to help get us there. Things age. What's in the news now? What's happening now, and how can I take what I had in my time and incorporate it in the now, so that you don't get caught up in the traps?

To my Christians and Muslim family, the Minister said stop talking Jesus and start living Jesus. He said it is not easy to be a disciple of Jesus, but we have to endure to the end. He said Jesus is more than a song. He is more than preaching a sermon. He wants us to become Him. Wow!

We think so little of ourselves. Let's just take that little that we think of ourselves and remove it, just for a moment. Hopefully, I can lock it away long enough. And imagine God using you, that He can grow you and me up into the oneness of Jesus and then from the oneness of Jesus, into the oneness of God. How does that make you feel inside, to be able to grow into that if we're willing to accept Him?

And then the Minister said, "You don't hear me." He said, "Let this mind be in you, the same that has been in Christ, Jesus." He is offering you the mind of God. We are refusing to take it.

When that chastisement actually starts to hit, it starts to make more sense. I tell you, this is from the Minister, as I prepare to close out. He says, "I tell you, let Him, have you. Let Him have all of you." Then he says, "Put on the whole armor of God. Get your helmet of salvation. Get your sword of spirit. Your shield of righteousness. Your feet covered with the Gospel."

Respect for life in the spirit of God's word. Let's put on the whole armor of God. Let's get up today. Let' submit to His Will today. Whatever negativity, whatever that whisper is that tries to give you doubt, push it to the back. Shut it down. Kick it out the mind, just like we do during fasting when we get hungry. We're not really hungry. That's that same Devil trying to get us to fall off course. So, let's put on the armor of God, let's respect the life that Allah has given us, and let's respect our body, that we will be victorious at the end.

6

Pain and Power

"You cannot go to new levels of consciousness, new levels of awareness, new levels of power and development without pain."

The Honorable Minister Louis Farrakhan

If it be the will of Allah, we will be going into the chapter entitled, "Pain and Power."

We thank the Originator for setting into motion the universe with the thought behind it to gain into it, perfection. He wanted perfection of Himself. People will argue that God is already perfect. Of course He is. Whatever stage of development He is at, He is perfect. He is present now to perfect.

There will be soldiers who create a perfect Kingdom of perfect peace with unlimited progress. We thank Him for seeing something in us.

There is no way we could have seen it in ourselves. His sight and His love were so perfect that He chose us. You didn't hear me. He chose us to make us the heirs of the Kingdom and to make us the heirs of Himself—a Nation of Gods.

We are on a continued journey, and this journey that we are on is a journey of continued demand. What will you give? And sometimes we may be overcome by duty. I can't do that. I don't have time. You may not even have anything to give from your pockets right now. But that is not what God is asking for. He is asking and demanding of us to perfect ourselves. The perfection of ourselves is the perfection of God Himself.

Hidden deep in our DNA is the original man; deep in our DNA, the Original God Himself. That's why when we hear in the scriptures that He made us in His image and likeness, because deep in us is Him. He's trying to bring it out of us, but it takes pain to do it.

The challenge is, we're struggling right now. We're struggling bad.

We're really going through some serious pain in our lives right now. And if you pay attention to my words, I said, deep in our DNA. Why did I have to say deep in our DNA? Because present in our DNA is pain! Our current condition in life is pain.

Lots of pain, a whole lot of pain we're going through right now. The Black man and woman, we've been through so much pain since we've been in this country they call America, and there's a slogan that says, "Make America great again."

When has America ever been great for us?

As individuals, some of us have achieved certain levels of success, but as a people, when has it ever been great for us? The pain of our parents, our grandparents, our ancestors and forefathers are in our present DNA. Their pain has become our pain. And when we get up and we're going through our day to day life, we're working out their pain that is deep-rooted in us. Not only are we going through their pain, we have been given the mindset of our former slave masters. We work out of the pain of our families, but we think like our open enemy. That's called an oxymoron. An oxymoron is when two terms or ideas that seem opposite are paired together.

Out of that mindset, we mistreat one another, and that mistreatment creates more pain.

There was a video of a guy on the subway, and he was mistreating one of our elders. Are you kidding me? Today, the NYPD Chief of Detectives said the search is on for this suspect. Subway riders captured the moment he kicked a 78-year-old woman in the face over and over. It was Sunday, March 10, at three in the morning, the 230 Eighth Street Station on the two and five lines in the Bronx. Police say as the train pulled in, a man approached the woman and attacked. She raises her arm trying to block the blows.

Wait in New York? Yeah, at the subway station.

I can't even imagine. I have grandmothers. I respect women. I was raised by women. On the video, you hear the voices of several riders and even see another passenger recording. But no one steps in to help. The man is able to get away right after the attack. Do you think there's anything that other people can do in a situation like that?

I would have challenged him. Trust me. I'm an ex-military man, and I would have confronted him. I would have stopped it.

I want you to understand that you and I are a cry and a yearning from our parents. You and I are a cry and a yearning from our grandparents, our ancestors and our forefathers, so how do you think they feel seeing this?

This hurts. I hate seeing this.

And the sad part is, we're so frozen. We're so made up in Satan's world that it has frozen our potential, and we are actually moving backward right now.

We're not thinking straight.

We are actually not in the right mind right now.

That bothers me, because I'm tired of hearing on videos the "oohs" and the "ahhs." Put the damn phone down!

That could have been my mother, my grandmother. If we're not willing to give our lives for women and children, what are we willing to give our life for? It's painful.

And the brother is probably going through something in this life, if you really think about it. And he was at that final straw when he snapped off on an older lady, but come on, man.

Study Guide No. 3 is titled, "*Overcoming Difficulty.*" Let me know if I'm wrong, but I'm pretty sure we're all going through a difficult part in our lives right now. Right? I'm not the only one who's been through some difficulty in their life, right? Okay, I just want to make sure we're on the same page before I go further. Because The Honorable Minister Louis Farrakhan said that, if Allah God has created man to face difficulty, then a difficulty factor is present that intensifies, as man moves closer to the goal. The difficulty factor is attached to everything of value. Is your life valuable? Was there a difficulty factor attached to our coming into existence? What was that?

If we go to Surah 21 as is suggested in our Study Guides, Surah 21 is titled, "The Prophets." Section number one, Judgment Approaches:

> *"In the Name of Allah, the Beneficent, the Merciful. Their reckoning draws nigh to men and they turn away in heedlessness. There comes not to them a new Reminder from their Lord but they hear it while they sport, Their hearts trifling. And they—the wrongdoers—counsel in secret: He is nothing but a mortal like yourselves; will you then yield to enchantment while you see? He said: My Lord knows (every) utterance in the heaven and the earth, and He is the Hearer, the Knower.*

I'm going to stop right there because I want us to understand. Most of us are caught up in March Madness right now.

Many of us are caught up in sport and play. That's what I'm trying to say right now. We're so caught up in sport and play, and we're so caught up in these situations. They happen so much, and they're flooding social media so much that we're becoming desensitized to them. We're becoming comfortable living in this type of pain! Pain!

One of the major parts of our difficulty is where we put our energy. Our energy is in sport in play. How can we grow into oneness with Almighty God Allah if we're too busy concerned about who's going into the Final Four? Who's going into the playoffs in the NBA? Oh, spring training is around the corner. This enemy keeps us so consumed with childish things. He distracts us with situations while he goes around the corner and makes other decisions.

This enemy.

In this beautiful guide, this beautiful book called the Study Guide: Self-Improvement, I want to quote a couple of parts from The Honorable Minister Louis Farrakhan. Do you mind? You really don't have a choice, but I just wanted to ask anyway. I'm going to lighten it up because this is a serious subject, so I don't want you to be down the whole time. But I want to make sure I hit some points in it.

On page 35 at point number two, it says the Holy Qur'an teaches us that Allah God does not desire hardship for us. Further, it is His desire to please us.

We go through a hard time, but He wants us to be happy. Even so, we can find no life form that came into existence without a struggle. Whether it is the lowest from of an insect or man himself, we see that overcoming adversity is a necessary part of life, since life cannot come into being without it. We must struggle. We must struggle in order to obtain our ultimate goal. Our ultimate goal is to meet with Allah God. The difficulty is an essential factor in the journey from being a speck of dust to being one with Allah God. We know struggle must take place by understanding that struggle causes us to do.

Review the lectures, Self-Improvement: The Basis of Community Development, paragraph 13. It says, without struggle, you cannot bring out of yourself that which God has deposited within you. It is something that has to be brought out, and it is a struggle overcoming difficulties that manifest your gifts and your sublime qualities.

Some of the struggles, difficulties and pain we go through are self-afflicted, meaning we are either self-afflicting on ourselves or someone is afflicting the pain on us. But if we really look at these books, Bible and Qur'an, there is no prophet nor messenger that did not go through pain. All of the prophets and messengers went through some form of pain, and their pain seems a lot worse than ours, which shows we become a little weak.

If we look at Abraham, God called Abraham up and requested that he sacrifice his son.

I got a question for you. Would you had sacrificed your son without hesitation? That's a hard one to do. "Hold on. Hold on, God. So you want me to just like... really? But God! You want me to just...You sure!?"

God will try you. He will send you through something to see will you really submit youself to Him, because Abraham did not hesitate. God was like don't even worry about it. I just wanted to see who was more important, him or me.

Then you look at our brother Job. Job lost his wife, his family, his crops and his riches. And Satan was like yeah, I'm gonna make him turn on you. But he was so dutiful through that struggle and pain that God doubled it back up for him. I got you son!

What about Joseph? Oh, Allah! What about Joseph? Man, Joseph went through everything. Joseph got sent to prison. He was a slave. His own brothers sold him. How your brothers sell you? Then he was falsely accused.

How about our brother Jesus? Jesus gets lied on. Jesus gets brought to trial for something he didn't even do. But how about this part: He gets betrayed by his own friend. Then, he's abandoned by his brothers. And with all that being said, Jesus gets crucified.

We're all going through something, but man if we actually go back and nurse in these scriptures, we will see our struggles are not as bad as we think they are. Oh, you didn't hear me.

"Man, my cell phone got cut off." Maybe you need a break.

"Aw man, they cut off the cable." Maybe you need to read a book.

"Man, I ran out of gas." Man brother, you do have a little belly. You might need to walk anyway. Sometimes we look at the glass half empty.

And I understand at the moment, it's frustrating. But outside of us being irresponsible, Allah will show us things if we take a step back and we look through the difficult factor and say, "Whoa, whoa whoa. Man, I was wrong okay, Allah, but how can I make this a blessing?"

"Man, I have to walk to work. That walk wasn't that bad. I actually feel good. I need to start getting back in the gym, now." That's how Allah works. The Honorable Minister Louis Farrakhan says, trials manifest weakness and store up strength.

So through our trials, through our tribulations, there is something in it, if we stay steadfast through it, because we're going to go through pain in the process as we're going through pain every single day.

We're going through a trial all through our lives, but the thing is, we cannot give up on ourselves. There's so much pressure on the Black man and woman today. Did you know that suicide in the Black community has increased? Did you know that in the Black community, we commit suicide twice as much as Caucasians?

And don't let me get on our children, man. Because of something somebody said to them at school, our babies are taking their own lives.

We become so comfortable in our pain that we don't realize that the pain is boiling over right now.

I lost a good friend of mine in January to suicide. My sister always tells me, brother, you always find a way to find a message in a situation. I'm trying not to beat myself up in situations most of the time.

As I reflected on my brother's death, he took his life at 36. At the time, I was 34. He's only two years older than me. He left behind two beautiful, amazing sons. Thinking about it hurts. It's not even the fact that he left behind the two sons that hurts me the most. It's not even the fact that he left behind a mother who loves him dearly, or brothers and family and friends who care so much about him.

What really hurts is that we would talk almost every day, and we have friends we would talk to almost every single day and we talked about *everything*.

I'm talking about baby mama drama. Brothers know what I'm talking about, but they don't want to acknowledge it because they don't want to get in trouble.

I'm talking about financial situations, transportation situations, goals, achievements, children, the whole nine yards. I'm talking about, we opened up about everything, but you never felt comfortable enough to say this is how I feel. Now that hurts, especially knowing the day before he decided to take his life, which does not belong to him. That's Allah's gift.

He and I spoke for two and a half hours and you didn't say, "Yo, bro. I don't want to be here anymore. I don't want to do this anymore. I want to take my life." Nothing. Nothing!

That bothers me because my mother does suicide prevention two times a week. He could have went to see mom. I would have called her immediately. But what happened? He decided to write a four-page letter before he did it, and he expressed himself in there. That hurts.

Many of us are one or two situations from being like that, but we don't feel comfortable enough to express it. "Oh, I don't want to look weak. I don't want to come off like I ain't strong."

It only takes one or two situations to get us to that point, and for some of us, the only thing keeping us alive is the love for our children or because we don't want to leave our mother, father or grandparents alone like that.

We're going through pain. We need each other. We need each other more than we realize. We need each other right now. So I have a question for you.

When was the last time you reached out to your friend, your brother, your sister, your mom, your father? That person you had a falling out with? "I don't talk to that person anymore."

When you go to the funeral services or the Janazah, many times the one who's going through it the worse is the one who's upset with themselves because they never got a chance to fix it. So seriously, when was the last time you checked in on that person? When was the last time you just called and checked in on your brother, sister or friend? And I'm not talking about reaching out with a motive. Because a lot of times when we call somebody, there's a motive attached. Brother Hannibal, what do you mean by that? I'm really only calling you because I need something.

We all got those people who only call you when they want something. You're nodding your head like yeah. I got a few of those. Ain't heard from you in months. Bro, how you been? What do you need? I know you want something.

But when was the last time we actually reached out without a motive? "I just want to check in on you. You were on my mind. How is the wife? How is your husband? How are the children? How is work? How has life been for you? What are you going through? You good? Do you need anything? Is there anything I can do to help? How are those bills being paid?" Many times, stress comes from bills, first. "I can't afford this man. It looks like I can't pay my bills."

We're going through pain. We're going through a lot of pain in our lives right now, and sometimes through our pain, we actually inflict pain on others.

You're not paying attention.

Sometimes through our own pain, we inflict pain on others. It's called lashing out, and we don't realize we lashed out.

When I was in banking, one of my managers said to us, "People don't leave a great company like this knowing all the great things they can get. They don't leave the company. What they're leaving is their manager."

Why are they leaving their manager?

Because they know I came into this with an expectation. I read through the descriptions. I read through the history of this place. And when I came into management, you are not fulfilling it.

It says we could do this but we're not doing it, so they get frustrated. They get dissatisfied, they become disgruntled and then they wind up going to find something else to provide peace. So the question becomes, how are we treating one another?

We have to treat each other with love. I ain't talking about that 'oooo oooooo' love. I almost hit you with that Young Ma song. But I'm talking about real love. I want for you what I want for myself love!

And we know when you really love someone, love can be painful. Love can be very, very painful, but we still have to bring genuine love. Let me tell you a little about some love real quick.

Our beautiful Mahdi, Master Fard Muhammad, loved us so much that He would study the whole world. He would study the whole world and find a people who are in dire need of God Himself. Do you know how painful it is to actually have to study your whole life, to travel 9,000 miles to a people who are deaf, dumb, and blind, to come and raise up a people who do not like each other, to raise up a people who are constantly fighting with each other, to raise a people who don't even look at themselves as humans and will bow to an open enemy but turn on a brother and sister?

That's painful. Let me tell you about some more pain. I'm going to show you how we even got here. Almighty God Allah created Himself out of triple darkness. Do you know how much patience that is? Do you know how much pain he had to go through to produce Himself so that He could produce us? That's called a trial.

I love the Honorable Minister Louis Farrakhan. I will give my life for this man, and I'm not saying that like, oh, that's what you're supposed to say. I'm being honest. I will salute my family and take a bullet for this man! This man has been through so much pain,

Near death experiences. Not just one time, not just two times but three times, and comes out and says, I want to see the people. Do you know what kind of pain he went through and goes through? He had to go through being lied on. He receives death threats. You think he ain't receiving death threats now!? But he's willing to give his life, and he's willing to endure that type of pain for you and I! That's called love! I'm talking about a man willing to die for us.

Aw Man.

We have to become a family. I know some of us don't know what family looks like. I'm being honest. Some of us don't know what family looks like, so because we don't know what family looks like, it's kind of icky to us. It's hard for us to adapt to a family environment if we're not used to being in a family environment.

That might have hurt some of you. Family goes through thick and thin with each other. And families are not perfect, but they are a form of perfection. There's no perfect family. I don't care what anybody says, because family goes through things. We don't get to choose our family. Most times we don't know the family is coming together. Oh, are we having a sister? You are pregnant again? I wish you would have asked the child if he wanted a sibling.

What I do love about my family, my family and I would get in arguments growing up. I can never get in fights because I have sisters, and we'd get in arguments growing up. My family and I would get in fights growing up, but when we left the house, you never knew. If we were beefing, if somebody ran up on one of my family members, I'm sorry. They getting it. And then we'd be like, "I'm still not talking to you though. Don't say nothing to me." And it's funny because you know, it'll be like "Yo, man look. I set up the Madden, bro. You want to play? I know that's your team right there." "Man, whatever bro. I don't care. You about to get this 'w' though."

Sometimes it's those situations right there. Ain't no "I'm sorry, my bad." Because you know at the end of the day, you love each other and you're willing to go through the trials and tribulations. It's only you and I, so when we get in fights, that breaks down our unity.

There was a video of one of our beautiful sisters in Dallas. A Caucasian man harassed her at three, four o'clock in the morning. He punched her in the face relentlessly. She told news that the left side of her face was swollen and that it would take her some time to get over what happened.

When I watched it myself, yes it makes me cry. All I could do was ball up my fists. He was fired. This makes me boil. I'm trying to stay calm, because I'm getting tired of this. We need real men, today.

She's thankful that somebody was recording it, but I want to know who's on the other side of the phone. I don't care if you got a gun, you gotta take me too! I'm tired of seeing women get mistreated. Let me tell you what I love before I get into this pain part.

In the Nation of Islam we have something called General Orders. There are 12 of them. Our 12th General Order is "to be especially watchful at night." I'm not going to go into the whole part of it, but I want you to understand that these General Orders don't apply just to the mosque. We have work to do, Muslims! There's a reason why the Most Honorable Elijah Muhammad did not want the woman out late at night. I'm not blaming her, because she didn't know.

But we as men got to bring men in so we can teach and train our community, so if she goes out, she knows she has a lifeline to call. Forget calling 911. You should have been calling one of us because we would have chased him down and handled it.

Our women are going through way too much in this hour. I'm sorry. But I'm tired of the videos and the "oooos" and the "awwwwwwwwws" and "I'm shocked.: How about you turn it into a selfie that says, "Wife, I love you. Children, I love you. But I may not be coming home today." It seems like we're asking for too much for men to stand up and be men today.

I remember hearing stories about Prior to '75. I wish I could have been around at that time when the dope fiends or the drug dealers or the gangbangers would be on the streets, and the MGT (Muslim Girls in Training) would come walking by and they would jump off the sidewalk.

When the brothers could pull up and put the Muhammad Speaks right there on the dashboard, and their car wouldn't get robbed or stolen. We have work to do, Muslims. Muslims, Muslims, Muslims, we have work to do. Our people are hurting right now, man. And it's going to get worse. That's what I need us to understand. We're already dealing with enough pain, and this is going to get worse. There is a split in America right now. He had his gun out. You could front on a woman, then you got your gun out, but she a woman man!

We need to do some housecleaning. I'm talking about everywhere. We need to get back in our communities and clean house. Our people don't know. Our brothers don't know. We have to teach and train. The Nation of Islam has been given the tools. We have the tools, and our people are going through this type of pain. Most of it is the result of injustice, mistrust, family mistreatment, insecurities, and everything else. When we see our brothers and sisters going through pain, we have to speak up for them. I'm talking about in general.

"Sis, how you doing?" "Things aren't going too well." "Does your family know?"

"Bro, how you doing man?" "I'm struggling." "Does this person know? What can I do to help? What do you need? What steps are you taking to get out of the situation?"

We have to do it the right way, though. So I want to introduce you to something: a beautiful book given to us by the Most Honorable Elijah Muhammad titled, *The Proper Way of Handling People*.

Now it's going to say for the Laborers and the Muslims in general, but I want you to understand that every single one of us is a laborer. You might be a manager at work; you're laboring over your staff. You have children; you're laboring over your children. You have brothers and sisters; you're laboring over your brothers and sisters.

Point number one: Have a genuine concern for our people. That's the first step. Because our people you know, my brothers in the hood, they know when you coming fake. "Aw, he fake. He don't care about me." Point number two: Make a person feel wanted. Man, this one right here can go a long way. "Look, we're not doing too good, but I really appreciate everything you're doing." The fact that they feel appreciated will make them work even harder.

Point number three: Make a weak Muslim strong. How about we switch it up like this? Make a weak person strong. Point number four: Let a person speak up. Do not suppress ideas. Let people relieve their minds of problems. Don't be quick to charge insubordination. Now I have some teenagers in my group home, and I've dealt with younger children before, so I'd be like nah, go do this. But I know they're teenagers now. I have to reason a little bit. I don't go straight to insubordination and "go to your room." It's over with. You're on restriction? No. Let's talk about it. What's your idea? Let me show you why that does or doesn't work. Let me show you, like I tell my boys. You have the small picture, the medium picture, the large picture and the big picture. You all think on a small picture level. I have to look at the big picture.

Point number five: Listen to people's problems. Now I'm not saying we got to open up a door and just be like bring your problems in. No. But if the people are going through something, I said many of us are one or two incidents from being suicidal. If we're willing to listen to the problem, even if we can't resolve it, that can be enough for the person to want to do better. Point number six: Remember that Islam simply means peace. It simply means peace. It's more than an expression of a handshake. It's peace, love and harmony.

Point number seven: The most valuable asset is the Messenger's followers. The Messenger's followers are the most valuable asset. I'm humbled for that one.

In our lives, we run into a lot of what's called unity. The Most Honorable Elijah Muhammad taught on it for years, and the Honorable Minister Louis Farrakhan has been teaching on it. Part of the reason why we as a people have not come up yet is because of disunity and division such as speaking a different language.

We must not speak the language of the people and that of the other laborers. We may deal with each other. When we're moving out on stuff, we have to be on the same accord. We can't say I'm gonna do this and do the total opposite of it.

Lack of education for all: We must make ourselves available to all materials and information we can access. Things change in life, and social media is not that old. The internet is not that old. "Aw man I'm reading the newspaper." Nothing wrong with that, but by the time you get the paper, it will already been on social media and everybody will already know about it. Keep up with modern times.

Lack of friendly understanding. That's a deep one. The difference in ideas, laws, and customs. Keeping the Messenger's Program as our go-to. We as members of the Nation of Islam have the same common goal, because our goal is the Messenger's work. Remember, a society of men or groups of men for one common cause.

Barriers to transportation: Strive to see each other regularly. If we're not around each other, how do we get to know each other? And transportation should not be the reason why we're not around each other.

Barriers to communication: Keep in touch with each other daily. Let the others know of your whereabouts. That means we can't be all secretive with each other.

The book talks about fundamental techniques. Don't criticize, condemn, or complain. Give honest sincere appreciation. Arouse in the other person an eager want.

Ways to make people like you: Become genuinely interested in other people. Smile! It's so easy to smile. Eye contact. Remember that a man's name is, to him, the sweetest and most important sound of any language.

I recommend we look through the Proper Handling of the People. It's something I implemented in my life once I came into the Nation. People wouls ask me, "Brother, you know when I was in banking, how are you going up the ladder so fast?" I was using this. This was part of my principle. I was using this and the principles of the Teachings of the Most Honorable Elijah Muhammad. We as men don't have our hands in our pockets. We don't slouch over. I would teach my team that without saying, "Well the Most Honorable Elijah Muhammad said..." No, I would just implement it. Just implement the principle and watch the success happen.

Now, the challenge for some of us is, we're going through so much pain that we don't want to even address this proper handling part.

I got a solution for that, too.

In 1995, our beautiful Minister delivered an outstanding speech, but in that, he gave us something called the 8 Steps of Atonement. If we properly use these 8 Steps of Atonement, we're able to work through these dramas. Here are the eight steps:

1. Point out the wrong. "Oh, I ain't never wrong." You're wrong right now. The first stage is the most difficult of all, because when we are wrong and we are not aware of it, someone has to point out the wrong.

2. Acknowledge the wrong. "Hold on! So you're saying I'm wrong, and I have to acknowledge the fact that I'm wrong?" Yes. In this context, the word acknowledge means to face the truth of the fact that we have been wrong.

3. Confess the fault. First, you confess the fault to Allah God, and next, to the person or persons whom your fault has affected.

4. Repentance means feeling control or self-reproach for what one has done or failed to do. So, we have to pull out the wrong, acknowledge the wrong and confess fault. Then, we have to go through the process of repentance for ourselves.

5. Atonement means we must be willing to do something to get rid of our sins.

6. Forgiveness. Wow. That's one right there. "I hear you, I hear you, whatever." But we won't forgive. We won't forgive. And then we hold on to the pain that the person came to atone. Forgiveness means to cease to feel offense and resentment against another for the harm done by an offender. It means to wipe the slate clean.

7. Reconciliation and restoration. It means to resolve differences and to establish or re-establish a close relationship between the previous divided person. After we go through that process, we got to be able to start spending time together to work through the issues again, so that we can continue to grow.

8. Perfect union with God. The result of completing the atonement process is achieving a perfect union with Allah God who is best at guiding us to freedom.

Those are the eight steps of atonement. In order to be successful with these steps and to achieve optimum results, both parties must do this. We must lower our guard. We must remove our egos. We must remove our pride. We must humble ourselves. We must be willing to get past our differences.

If we don't do this correctly, we will actually create more pain, and that pain creates more hurt. We are at a time when we should be coming from behind the sycamore tree. The challenge is, many of us will come from behind the sycamore tree. But if we do, we're coming out with too much pain and hurt, and that pain and hurt create bad motives.

Those bad motives create bad intentions. So most of us won't even come from behind the sycamore tree because we are in too much pain to come from behind it, and that pain that we're dealing with has created a ceiling cap in our productivity in life.

Until we atone with ourselves, how can we become more productive in our day to day? We must resolve it in order to grow. We must resolve in order to help others grow. The Honorable Minister Louis Farrakhan said this to us: How do you know that your faith is weak and shattered? It is when God calls you from something that is hiding you—buoyancy. That is similar to asking to come from behind a sycamore tree. You are going to be tried. Anytime we step out on something, we are going to be tried. So we step out trying to resolve an issue with an individual we have a problem with, and they may not be ready to atone yet. That's a trial for us.

But if we're sincere, if we do it, if we're genuine with it, we can still work through the process and the steps, and when they become ready, we're still ready to receive them. People are fragile nowadays. We have to be very careful in how we are dealing with people, because we are dealing with people while we're dealing with the end of this world. We have to make it easier for people, and we have to encourage them. Many of our people are easily discouraged. Evangelizing is not all of the work, and standing behind the rostrum speaking is not all of the work. But it's pastoring to the people. It's talking on subjects that you know. We have to strengthen ourselves up. In order for us to labor for our people, we have to be able to fill, address, and solve their pain and problems.

How many of you have seen or gone through a few trials in your life? And as you started going through those few trials, you just gave up. "I won't do this no more. I'm done. This is too hard." It's hard trying to be right in this world. This is Satan's world. He's made everything fair-seeming. They're talking about legalizing LGBTQ+ history in grade school now. It's hard to be right when you're in a world like this, and that's why we need each other.

There was a song: *"Lean on Me."*

Lean on me, when you're not strong. And I'll be your friend. I'll help you carry on. (Lean on me). For it won't be long, 'til I'm gonna need, somebody to lean on.

You know the song. I had to sing that song in grade school, but I need us to understand that there are some valuable points in that song.

Where I may be weak, you may be strong, and where you may be weak, I may be strong. And if I'm not strong, give me the opportunity to find somebody or a group of people who are strong enough to help you work your way through.

We have to be able to lean on each other, because that's all we have. The Honorable Minister Louis Farrakhan said if we stay the course like Elijah Muhammad did, he stayed the course and was made into a god. The Minister is one of those students who stayed the course, no matter what the devil did. He stayed the course. Guess what? He said, "He made me into himself."

You can't be faking this. I attend Muhammad's Mosque #32. If we went to this beautiful book Holy Qur'an, Surah 32 is titled "Al Sajda," which means adoration, deep love and respect, worship.

Muhammad's Mosque #32 is a beautiful mosque that was numbered by the Most Honorable Elijah Muhammad. He loved the city and mosque so much that he has a house here, a home here.

The Minister said that this used to be a great mosque, but he said it's not that right now. I'm not trying to bash the mosque at all by this statement, but he talked about what this mosque used to do. And it still can do it. But we need help. Help. We can't do it by ourselves. This mosque was number one in study, number one in love, number one in productivity, but we need help to do it. Us working together, we can produce that to be number one again. Us working together allows us as a unit to come from behind the sycamore tree. Us doing it together allows us to become better helpers in our community. Philippians 4:13 says, "*I can do all this through Him who gives me strength.*" You and I need to be surrounded by people who support us. It's time for us to unite with those who want to do better.

Isaiah 40:29 says *"he gives strength to the weary and increases the power of the weak."*

7

Corrupted By Our Own M.O.

"There's nothing stopping us but our ignorance and our unwillingness to fight negative forces."

The Honorable Minister Louis Farrakhan

Master Fard Muhammad didn't just come and make Himself known. He didn't just come and knock on the door and say, "Yo! I'm God!" But what he did is something that we can really understand and study. It's the fact that he actually researched and studied to find a people who were removed from the land that not of their own.

He came in and out of this country for over 20 years, just to have a better understanding of who we are. He left the comfort of his own home and traveled **9,000 miles**. I don't know if you really understand how **far** that is.

Most people don't want to go five miles down the **street**. But Almighty God Allah traveled 9,000 miles to come to a people who are considered deaf, dumb, and blind, and he came to raise them up to their rightful place.

He doesn't just focus on the colt, the young professionals. He took one from among us who did not go beyond the fourth grade of **education** to show us how beautiful and how strong **his** works is.

He raised the Most Honorable Elijah Muhammad to be our Exalted Christ, and the Honorable Elijah Muhammad put in that work for over 40 years; 40 years of **blood, sweat, and tears!** And he asked Allah for help.

Allah gave him a gift at Saviours' Day 1955! His gift was the Honorable Minister Louis Farrakhan, who is the divinely guided **one** who would uphold the torch for Almighty God Allah. We are truly blessed **today!**

We could be here at any time, but Allah gave us **now!** We have a man who is despised by the world, who has done everything he can for us and has given us all that he has.

This isn't easy, but it's what Allah has placed on my heart that I must address. Insha'Allah, with his guidance and grace, I'm going to give you something to the best of my ability.

We are on a continued journey, and this journey that we are on is a journey of continued demand. We can't go on a journey and then expect to chill out like we're on vacation.

What will you give? What will you and I give to help fulfill what Allah wants of us? Sometimes we may be overcome by doing. I can't do that. I don't have time. I don't have money in my pocket, so what can I do to help?

Believe it or not, that's not what He's asking of us. He's asking and demanding of us to perfect ourselves, because the perfection of ourselves is the perfection of God Himself. When we're confident in building that true love and essence in God, that strikes fear in our enemy. That strikes real fear in our enemy. Why would our enemy fear us building confidence in God Himself? Because he knows who we are. But our M.O. our modus operandi, has been corrupted, so, we don't know that we are God's chosen children.

I went to a funeral, and when you witness death, it puts life back in perspective. We only have one life, and Allah gives us the free will within His permissive will to do as we see please with that life. We have an opportunity to grow into Allah Himself as He wants of us, but sometimes we're afraid to do that.

That's why I'm taking on this subject, 'Corrupted By Our M.O.,' 'Corrupted By Our Modus Operandi.'

Let's define a few words in the title of this chapter. Do you mind? You really don't have a choice, but I still had to ask. (Laughs)

The first definition is **modus operandi,** or M.O. It's defined as: *mode of operating or working; procedures; method of operating; the way someone does something; a characteristic method.* An example the dictionary gives is: *Her modus operandi is buying a new car, always including a month of research.*

Her M.O. is she always does a whole month of research before she makes a decision on purchasing a car. Many of us do not know our modus operandi and the way to function through it. Many of us don't know! It's usually identified by outside sources such as family, friends, associates, etc.; people who have indicated it to us by their interactions, perspectives, and/or track record of us.

People have viewpoints of you, and sometimes you do not understand why. Why does that brother have a problem with me? Why does that sister have an issue with me? Many times we are doing things that we think are correct and beneficial to us, but in actuality, we are making the same mistakes over and over and expecting different results.

We do the same thing over and over and over again, expecting different results. What is that called? Insanity! We have an insane M.O. and don't even know that we have it, because we're doing the same thing over and over and over expecting a different result. We've been corrupted.

So, let's define other words: **corrupt.** As an adjective, it's defined as *guilty of dishonest practices, as bribery; lacking integrity—*that's a key one right there*—crooked; debased in character; depraved; perverted; wicked; evil; made inferior by errors or alterations; infected; tainted; decayed;* As a verb: *to destroy the integrity of; to cause to be dishonest;*

disloyal; to lower morally; perverted to corrupt; to alter; to infect; to be tainted.

Many of us have been tainted in our lives and don't know that we are. We make many decisions in our life based on our upbringing and how we were raised.

I was at a funeral, and the Bishop was speaking. He mentioned something in the aspect of, we're on the same road, but we're going two different directions. And at that time, he was fishing! I mean, he's trying to get converts. I'm being honest with you. But, it was a valid point in there. We're on the same road of life, but we're going two different directions.

Some are in the direction of the fulfillment of God and what He wants of them, and some of us are in a direction of the fulfillment of Satan. In either direction, we can that we have a corrupted M.O. Why am I bringing this up? Think about it: If our thoughts are clouded, then our decisions are clouded, which means our M.O. is corrupted and clouded. That means our actions are actually corrupted, and a lot of times, we don't even know we're doing wrong.

Have you ever had a computer that has been corrupted or am I the only one? I'm serious. You're on a computer, working on homework, and it just crashes on you! And when you load it back up, it's moving crazy slow. That's corruption, right! Now, you have to call somebody in to fix it. That's that outside source that has to come into the inside of the computer and fix it.

Well, a lot of times, we don't know we're corrupted, because we're in the midst of the corruption. Sometimes you need an outside source— Almighty God Allah and His Messenger—to put us on a straight path so we can line up and see, dang! I'm corrupted right now!

We don't always know when we've been bit by a snake. We got that venom in us, and it's been eating at our morale! Well, where did the snake come from? Who is the snake? Who is the snake figure that we're dealing with?

Our M.O. is established by our character, our personality and the way we function. It is also established by our upbringing, our environment and our influences.

We are taught that our children should not be watching cartoons and such with talking animal figures. That becomes an influence on our child. We could be easily corrupting our children and don't even know it's happening.

It's also established by our actions, our thoughts, and the way we operate. The decisions we make today will impact our lives ten years from now! Let's take a moment and think back 10, 20, 30 years. Some of you been doing the same thing for some time now, so it's kind of hard to weigh it, but 10 plus years ago and the decisions you made then, are you still reaping some of those decisions? Are we still having to deal with some of the bad decisions you made in your past? "I got a felony. I can't get a job. I got a felony 15 years ago. I can't get a job, but it was a decision that was made that led me to that felony that's impacting me **now!**" So, we have to figure out how to maneuver outside of it.

Our past and our current M.O. is either benefitting us or it's harming us **now!** And the decisions we have made in our lives and the perceptions people have established about us is determining how we move forward.

I work in a group home, and I enjoy it because I get to be a mentor, a coach, and all of the exciting things you get from working with children. I get to help uplift these young men and make them prepare for life. They're already great people, but I get to make them a little bit better, right.

And I have this one little brother, so smart, so intelligent. But he always gets caught up in an environment with the wrong crowd. Every time! He says, 'I wasn't smoking weed.' But he's always in the environment where there's weed involved.

Even though he may not get caught with the contraband on him, I'm always getting a call pertaining to a situation with him, a bad crowd and there'll be weed involved. And when he gets in trouble, placed on restriction, or whatever it maybe, he'll say, 'Man. Mr. Hannibal, I'm sorry. I'm going to change!'

Alright. Sound good. You know, after two, three, four or five times of him crying wolf, the last time he said it, I said, "Can I be honest with you? I don't believe you right now. With the M.O. you have, I don't believe you right now. Until you change your M.O., it's hard to believe, because a month or two later, I might get the same phone call."

A lot of times, we find ourselves in situations and we think we're doing something different, but we're actually doing the same thing expecting different results. It's hard to trust someone who has a bad M.O. I'm just being honest. Let's be honest.

If I asked to borrow some money from you. Think about it. If I asked to borrow some money from you and I never paid you back, would you be happy? You know you would be pissed! You would be slandering, talking behind my back. "That n——r owe me money." Let's be honest.

And we are going to add to that. Let's say you go on my social media, and you see I'm having a grand time! "Oh, he in Morocco!?! That brother owes me $200!" You would be pissed! You would be so upset. You'd have me out here looking like Lee Daniels and you Dame Dash. You didn't catch that. That's alright. You don't know Lee Daniels owes Dame Dash $2 million, and he had to confront him? "Yo, you owe me some money man!" It looked like they were about to scrap, too.

But the problem is, which becomes part of our M.O., this M.O. that we have established damages relationships. It also damages the success of organizations. I broke my **word.** If we just thought about that and how many times we broke our word for somebody, we might have some corrupted aspects in our M.O. right now. I committed to doing something and I did not follow through. I promised something, and I broke that promise. I lost your trust.

In Supreme Wisdom, it says: *"Have you not learned that your word shall be bond regardless of whom or what?"* The answer: *"Yes! My word is bond and bond is life, and I will give my life before my word shall fail."*

Right now we're not trying to give our lives, because if our life was on the line, we'll be purifying some of that corruption in our own M.O.s. I'm speaking to myself! I know you are perfect. You are perfect.

If we live by that motto, we would actually break the corruption of our M.O. and actually start purifying ourselves. That purification as a unit actually creates a standard for other individuals to elevate through. If other people are around you see these are the standards you live by, either they're going to want to step up or they're going to step out, which means they exposed themselves as being corrupted or as one of Satan's dumb devils.

Because we would know, no. No. No. No. No! My word is bond. This how we function. Well, man, I can't do that. In the scriptures, they praised and they said that they were with him, but then they went behind closed doors and said they not with God Himself. We know they're out there. We know they're out there.

I may not even know that I have this habit of breaking my bond. Sometimes we don't realize how many times we broke our bond with someone. It becomes second nature because we do it so often. To some of my Muslims, when we start saying, "Insha'Allah"... (Laughs) Uh, oh! I might have started something. I might have started something. When we start saying "Insha'Allah," that's like "I don't know. I might show up."

We used to be like, "Yes sir! I'll be there!" Now, we're, "Insha'Allah." "Mashallah? Alhamdullilah!" That's usually the response when you do show up. I gotta bring a little humor. I know this is a serious subject.

The victim in me gets mad when I ask for something and you won't give it to me. I break my bond. I got a corrupted M.O., and I want something from you and you won't give it to me. Now I'm pissed. I'm playing the victim, but what we don't understand is that victim mentally in us is actually a little Satan in us. And we may not even be aware that he, Satan, is sitting in that little place, interrupting the way we function. If we go back to the computer, Satan is the virus inside of our minds.

Satan told God that he would be in front of us. He would be behind us. He would be on our left side and our right side. And if we think about when the Son of God was going to see God, he was accompanied by the Devil himself and did not know that the Devil was with him.

So we have a devil that's been coming along with us, and sometimes we don't know he sitting there corrupting every move we make. We may have the right intentions, but for some reason, it always comes out wrong.

When we start taking on the ways of this world, we start taking on the M.O. of this world. Well, whose world is this right now? Whose world is this? When we take on this world, we're taking on Satan's world, and that means we're taking on the M.O. of Satan! And trust me, he's putting in work trying to exalt us in his ways.

Even when you go to scripture and we look at Judas, Judas had a noble motive when it came to the woman rubbing the feet of Jesus with the oil in her hair. And Judas would say to Jesus, well we could take this oil and sell it and give that to the poor. That sounds great! That sounds great! Man, you know you're right. We could do that. But Jesus reminded him, brother look, you're only going to have me for a little, but you'll have them for a long time. Let me have this for a moment. But what he was also exposing in that was, I see you. I see you! I'm not going to expose you to them, because that's not for me, that's for you and them at that time when it comes, but I see you.

It wasn't that Judas really cared about giving it to the poor! He was dealing with something called jealousy and envy. That's corruption right there. Your own A1 is jealous and envious of your success! Sometimes we could be corrupted and not even know we're corrupted. And he got so jealous and envious that he would even turn God's man into the law! You're supposed to have my back.

If we go to the serpent in the garden from Genesis 3:4-5, the serpent said to the woman, "*You surely will not die!*" Dang! He got that much clout? "...for God knows in the day you eat from it, your eyes will be open and you will be like God, knowing good and evil." So they ate from that tree and became corrupted.

Then you go to II Corinthians 11:3:

> *"But I am afraid that just as Eve was deceived by the serpent's cunning, your minds may somehow be led astray from your sincere and pure devotion to Christ."*

Allah God wants things so easy for us, so, so easy for us. He wants things simple and pure. And if things seem to be a little extra harder than it should be, we might need to take a step back and figure out why isn't this as easy as it should be. Maybe I'm trying to do too much. Maybe I have some negative influences around me that's corrupting the way I operate.

Jesus had the same situation talking to the Jews. In John 8:44 he said:

> *"You belong to your father, the devil, and you want to carry out your father's desires. He was a murderer from the beginning, not holding to the truth, for there is no truth in him. Where he*

lies, he speaks his native language, for he is a liar and the father of lies."

We have truly been corrupted by these four devils. You know Nas song Affirmative Action? AZ has a line where he says: "lust, envy, hate, and jealousy."

If we really think about it, those are different demons that we're fighting every day of our lives. We're fighting lust, we're fighting envy, we're fighting hate and we're fighting jealousy. When they enter the mind and the hearts of a person, they corrupt the thoughts and the actions of a person. But we don't realize we've been corrupted.

When we're losing power, it's natural to try to take control of everything around you, even though we should just step back out of the emotion and be logical. "What's going on? Why am I losing this power?" But when we've been corrupted, we do not understand why we're losing the power, so we react a certain way, which causes more mayhem than it should

Every time we open the scriptures and study the works of God and His words, we see His prophets, His messengers, messiahs, and servants. We're able to learn what M.O. he is requiring of them, which is the same M.O. He's requiring of us. All we have to do is compare how they were living and measure how we're living ours. Does that make sense? I just want to make sure I didn't leave you.

The only way that we can overcome the inner pressure and the outside is through our faith in God and our efforts to live the life that He prescribes. What I love about Almighty God Allah is He has the Best M.O. He's got the best one! Allah is the Creator of the heavens and the earth. There's an action word in that sentence. What is it? Allah is the *Creator* of the heavens and the earth. The action word is Creator. He creates. Not only does He manage our affairs, He creates the circumstances that we maneuver through.

Many of us just manage our affairs. We just manage whatever Allah puts in front of us, but there's a difference between management and leadership. Management takes something that you give them, and they just maintain the status quo. They might take it a little bit higher, but they're not going to do too much more with what was given to them. But leadership, a leader will take nearly to nothing and find the true essence in it and expands it out beyond whatever they were given.

Allah creates through leadership, because He took a nobody like us and as we look up, we watch ourselves be lifted up day by day in **Him**. That's leadership. And when we take on the mind of leadership, that puts us in the mind of a creative genius to create and manifest as God desires of us. That takes us on a process to get on that Dragon Ball Z Super Saiyan level. You don't know anything about that! But it does.

That removes fear from our entity. We can't be afraid to look in the mirror and challenge our fears. We must challenge the fear of failure. We can't be afraid to fail at things. We must challenge the fear of the unknown. I don't know how the outcome's going to be, but we must challenge the fear of success. "I'm afraid to be successful," and if we really go to the root, many of us are afraid to be successful. And a lot of that comes from a corrupted environment, a corrupted upbringing.

I remember one day Student Minister Tony Muhammad had said in a meeting during the time we were going into Dianetics. He explained how when he was growing up, he was told by his family he would be nothing, so he didn't want to be anything. But as he went through Dianetics, he started seeing all that charge come off of him.

Sometimes we grow up and we as parents may say stuff to the child out of the anger that we have towards the other parent. "Your father wasn't nothing. You won't be nothing." That's the instilled engrams in that child. We have planted a virus of corruption and changed their M.O. so they don't want to grow up and be nothing. "Your father went to jail. You're gonna go to jail," and we take on that valence.

The Holy Quran mentions very little of love, but it mentions duty. In this connotation, if you tell someone that you love them, love becomes a verb. Duty denotes some activity that expresses the love that you have. So when we say I love you, I have to be able to show I love you. "I want that woman to be my wife. I love her." Well, brother, you live with your mama. What are you going to do about that? And brother, you're catching the bus right now. "I don't know!" Man, brother, you're staying with brother so and so and so and so. "I don't know!" That equation ain't adding up. That love ain't adding up!

Sometimes we don't realize. "Aw man. I thought that was cool." Corrupted. My M.O. jacked up. Brother, you got a bad M.O. brother. I'm just being honest.

Allah-u-Akbar!

Now you and I can identify our M.O. It takes some work, but it can be done. I recommend that we do it and we learn about ourselves. This is what we need to do. That's what I was leading to. I'm giving the layout of how we can fix our M.O., Insha'Allah. Hopefully, it goes to Masha'Allah, and then we can end with Alhamdulillah. (Laughs)

We must study the type of person we are, first and foremost. We must study self. We must study the characteristics we possess. What kind of character am I? We must study the environment we create and the influence we have on other people. As we start going through that, we can see: how do we respond when people ask of us? Are we bringing hope and positive changes in the lives of ourselves and others, or are we causing mayhem?

If we're in a situation and for some reason nobody ever invites you nowhere, you just might have a jacked-up M.O. Every time I invite this brother, he always talking about how much he hated the mosque. Yeah, brother, I don't want that negativity. You got a negative M.O. Every time we try to go out and get something to eat, he ain't never got no money. Hey, I have friends like that. You got a broke M.O. This is real life.

We actually have some courses that help to establish and build strong, positive M.O.s. We do! We actually have courses that do that, and if I were to offer these courses to you, would you be interested in joining and going through the process? If so, raise your hand. Okay. All Praise is Due To Allah. I got you on a hook. All for the low price of $9.99. (Laugh). There is no charge.

I'm going to show you. Are you ready? Alright. Alright. Are you sure you're ready? It's a great course. Alright. We have these courses every Wednesday and Friday at 7:30 at Study Group. This can be found at any Muhammad Mosque and Muhammad Study Group.

If we were really honest about fixing our corrupted M.O. and building a positive and stronger M.O., we would understand the value of Wednesday and Friday night Study Group. Why is that? Because it's called Self-Improvement: The Basis for Community Development! The whole course is self-improvement. Self-improvement is the process of purifying ourselves to remove the corruption that's been living inside of us and to get rid of the little demons and devils and Satan that's been in us for so long. As we go through these studies and we line ourselves up with the thinking of the Most Honorable Elijah Muhammad and the Honorable Minister Louis Farrakhan, we start cracking atoms upon one another. We start learning the thoughts and the minds of each other. We start seeing certain charges come off of us. We're actually going through a purification process.

For those in the Nation who been in for some years, remember when you first joined? You were at every Study Group. Energy was crazy high. Can I say crazy high? I'm going to say it anyway. The energy was really high. You enjoyed yourself. You didn't want to go home. We were removing the bad ways of your life, and we were purifying ourselves, so when it came to Saturday morning, we were out in the field, brothers. When it came to Sunday morning, we're at the mosque all day, brothers. But it starts with studying self.

Right now if we can't fill a mosque or a building, that says there's something corrupting our own M.O. I know. I'm going to get off that subject. I might get beat up after you read this. Let me leave that alone for a minute, which I know I'm speaking the truth because I'm a victim of it myself. I said victim, right. That's a Satan living in me, instead of taking ownership, how quickly it came out.

I'm going to take the last two paragraphs of "Building Human Potential" out of the Self-Improvement Study Guides and read to you. You don't mind, do you? You really didn't have a choice, but I am going to anyway.

> *"If Malcolm X, with an 8th-grade education, accomplished what he accomplished under the guidance of The Honorable Elijah Muhammad, read every book in the prison library, beginning with the dictionary; if individuals and people can manifest hidden beauty and potential through reading, then each one of us must challenge our aversion to reading and begin to READ, READ. "READ IN THE NAME OF THY LORD WHO CREATES, CREATES MAN FROM A CLOT. READ AND THY LORD IS MOST GENEROUS, WHO TAUGHT MAN BY PEN, TAUGHT MAN WHAT MAN KNEW NOT..."*

Reading and Writing (use of the pen) are two lost arts among our people. If there is one among us who cannot read, that is one too many. If one of you is unable to read, then we shall establish a reading class.

So we will get a reading class if some of you can't read. We will make that happen, but there's a lot of art here that we are struggling in that's allowing us to be corrupted because we're not opening these books. When we open up the books to see what Allah God is manifesting for us, we can see what's happening in the world and say, "Whoa! It's right here!"

Then as we read, we take out a pen and paper, and we start jotting down things that we're learning. We go to a dictionary and pull up words to get a better understanding. As we start going through that deeper understanding, it starts to remove the corruption, the viruses that are living in us, the parasites that are living in us, the jealousy and envy that is living in us.

All we have to do is start reading and writing. That type of guidance and study helps to develop quickness, fast-moving, cleanliness internally and externally, right down to the modern time, but we can't procrastinate with that if we want to grow and purify ourselves.

My big brother, brother Nuri Muhammad said, "Procrastination is anti-God." I don't think you're paying attention to what I just said. Procrastination is anti-God. We are taught that we are in His image and likeness. We can't grow into His image and likeness if we're procrastinating on our own self-development. The Holy Quran 18:23 says, *"And say not of anything I will do that tomorrow."*

We can't have slowness. We can't be sloppy in this. Being mindful of our thoughts and actions help us to move faster. Being mindful of what we take into our body helps us to become cleaner. We can't study and then take in toxins, because now what we study becomes corrupted by the toxins.

That allows us as we study to submit to do the Will of God, and if we're submitting to do the Will of God, that allows our admission to become a god. You didn't hear me. It's alright. It's alright.

Our submission to do the Will of God is our admission to become a god, but we have to be willing to submit first. "Oh, I got there by myself. I didn't need God's help." Once you give yourself totally to God—this is from the Honorable Minister Louis Farrakhan—"Once you give yourself totally to God, absolute love for Him, that's the beginning of the release of your power." You must love Him who gave it all to you!

We make ourselves more powerful than God is. At least that's what we think. That's a corrupt M.O. That's the beginning of purifying a corrupted M.O.

Closing the Gap page 47 says:

> *"For Allah God so loved the world that He gave His only begotten son. He gave, He sacrificed him, and the son was willing to be sacrificed. I have no life of my own. My life is for the redemption of a people and that is pretty hard. However, that is the necessary requirement to effect resurrection, redemption, restoration, and reconciliation of the soul that is lost."*

> *"When a person is like that, he has no sin. He has shortcomings for sure and he may commit sin, but by his long-suffering and continuing to pull on the good nature of Allah God on the people to make them better and better and better, Allah God just wipes away the sin that He has and throws it away into the sea of forgetfulness and covers his sin. Because of the work that he does of redemption, that is why Jesus is looked at as absolutely perfect and sinless."*

We're going to commit sin. We're going to get viruses. We're going to have shortcomings. But if we're willing to suffer and continue to work harder to try to build up ourselves and if we're willing to challenge the different things that are causing our shortcomings, Allah God Himself will wipe away those sins.

Have you ever made a mistake and you knew you were going to get in trouble but then you didn't get in trouble? Sometimes you have to weigh the positive to the negative. We can't always beat up on ourselves on the negative things that happen in life. Those are shortcomings, but did you try? Did you give your all? Did you fight against that fear you had to do it in the first place? Then get up and keep going.

Our M.O. has had a major impact on why we won't unify with one another. Yeah, I said it! Who trusts someone who has bad credibility? When I talked about money earlier, that's bad credibility. When will we realize how beneficial we really are to one another? Right now we don't see that value in each other yet. Allah is still forcing things in place that's forcing us to have to work together, but we still don't see the value in each other, yet. All these businesses are shutting down right now because they're saying and doing things that are pissing us off, especially with the police brutality, and we could have shut them down years ago.

So Allah is intervening in our affairs to force us to come together. I'm going to put my sister on blast. We bump heads all the time, but when we got a whooping and mom was like you better fix it, we fixed it! Allah is going to have to give us a whooping if we do not figure out how to get along now, and we do not want that chastisement. There's no future in us trying to make this America the dream that it wants to be. It's a straight-up illusion, and it's not worth it for us. God wants to separate us and give us a land of our own with Him as the ruler over it, but the enemy doesn't want that, so he's constantly dropping viruses to distract us and to see if we'll bite at the bait.

There are more people like Mr. Papa John's. Yeah, I know you heard about Mr. Papa John's (John Schnatter)! He used that good old' n-word, if you didn't know. What's happening with somebody like that, they're continuing to come out because something is deep-rooted in their heart on how they feel about us, and Allah is forcing them in situations where they can't hold it in anymore!

His M.O. is greed! What he failed to realize when he went into that contract with the NFL so he'll be the endorsed pizza company, he didn't realize we were serious about boycotting the NFL! I know some of you watch the game. It's cool. I know some of you do. Your team got into the playoffs. I get it. But what he didn't consider was that we were really demanding a change. You are upset with Kaepernick for not saying anything, but he took a knee! He ain't running out on the field acting out, but he just sat in his own area being peaceful.

Can I give you some stats real quick? I love giving out stats. So, we know since Kaepernick, we started boycotting the NFL, right? In 2017, Sunday Night Football's results came in at 18.175 million ratings, right. But they're down two million. So when I saw that large figure, that doesn't seem like a lot, but did you know the NFL is the highest watched and the most-watched sports/entertainment source in the world? For the ESPN Monday Night Football, came in at 10.757 million. It's down one million view ratings. When you look at Thursday Night Football, it's at 10.937 million. It's down nearly two million! And the experts in this space reported that the NFL's regular season ratings overall were down 9% versus its audience a year before!

If we think about the boycott we had leading through Christmas, we're taking the same stand against the NFL.

And what's happening is as we boycott against the NFL, they lose money, right? The different people who would normally endorse or try to buy contracts into the NFL for ads, they stepped back because they know they're losing money. It's called the domino effect. That's the reason why Mr. Papa John's is pissed! Because he fell into that domino effect, and he didn't gain from it. He reaped what he sowed.

He had a corrupted mind of greed. His M.O. is greed! Now he's upset. He's like, "Them niggers messing up my money." And the next thing you know, we were like, "Oh really! I ain't like your trashy pizza anyway!" That's good! Now everybody like, yep! No Papa Johns!

Now the question becomes, are we going to increase Domino's revenue now? Are we going to increase Pizza Hut's revenue, or are we going to say, you know what? How about we start making our own pizza?

Allah-u-Akbar!

That's the real move right there. How about we start making our own pizza? I mean, technically, I know shouldn't eat so much pizza, but it's hard to give it up. I'm a pizza fanatic, so don't let me be back east. That's the first place I stop when I touch down. I can't help it. (Laughs) I gotta bring a little humor. I have to bring a little bit.

Think about this. What if we started purifying our M.O. and the people who had noticed that we had bad M.O.s started seeing a different M.O. out of us? What do you think that will do to them? Many of us can bear witness to that.

Before some of us joined the Nation of Islam, we might have sold drugs, might have been addicts, might have sold their body, might have done a lot of different things that would not be pleasurable to talk about, now. But what they received from these teachings helped to purify the way they used to function. They wanted to change their M.O., and through that process, friends and family may not have accepted it. They may have talked negatively about them, disowned them from the family, stopped inviting them to the family unions and the cookouts. They got tired of him talking about taking that pork off the grill.

But one thing they do know anytime that good old believer did something they weren't supposed to do, they were quick to bring it up. "You know you ain't supposed to be doing this." That's because they're always paying attention. They're watching the change manifest in front of their eyes. They just may not be ready to do it yet because they're watching you and us to see, if what we are doing is the right thing? Is he going to make it? Is he gonna last? If he could do it, then maybe I can do it. Sometimes we're the biggest examples and don't even know what example we're displaying. But I tell you, this is the place for you. I tell you, this is the place for you. It takes work. This is not something that'll be done overnight, but with our heart and our mind, we must identify what it is that's keeping us from our success.

The standard M.O. of the Nation of Islam is the M.O. of a Savior. I want you to think about that. Our standard M.O. is the standard of a Savior. That is our standard. And the Honorable Minister Louis Farrakhan is our measuring stick. When people see and meet us, they should see the Honorable Minister Louis Farrakhan. They should see the Minister manifesting through us.

When you see the Honorable Minister Louis Farrakhan, you see the Most Honorable Elijah Muhammad. And when you see him that means you're seeing Almighty God Allah Who came in the person of Master Fard Muhammad. The Minister is the direct connection. He is the lead wire to God Himself, and if we're lining ourselves up to the Honorable Minister Louis Farrakhan, that means purifying ourselves. All the bad decisions we made in the past can be wiped away like sins thrown into the sea of forgetfulness.

The Honorable Elijah Muhammad wanted us in a vanguard position. He didn't want us to follow others. He wanted us to be what the Qur'an says. *You are the best nation raised among men. So you enjoin good and forbid what is evil.*

Your standard of M.O. comes from Genesis 1:26-27, where it says, *"God created man in his own image."* He created male and female in His image. Your M.O. is to become a god. I know that seems so far out of reach. It seems so far out there, but it's not. It's not. The first step is actually studying self and developing self, but as we develop, we master self. And as we master self, we're able to master the obstacles that are put in front of us, and they don't shake us or wave us away. They become ease, and we maneuver in peace. And once we start mastering these things, Allah God continues to exalt us, so that His power is amongst men. You don't have to believe it, but I'm telling you. We cannot continue to read these scriptures and not see ourselves in them. We only have one life, and Allah has given us everything we need to grow into Himself and what He desires of us. We just have to be willing to submit to it.

The Honorable Minister Louis Farrakhan said feeling unworthy of God's eminent grace puts our mind in a state of humility and deep gratitude for that grace. If you keep that state of mind, you will continue to grow in strength.

We need some soldiers. We need some soldiers because there's a need in our community for universal change. That change starts with the men. We have to step up and change the M.O. of our community, because until we change the M.O. of our community, we will not earn back the respect from the women and children of our community.

Being a man of God means being a man possessed of the knowledge, the spirit, and the power of God anointed to do His will. To build a people, we first must make man. So every man, no matter of his color, no matter of his race, every man in order to be a man must be a man of God or he's not a man at all.

Let us make man today.

There will always be an obstacle to any great desire that we have, but it's the overcoming of obstacles that bring joy to the accomplishment of our desire. We must put on the armor of God so that we will be able to stand firm against the schemes of the devil.

We are all caterpillars in this world. We're all crawling through this world looking for a better life. But the caterpillar has to build a cocoon that he can rest and better himself. That cocoon is the Nation of Islam. That's the cocoon that we caterpillars have to develop in. When you look at those who came through the Nation, you will see that they grew from caterpillars to butterflies and look at their wings, they're like angel wings, their wings are like birds. And those wings are expanding. They're coming out so strong that we're able to rise above the ways of the world, and as we rise up, we're able to look down at the distraction, and come down and swoop up our people! We are God's chosen people. We have to accept it and grow into our true potential!

8

Living Our Best Life Part 1: Islam, Peace & Harmony

"If our thinking gets in harmony with the Will of God, gets in harmony with The Time, then our actions follow suit."

The Honorable Minister Louis Farrakhan

I'm humbled today. I am truly humbled that you are enjoying this book.

Today we plan on living our best life. We should be in high spirits today because the Original God Himself gave birth to us so that we can birth the nations. That's what makes me excited, because when you look at the Honorable Minister Louis Farrakhan, you can see the Original God manifesting Himself through that man. When you see him, you see a free man. You see him living his best life; the best example we have, and what I love about this man is that he's made the people and the community his mission. He's made his devotion to God and living the examples of what God wants as his best life. And that's why when you look at the celebrities, the ones we idolize, let's be honest. When you look at the celebrities we idolize, they idolize him! But we have him in our midst and we idolize them. And what he's doing is introducing them to Almighty God Allah.

I want you to see these pictures real quick.

You got your brother 2 Chainz. That's his name. Platinum artist.

You got our brother Sway. I know you who he is.

You got my brother DMX next to Taraji P. Henson at the Big Three game. The Minister in front row seats.

The Migos. These people love the Minister.

Our brother Eminem. Do you see our brother?

Kendrick Lamar; all my West Coast people.

Then you see Jermaine Dupri, Rick Ross in the picture. This is actually a Holy Day of Atonement in Atlanta, Georgia.

Then you see Kanye and Kim Kardashian.

When we look at the Honorable Minister Louis Farrakhan, we don't see who he is, but the people see who he is. The fear that they have is what's keeping them from connecting us to him, because they're afraid of losing their money. Let me get into this chapter, man.

In the title, "Living Our Best Life," in the sub, it says, Islam, Peace, and Harmony. When you take Islam and you put peace, I could have just chosen one or the other. Since Islam means peace.

Islam is an Arabic word, right? Okay. And Arabic is a rooted language, right? And in Arabic, they have rooted letters that represent a word, and it gives the true meaning of that word. So when you get into Arabic, there are rooted letters that represent Islam, which is SLM.

When you see SLM in any word coming from an Arabic rooted word, it means peace. It equals peace, right? So when you go into these other words... I want you to understand that people have been programmed to think negatively of us and people have negative thoughts towards Muslims because they don't understand what it really means to be a Muslim.

When you look at SLM I said it means peace, right? So we're in agreement SLM equals peace. Well, when you see 'Islam,' that means peace. When you see a Muslim, it has peace in it. When you see Salaam, you hear someone say As-Salaam Alaikum, 'Peace be unto you.' Shalom, Peace. Hold up. Jerusalem is the city Jesus was born in. Founded in peace!

All Praise is Due to Allah.

We find ourselves upset with one another because we lack the understanding of who we really are. We are Muslims. "I ain't trying to hear all that." So you're not trying to hear us speak peace to you?

When we find ourselves living in peace, now check this part out. When we find ourselves living in peace with ourselves, we actually find ourselves living an Islamic life. I know that's too much. I'm sorry. Let me slow it down a little bit.

Islam equals peace, SLM. When we find ourselves living in peace with each other, that means we're comfortable and confident in who we are. We actually find ourselves living an Islamic life. That's why when you travel overseas into these Islamic countries, the crime rate drops. The killing drops. As you get off the plane, the stress of America comes off your shoulders. As soon as you come into these Islamic countries, you find yourself at peace and harmony. It becomes easier to live your best life.

Do not allow these media outlets to create your narrative of Islam without researching for yourself, and for a fact check, Wikipedia does not count! I'm being honest. (Laugh) Because there's actually a group. I'm not gonna throw names out there. There's a group that actually has hired informants to work Wikipedia to create the narrative. I ain't trying to put nobody out there today. This ain't that subject. But I want you to think about that.

The goal of living our best life is living our full potential, our full purpose, and a life with peace and harmony. And when we get to that point of peace and harmony, we're no longer easily distracted by other affairs. We're no longer easily angered by people and circumstances, because we're happy with who we are. Living our best life as a child is different than living our best life as an adult. Can I get a bear witness to that? As adults, we become very materialistic.

We're frontin' now. I gotta have the best looking car. You see that new rolli I picked up? You see how big my house is? We've become very materialistic, and we look at that as "I'm living my best life." But that's an illusion. We've become so concerned about what everyone else thinks about us that we become very insecure with ourselves and who we are. My brother Will Smith. Yeah, Will Smith said: *"Too many people spend money they haven't earned to buy things they don't want to impress people they don't like."* I mean come on Fresh Prince. Keep it real.

How many of you have done that before? Please don't raise your hand as you are reading this. Please don't raise your hand. But I do want you to think about it, because we all have done that, been in the store, went and bought something, and said, "Oh I can't wait 'til I get to school so I can show 'em I got the new J's!" Who are you trying to show? "Aw I gotta get that car off the lot man, that's the best car they got. Man, oooo, it's sitting on 24s." Who are you trying to impress? So we find ourselves going broke trying to impress everybody else when who we should be impressing is Almighty God Allah.

I remember when I was younger, and this is going into elementary school days so you talk about some years ago, and I would get so excited when my mom would take me to Payless. I'm being honest. I would get excited when she would take me to Payless or Wal-Mart. I was in a family. Around that time, Nikes was out, but Nikes weren't popping like that yet. Converse was more or less the shoes, the Chuck Taylors. Jordan hadn't dropped his shoes yet. They're about to come out. At that point in time, I'm not caught up in the materialistic part of the world like that. I couldn't wait to get to Payless because when you got to school you couldn't wait to show off the Ninja Turtle shoes. (Laughs) "Awww you got the new Batmans on!" "Aw man, you rocking with the glow in the dark. Them LA Gears." See man, you don't know what we're talking about right now. I'm just saying, you couldn't wait to get them checkers out of those fancy printed shoes, them canvas shoes so you can go to school, but you didn't look like everybody else. You weren't walking around with the normal white strap shoes that the nurses wear. (Laughs) And back then, you bought some Ninja Turtle shoes, they might have cost you 10 bucks. We didn't know that. We were happy to have them, because that was big to us.

Do you have children? Have you ever just sat back as a parent and watch your children be themselves? Like really watch them be themselves? They're playing and being themselves and their creativity and imagination is at high alert. You just sit there in awe like wow! I can't lie, I get jealous sometimes. I look at my daughters playing and they're just free to the world, playing with a little Barbie's and stuff and talking to themselves and their whole imagination's having fun. And you look like, man, that looks like fun! I am sitting there like, man, can I be a child again? Nope. No bills! They don't have that responsibility that you have as adults. They still have that freedom of expression. They still have that innocence of life. They still have that excitement. And the funny part about it, they're living their best life. For that stage of life, they're living their best life. You have to force them to come up off of whatever to come to do what you need them to do because they're having so much fun being themselves, discovering who they are.

If you ever get a chance to read the book "Closing the Gap," towards the end, there's a part where Brother Jabril asks the Honorable Minister Louis Farrakhan what's the meaning of fun to him. And he talks about fun is learning something new. And as you learn new things in life, you start having fun doing it. The children are having fun discovering the different parts of that little world of theirs. It might only be an 11 by 11 square room, but they're enjoying themselves. When we find ourselves and we find a way to determine ourselves as we should be, we will find ourselves having the same fun.

I was talking to Louis Farrakhan, Jr., and may the blessings of Allah be with him, and we were talking about children. It was the week before he made his transition, and he was telling me and one of my brothers how free they are as children and how we as adults damper their spirit early in their development with our own fears. If we really started taking notes of yeses and no's, we'll find ourselves telling our children more no's than we say yes and encouragements. So by the time they become adults, they're already going into things expecting to hear a no instead of "you can't tell me no, because I've heard yes my whole life."

We find ourselves robbing our children of their own best life because of our own insecurities and because we did not have certain things when we were growing up. And many of us find, if we go back and look at ourselves, we were robbed of our own childhood, because our parents did it to us. We did it to our children. And then we're teaching our children to do it to their children. The cycle never breaks. We take it out on our children the same way our parents took it out on us.

Part of our best life is giving the future something better than what we actually had. Now, this is the hard part of that statement, because a lot of us lose our creativity to live our best life. We lose our creative genius and our imagination because we find ourselves bogged down so much trying to provide for our children so they can have a better life. But while we're trying to provide for them, we're also taking away their mental, because we're beating them down with so many no's. When they grow up, you may have given them the world, but they are not appreciative of it because all they kept hearing was no. And that becomes hard for us to do when we actually don't see value in ourselves. We don't see value in ourselves. We live in illusions.

We see the divinity of all of Allah's creations. We see divinity in nature. We see the divinity in animals. We even see the divinity in the universe. But we do not see the divinity in ourselves, and that's because we see ourselves lesser than. Allah has made everything subservient to us, but we don't see divinity in ourselves. Allah has put everything beneath us, but because of how we see and value things, we've put everything above us and we made everything else better and more powerful than who we actually are. We are His greatest creation. We are Allah's greatest creation. He created the heavens and earth. He created the oceans and the mountains. He gave us lands and rivers. He gave us trees where oxygen can connect to us so we can breathe. He gave us the produce so we can consume and live, and all that is nothing in comparison to Him creating you and me.

Allah-u-Akbar!

When we learn who we are and start actually living our purpose, we will find ourselves free, living our best life.

Social media is a great tool, but to get on social media, you have to go on the internet, right? And you don't have to type this in too much more nowadays, but before you typed in the name of the site you're going to, there was a period before the word and what was before that? www - the World Wide Web. Social media has become a web. If you ever watch any documentaries or if you were just like me as a child—kind of bad, taking flies and throwing them on the spider web or finding ants and throwing them on a spider web. I did that kind of stuff. You watch how the spider comes out and attacks the ant. You only got a few seconds to get out that web. And what happens is the spider actually injects something into the brain to numb the insect before it actually takes the insect into its house.

When we get caught up on social media, the World Wide Web, we have to be very strategic on how we maneuver, because as soon as we get on there, that means that the enemy, that spider, is looking to inject something into the brain of the consumer. And once they inject their ways of their social equality, we fall victim to their ways of living. Don't get caught up on everything you see on social media because it is an illusion. Don't compare your best life to somebody else's best life, your circumstances to their circumstances, your upbringing to that upbringing.

You're two different people. We're not one and the same. Every raindrop that comes from the sky is not the same raindrop! Every snowflake is not the same snowflake. Allah has that much detail, that everything has its own independence. What you do and what I do from social media is really the best part of our lives. You didn't hear what I just said. What you and I do away from social media is really the best part of us living our best life.

Social media really just shows the tip of the iceberg of what's really going on in our day to day life. And it's funny because we get so caught up in the illusion of how people live their life that we find ourselves competing, "Oh, they could do it. I could do it too," not knowing what's really transpiring in their life.

"The grass is greener on social media." We all fall for this. People look like they're having a great time on the beach. "Man, I'm just enjoying myself. Two in the afternoon, I don't have to work." He got him a nice little brew, got a towel behind him, no shirt on, like enjoying getting a little tan type piece, right? But then when you go to the picture to the right, the reality is, "Well, I'm really not enjoying my life. I'm really not doing what I think I should be doing. I'm really not where I want to be in life. But I got to put up the front for people to think I'm living my best life."

Not thinking about the fact that he opened his eyes today. The fact that he's still got all his limbs and he can move around today. The fact that he was given another opportunity to do something better in his life today was really him living his best life at that stage of his life. But we get caught up on the illusion. Have you done that before? Don't say nothing. Don't say nothing.

You get your food. You clear the table. You take that nice picture and post it on social media, but it's just a glimpse. The real achievements are what we're doing away from social media. It's that process of achievement that is really the best part. You're not paying attention. That process that we go through, those late nights when you want to go to sleep but you got to get it done. When you are doing what you really love and you feel that real purpose in life, when you don't mind missing sleep because you're enjoying yourself, when we're actually tapping into that creative genius and we're really developing our gifts and talents, that is really the process of living our best life. But I want to go back a little bit more on that iceberg piece because when you see the Honorable Minister Louis Farrakhan, you would consider him a successful person. A very successful person, right? I just showed you pictures with him and celebrities and it's not him saying, "Yo, come take a picture with me." It's not even like that. They want to come and take pictures with him.

You know, I heard there was a concert recently. It was a sold-out concert. And when the 65,000 people in attendance heard the Honorable Minister Louis Farrakhan was there, the crowd erupted. He didn't go and say, "Yo! I'm in the building." He came to enjoy a concert. I want you to know when you see the Honorable Minister Louis Farrakhan, this is all of us, if we really think about it.

Back in the days, he struggled; I mean really struggled. He lost plenty of jobs. He even had holes in his shoes. Imagine walking through New York and Boston with holes in your shoes. He only had one suit to his name. His family struggled so much that he and his wife, Mother Khadijah, would go to the market after it was closed to pick up the food thrown out to take home and feed their family. So when you look at it like that, don't judge that man.

There was one time when Mother Clara, may Allah's blessings be upon her, the wife of the Most Honorable Elijah Muhammad, went to visit him, his wife and family in Boston. And when she came to the home, she saw how poor they were living. Then when she went back to see the Messenger, she said to him, "I've never seen poverty like that. But they seem so happy."

That shows it wasn't the materialistic things that brought him joy. It wasn't having the best things that you can buy that showed him joy. It was him living the best that he could be. It was him making sure he gave what he could for his family and his Nation. That's called Love! Love fills the heart. Love fills your being. We have to learn how to love ourselves. That's really our problem as a people; we don't love ourselves. We don't even know ourselves. How can we expect others to love us if we do not love ourselves? That's a struggle. That's an everyday struggle, and it's not all our fault. We've been made like this. We've been made in America. We have taken on the mindset of America, not the mindset of God. So God had to come and intervene in our affairs.

The Honorable Minister Louis Farrakhan's devotion and dedication to being one with God is what makes him the man you see today. His devotion and dedication to being one with God. Guess what? That's the same thing he wants for us. He wants us to be in oneness with God, but it takes real devotion. It takes real dedication. It takes going through the struggles of life to connect to that oneness, through all the distractions.

Now, you know, I like living my best life. I was at the J. Cole concert living my best life. I enjoy J. Cole. If you haven't listened to him, I recommend you listen to him, because he keeps it real. He was talking to us during the concert. He don't have a whole bunch of hype men. It's just him. He was telling us how he never saw himself being able to perform in these big massive arenas. He was like, it was never in the thought process. At the level he was at, he was doing clubs for so long. He never saw himself going higher. And he had great music as he has now, but the challenge he was hearing from everyone was, "I know hits.

I love his music, but he needs that radio hit that everybody can rock out with." There's a reason why I'm bringing him up, because he went through years of the process to get to where he's at today. He didn't give up on himself.

He said, overnight successes are one of two things, because many of us want to see overnight success, right? I want to drop 10,000 today and make 50,000 or 100,000 tomorrow," you know if we got it, but he said this: the first one he said is, it's not real. Which means if you see an overnight success today, they won't be here that long tomorrow. And he said the second reason you see no overnight success is that there was a process that took place that we didn't see. We just see the outcome. We didn't see the activities that were taking place to create the proper effects that will give them the results they have today. So when we see people on social media and the attractions they have from their followers and likes, we think it came easy. And if you talk to any person, especially YouTubers, they'll tell you they were posting videos for years before they had their real break. We must be willing to go through that process. Are you with me? Okay.

We've become microwave chefs. We go to the store, grab a TV dinner and throw it in the microwave. What you have for dinner? "Eggplant parmesan, brown rice, and some broccoli. Man, I was throwing down today." Ting! Three minutes later.

We've become microwave chefs. We want everything instant right now! "Man, I gotta go get it. I need it now. I need it now." Not knowing it takes a process.

We have to become real chefs.

I know some chefs. And if you know a real chef, a real chef will tell you. "Yeah, I gotta go to the market today. I'm gonna go pick up this today and tomorrow, gotta grab this, and the next day, gotta grab that." A day or two early, they're actually cutting up and prepping the stuff. Then they actually take the meat or whatever they're cooking, they marinate everything and put it in the refrigerator for a day or two, or they actually let something sit for a few hours to get the meat tender and ready. Then they start bringing this stuff together. Once they get into the kitchen with the fruits and vegetables and the potatoes and the meat, it still takes a long process to complete the dish. We're not talking about a three-minute instant microwave chef moves. You're talking about someone who understands it might take me a week to really prepare for what I need because I can't just go to one grocery store. You go to this store and they may not have everything. You travel to the other side of town to another store. You at the farmers market at another place. You gotta go get your milk somewhere else. They're willing to go to each place to get the best materials. Allah-u-Akbar!

That's a real chef. They know they don't have time for errors. Everything has to be precise, right on time with no distractions. They take their time.

That's how we have to be if we want to live our best life. We have to understand it's not going to come tomorrow, but it's going to come days, weeks, months, and even years later. We plant the seed now and we water it. Then, we come back and water it some more We make sure the sun is lined up properly for us and we put the plant in the right place. The sunlight brings the nutrients. While the seed is deep-rooted inside the earth, it starts to sprout out. Then you start seeing some of that best life coming to fruition.

It doesn't come right now.

The challenge is, we're insecure about ourselves. We're not confident in who we are. I am going to reference Fresh Prince some more, Mr. Will Smith. He said this. *"Do not chase people. Be yourself, do your own thing and work hard. The right people - the ones who really belong in your life - will come to you. And stay."* When that overnight success comes, people come running around that corner. Those phones start ringing.

You know, if anybody hit the lottery I'm calling you. (Laughs)

The people you don't see, they start calling and they start coming around because they see success now. I love my little brother because I watched him in his process as he does music. And as he's starting to really get a little more head waves and more buzz, the people who would not listen to his music, who he'd be begging, "Yo just listen." "I was always a fan." And he was like, "No, you weren't. You weren't there when I was struggling. I just needed help in this area. I wanted to use your studio, and you were pushing me away."

We have to be confident in ourselves. The one person Who will always be there in your life and is waiting for our call is Almighty God Allah. He's waiting for us to call Him up, and if you need the number, I'll give it to you. It's an easy call, too.

What I love about Allah, He's like your mamma or your dad. When you ask them for something, they're like let me think about it. And you don't know if it's going to be a yes or no, and you're waiting and you keep coming, asking and asking and asking. Allah is like that insurance check. That insurance check, you're waiting on it and you almost forget about it and out of nowhere, it's like ding ding! And you're like oh! I got that money!

I just got an insurance check. So that's what I'm talking about.

But that's how Allah is. When you least expect it, when you almost forgot it, when you were ready to give up on it, He comes to your aid. He comes to give you what you need to be successful. When you're like, "Man, I can't reach that checkpoint," he gives you that boost right at the last minute. And that's what I love about Him. But in order for us to really allow Him to do what He needs to do, we have to allow our old ways to die off.

When our old ways die off, Allah can really manifest Himself in us. As long as we're fighting against what Allah wants for us, we're always going to be chasing something. We're always going to be comparing ourselves to what everybody else has instead of recognizing the everyday blessings we get from Him. We have to look at the real priorities of what we have in life and not be distracted by everything else.

Here's an excerpt from the Honorable Minister Louis Farrakhan:

> "You go downtown Atlanta, you see a pair of shoes you want. So you put your little money aside and you get your shoes and your ooooohhhh! Don't I look good! Ooooo God! Look at them shoes. Stillettos too! You get the things in life that you seek: a new car, a fur coat, a new apartment, a new house, and you're only happy for a moment; for a moment, because nothing that you have is there to fulfill your purpose. Nothing that you acquire can give you the joy that only working to be what God created you to be will give you!"

The Honorable Minister Louis Farrakhan! Fire, right?

We find ourselves chasing money and buying all these things for the moment, next thing you know we don't want it anymore. An example is when you buy your children toys. When you start buying your children some toys, you be all excited like "Oh, I can't wait to get this home." And then they play with the box! Oh, that hurts me! They only play with the box. "Do you know how much I spent on this?" But that's not important to them. Our own children show us every day what it's like to live the best life. It's us trying to compete with everybody else. "Oh, I got him the super duper hot wheel." You know what I mean. "That one got hydraulics and stuff in it." Really!?

It takes real discipline and dedication for us to actually live our best life. It's not going to be an overnight thing. And within that dedication and that devotion and that discipline, we have to stop being afraid of what could go wrong and start being positive about what could go right. When we start thinking about everything that can go wrong, we find ourselves not even doing anything anymore. We wake up excited. "I can't wait! I'm going to do this today. I'm about to be successful."

"But then you know, man, then I got to deal with this, then this is going to happen and what if that doesn't work?" Next thing you know, that motivation goes right back out the window. We have to understand that if we desire something, we're going to be tried. And when God wants you and I to grow, he makes us uncomfortable. So anytime we find ourselves in an uncomfortable position, it's for one or two reasons: either we did something stupid or Almighty God Allah is preparing us for something better. And we have to take a step back and look and say what did I just do and how is this impacting my life? Why am I in this uncomfortable situation right now? Why is this harder than it normally?

That's when you know you're in the right process. When it's uncomfortable and you work through it and you start seeing the light at the end of the tunnel. You know you're in the right process. And it's time to learn who we are and learn how to live our purpose of life. Social media, that's cool. The material things we get, that's cool. Those are little perks. But when we live up to who we are as a person, we're comfortable with the skin that we're in and we're comfortable with what Allah blesses us with; we're happy with the fact that you went from walking to catching the bus to actually having a bucket.

I'm being honest. You ain't seen my car. I'm driving a bucket! But at the end of the day, I'm thankful that I get my children from point A to point B. I went two years with no AC man. Whew!!! But then I looked at my children in the backseat fanning all day. I used to have to freeze ice to put in the car. After seeing them like that for too long I to make that investment. So I had to work harder so I can get the AC fixed. Because you know, if you don't get it fixed in the wintertime, the summertime prices are so high that you feel like you are buying a new car. Nah, I gotta bring a little humor to this though.

But we have to find out who we are. And for many of us, social media is not our purpose. I know that hurts. I know, my bad. Oh, sorry. It's cool, though. I mean, you get some likes. It works, but it's not our purpose. It's a tool to utilize to achieve our purpose in life, but it's not our purpose.

Social media becomes a drug for many of us. When we post something, we're running back to it every two minutes seeing how many likes we got. How many comments did I get? Did anybody share it? What did somebody say about it? (Laughs) That's the trap of the web because once it got you, it got you. Then we have to take time away and figure out how to cope in real life. We get so consumed in social media that we don't know how to talk to each other anymore. We don't know how to look at each other anymore. How are you doing, brother?

There's nothing wrong with social media. It just has to be used properly, but if we learn who we are as a person, social media is fun when it comes. We have to come from behind that sycamore tree. We have to come from that hiding place we've been at. That's the fear of wanting to be successful in life. We're afraid of the unknown that may occur. We're afraid of losing or failing if that comes. We're afraid of success, if it comes, we won't move or really live our best life, but we'll post a picture online as if we're really living our best life so people don't have to bother us about what's really going on inside.

If we learn how to enjoy the pressure, the real pressure to living your real life; if we learn how to enjoy the public pressure of putting in the work, it will make the achievement more enjoyable. I don't know if were on social media this week. I was on this morning. I'm on social media.

I don't want you to think I'm bashing social media, but there is a video of these two heavyweight boxers. Dude's in the corner gassing himself up. He hyped up, looking at a camera, like yeah yeah yeah yeah, it's about to go down. Next thing you know, the referee called them in and was like ding ding! He climbed out of the ring and walked out of the building. Allah is my witness! He wasn't ready to endure that pressure. He did all that training. He did all that training in his life to get ready for that fight, and when it came down to really going to the next level of achieving what God might have for him, he walked right out the ring.

Many of us do that in life. We get a little pressure on us, and instead of going through the fight in that process of overcoming the pressure, which is going to strengthen us mentally and physically, it's going to allow us to overcome the obstacles in front of us, we walk away and then we get upset. We sit in the same cycle of life and don't understand why we can't get out that cycle. Every time Almighty God Allah gives us an obstacle, we run from it.

We have to find love in the process. We have to take it day by day, step by step. If we're looking to enjoy our lives, we have to be willing to set a tangible goal, weigh out an event and establish small steps of achievements. And if we establish those small steps of achievements, we find ourselves enjoying our best life at that stage of development. When we actually get to the bigger stage, that arena J. Cole's talking about, it becomes more personable. The enjoyment is so much higher. And just as the Honorable Minister Louis Farrakhan was talking about, it doesn't just fade away so easily, because we know we worked hard to get it.

That love Allah has for us is for us to be successful. He wants us to be the best we can. But we have to be willing to remove the fear so He can manifest Himself in us. And if we do that, we will be able to live a real meaningful life that gives us obstacles that are easy to overcome. It allows us to enjoy who we are as a person.

Do you know how you know you're living your best life? You find yourself happy. You find yourself not just content, but you find yourself in peace and harmony. You're not distracted by everything that comes your way. You're not easily bothered by everything that comes your way. You're not angry with everything that comes your way.

If I'm living my best life and you're living your best life and we bring our best lives together, that's power. Because if I'm comfortable in my skin and you're comfortable in your skin and we bring our energy together, there's nothing that can hold us back. And if I got my best life and your best life, and we bring it together and start a business, now we have success. If you take your best life and my best life, and we bring it together for marriage, we have success. Your best life, my best life, that's family. Your best life, my best, that's a better community. We post pictures online, but how is our community looking? That's what I love about the Honorable Minister Louis Farrakhan, because his devotion is to the people, and when he sees us grow, that makes him happy!

Let's talk about the haters now. We got to talk about the haters. We all know we got some. You probably getting hated on right now. No, I'm serious. Me? I love my haters. I truly love my haters. To all my haters who are reading this, thank you. No, I'm serious! Thank you. Thank you for being my hater, because you are amazing. I know you weren't expecting that, but I get it. What I love about my haters is they keep me on my deen. My haters keep me on point, because I know they looking for my downfall. Your haters become part of your motivation, because you don't want them to see you fail. Even though you're not doing it for them, you don't want to even have to look at them when they see you fail. So I love my haters. Thank you. When we get to the point when we can enjoy our haters and we're in a good spot in life, we are more successful.

I'm going to give you some advice. Go so hard in your best life. Go so hard being the best that you can be as a person so that even your biggest hater becomes your biggest supporter. I love it when my haters start supporting me, because I've had it happen plenty of times. I looked up and was like, "Really? You gave me a compliment? You were just talking about me behind my back the other day, though." But we have to understand that we're all going to have people who are going hate our success, who are going to be jealous of what we're doing in life, who are going to be angry with us for going further along in our process than they are in their own process. You can usually tell who they are because they're going to be very critical of your moves; not in a good way, though. They're criticizing every little thing that you're doing. But this is how you prevent them from winning. My big brother Nuri Muhammad said four ways to avoid criticism: be nothing, do nothing, say nothing, have nothing.

You're doing that? Your haters winning all day. But if you're trying to live your best life, you're not trying to not do anything. You're not trying to not be anything. You're not going to just not say anything. And you're not going to just not have anything. You're going to work hard to be everything you can be.

You're going to work hard to be what Allah wants of you. When we are really being the best of what Allah wants of us, we become Allah's angels to the world. Did you know you're an angel? We don't see ourselves because we don't see value in ourselves like that. We're so consumed on what everybody else thinks of us. Have you ever had somebody come to you and say something positive to you about what you did for them and you didn't realize you did it for them? Or they recognized something you did and was like, man, thank you like you really helped us in a situation and you were like I don't even know who you are? That's Allah using you and I, even with our own impediments and shortcomings, because even through our own shortcomings, he allows us to help others out. You never know who is watching you.

One of the biggest haters was Pharaoh. If you study the Book of Moses, study Moses, and Aaron. But the difference in today's Pharaoh is he's actually already let us go. It is you and I who won't let Pharaoh go. Pharaoh's already let us go, man. Because we're so attached, it's like we're out of slavery but we still have a slave mentality. The only thing we know is what the slave master told us and gave us. But we have a man, the most Honorable Minister Louis Farrakhan who is trying to show us another way. Until we let the ways of this world go, we will not be truly successful and we will not fulfill our own purpose in life. We have to stop trying to compete with what this world standard is. We all are origins from the originators of the heavens in the earth. Everything is subservient to us. Stop competing with everyone else. It's hard. I know it's hard because we're in this world. We have to live in this world, but we don't have to be of this world.

Stop letting people who do so little for you control so much of your mind, feelings and emotions. We have to make all of our fears fear us. That's real work, to make all of your fears fear you. We're going to be feared and we're going to fear things in life. It's going to be kind of hard. "I don't know if I can do it."

Can I be honest with you? I've been honest this whole time, but can I tell you a secret? I was fearful of writing this book. I honestly was. I've been worried. I'v been anxious. I was scared. I was like Allah, man, I don't know what I'm doing. I am just a little servant. Who's going to read this. Why am I doing this to myself? I'm being honest. But even in this process, I always know He Allah has my back. Even down to that last second, I know He has my back. And I've had plenty of projects like this where I was like, man, why am I doing this to myself!? Man, I should have just done this and be done with it. But I know I want to challenge myself to be better, and every time I get like that, Allah blesses me. So I have to challenge myself to overcome my fears.

I'm not perfect. I got plenty of flaws, but we have to make our fears fear us. We have to be serial fear killers to our fears. We have to be sniping them into pieces as soon as they arrive because even in our trials of learning who we are, that fight will remove those fears. Our haters live off of our fear, so we can't let them see us scared. Sometimes we just have to remove the haters from the equation. So if you're on social media, sometimes you hit that block button. "Aw, nah I'm good. You got too disrespectful. You distracting me." And when we do that, we have to tighten our circle with people who are self-driven and want more for us as we want more for them. If we do that right, we'll become more grateful with what Allah has for us.

Let's get into that part that is really going to take us into living our best life. We have to become more grateful of Allah's blessings.

We have to truly become more grateful of Allah's blessings. You don't count your breaths. You don't count how many times your eyes blinked to block the dust from getting in there. We didn't count how many times a heartbeat, but we're still here and Allah is blessing us every day.

We must truly love ourselves more. We have to love ourselves. Psalms 28:7 says:

"The Lord is my strength and my shield; my heart trusts in him, and he helps me. My heart leaps for joy, and with song I praise him."

We have to always give God the credit for making you and me who and what we are. We don't do anything in this world without the grace of Allah. And this is how we thank Him. We have to take time to pray or meditate to center ourselves and reconnect with a stronger connection to God. We must reflect on the many blessings and accomplishments we've already achieved in life. We must become more thankful for the everyday opportunities to do more. We must accept who we are so we can work on bettering what we can become.

To my dear sisters, I want you to know something, because I know you go through a lot on a day to day, from a child to an adult. You are the most valuable blessing in life. Now don't let this get your head bigger than it is, because I know some of you got some big heads. But if you really think about it, Allah worked to bring into manifestation a reflection of His best self, His best life, and He produced you. You are the Second Self to Allah. Through the womb of the woman, we produce nations. You are truly royalty. You are queens. You are gods. So please protect this. Protect this.

From that fitted hat to that headpiece, wear your crown. Be who Allah wants you to be and watch. Through you, the Nations' thoughts will change on how to do stuff.

Dr. Ava Muhammad was doing a lecture one day, and she asked the question of what was most important: food, water or oxygen? And she said with food, you know, you haven't eaten all day. You have to eat. But if somebody told you, you know, we're feeding a little bit later, you can postpone that. Because you know, at least you're eating. With water, we got to have water to live. But if you manage to go a little bit longer with no water, you'll still be alright. But oxygen. Oxygen. If somebody cut off your circulation right now, we'll be fighting for hell to get it back. That's Allah's blessing to us.

The fact that we open our eyes every day and we don't die in our sleep, Allah is protecting us. And if we do what we're supposed to do every single day to try to be a better person, Allah will show us a better life.

I'm going to give you an assignment. We're talking building a Nation. It takes 21 days to change a bad habit, right? Here's the challenge. I want you to do it, and don't hate me when I say it. I want you to take 21 days away from social media. (Laughs) Now, don't jump me. I want you to take 21 days away from social media. If you ever participated in Ramadan, I usually do 30 days away from social media during Ramadan. If you take those 21 days away, watch what Allah will reveal to you. Trust me.

During those 21 days, this is what I want you to do. I want you to reconnect with God or whatever higher being you serve. I want you to focus on your prayers. I want you to focus on your communication with Him.

Step two, I want you to study yourself. Study what triggers you and what makes you happy. What upsets you? Why do you get bored? What shows do you watch? I want you to study who you are.

Step three. I want you to find something you want in life, and during those 21 days, I want you to put all your energy in it, everything you have. Not all your money to pay bills. I don't want you coming to me after reading this saying you are broke because of me.

And this is the fourth step I want you to do. I want you to block negative people and remove the distractions during those 21 days. Watch how Allah God will move you during the 21 days. Now, I'm going be on social media looking at you. (Laughs) But try it. Try it. Don't wait until Facebook blocks you, Instagram gets boring, TikTok runs out of dance routines, or Twitter puts you in Twitter jail. Do it yourself. Step away.

You'll find yourself addicted like it's a cigarette. You'll find yourself with an itch... Try it. Those first couple of days are going to be hard, but as you get comfortable, you will see you have more time. Do you feel like you don't have time to do stuff? During those 21 days, watch Allah show you so much time that you've always had that you consumed toward social media.

When you find yourself living your best life, that means you'll find yourself living in peace and harmony. When you're truly living that best life, you will actually find yourself living an Islamic life.

So this is what I'm going to ask of you. You picked up this book and you are reading it. I pray I didn't say anything that upset you. If I did please forgive me. It was not my intention. But if you are not in the Nation of Islam, I want you to try us out for 90 days. Try us out and look at what Allah has done for us that he can do for you. And during those 90 days, make sure you cut off your social media. Remove those distractions, and see how Allah will bless you with a better life. I can guarantee if you do it right for those 90 days, you won't want to go back to how you once were. I promise you that. You will find the stages of your life from that point forward becoming a better life day by day than what you're currently in right now.

9

Living Our Best Life Part 2: Have No Regrets

"Be of good courage. Be strong. Be not dismayed. You can't have doubt and accomplish your vision."

The Honorable Minister Louis Farrakhan

I'm thankful because there are certain things that Allah has blessed me to see that may be a little bit different than other people. And sometimes I take on subjects that may not be the norm for everyone. Allah has shown me some things and this one is heavy on my heart, I have to let it out. And I'm thankful for these opportunities to show you what Allah is showing me.

I want to recap a little bit. In the previous chapter, we reflected on our childhood, and we talked about when you were a child, how you used to live your best life as a child. And if you're a parent, you see your children and you watch your children enjoy their lives, especially the young ones, when they're discovering things about themselves.

I talked about how we build up our strengths in oneness with Almighty God Allah through that process of challenging our own creativity.

Then we got into social media, and that seemed to be the hit for a lot of us. Because we know that many of us have got caught up in that web of the social life of social media, and we've got caught up in the distractions of the illusion of what people may post about themselves. We find ourselves comparing our lives to their lives, not knowing that it's not greener on social media. And we get caught up on what other people are doing and we think, man, their living their best life but we don't know what's happening behind the scenes.

To my young brothers and sisters who listen to music, as you may be aware, an artist by the name of Mac Miller just made his transition. He passed away.

Now, when you listen to different people speak of him, they were talking about the type of music he gave. And most of the music he did, he did it while under the influence of whatever narcotics he was taking. He wanted to clean up his life. And in the process of cleaning up his life, he found the last album he just dropped. He mentioned that he was sober the whole album, and he laid out this album. But there's something I want us to see because we look at the fame of a person not knowing he was really struggling with something on the inside.

So we look at the glimpse of the iceberg, but we don't know what's going on under that water. We get caught up on what's being posted on social media, but we don't really know what's going on in those closed doors.

They said he made his transition off of an overdose, which means he went back to that struggle he was struggling with.

In the previous chapter, we talked about removing distractions. A lot of times we have decisions and moves we want to make in life, but we find that there are a lot of distractions in our way of success. And sometimes those distractions can be our own family, friends, co-workers or even ourselves.

Then we talked about blocking them haters, because we all got them. We all have them, right?

We can't live our best life if we're not grateful for the many blessings Allah gives us, and that's really what I want to tie in.

The more we become grateful for Allah's blessings, the more Allah can grace us with more of His blessings. And the challenge we have on why we become ungrateful to Allah's blessings really is because we don't love own selves. We've lost the love of ourselves, and we have to learn how to love ourselves more. Now, I'm not talking about that egotistical love, that boastful love. I'm not talking about that love. But I'm talking about that dutiful love, the love of wanting to please Almighty God Allah for blessing us every single day of our lives type of love.

Psalms 28:7 says:

> *"The Lord is my strength and my shield; my heart trusts in him, and he helps me. My heart leaps for joy, and with song I praise him."*

The Honorable Minister Louis Farrakhan said to us to always give God the credit for making you who and what you are. Well, how do we do that? How do we do that? We have to take time to pray. We have to take time to meditate. We have to take time to center ourselves and reconnect with the stronger connection to Almighty God Allah.

We get so bombarded with the stresses of our lives that we wind up disconnected to the lead source and die. We get so consumed with the stresses of our lives that we wind up becoming polytheists, because we make the stresses a god over God Himself.

We must reflect on the many blessings and accomplishments we have achieved in life, not putting them too high, not putting them too low. But acknowledging the steps and checkpoints in our lives that Allah has given us that has allowed us to move forward in the process of betterment. We have to become more thankful for the everyday opportunities we're given to do more. We must learn to accept who we are. When we look in the mirror, we have to accept who we are and where we are in our lives. "Am I where I want to be at in life, or have I come short of my goal?"

When we learn to accept where we're at, that opens us up to be able to take on the process of bettering who we can become. I have to take a moment to focus on my sisters. Do you mind? Do you mind, sister(s)? I'll be short then.

I need you to know you are one of the most valuable blessings of life. You are one of the most valuable blessings of life. Now you don't let that get to your head too much, because I know your heads get big pretty easy (Laughs) I'm being honest. Allah worked to bring into manifestation the best part of Himself. And when He did that, He gave us the woman, to be exact. You are the best part of Allah, but the hard part is, sometimes my dear sisters don't see that in themselves. My sisters have lost value in themselves. When He produced you, He made you royalty. When He produced you, He made you queens. When He produced you, He made you gods.

So, my sisters, you will have to protect what's here. Here in your head and heart. Because there's a crown Allah has placed on your head, and I see it in social media most of the time where the crown comes down by the statements, the pictures, and the videos that are posted.

I pray to Allah that He uses me to show you how thankful you should be to Him, because there are women out today spending 10s to hundreds of thousands of dollars for a new body. Why? Because there's something that has happened that's made the Second Self of Allah see less value in herself. Did you know that the cosmetic plastic surgery industry is worth $16 billion as of 2016? Our beautiful women are getting butt implants, lip injections, breast implants and tummy tucks.

I'm not trying to bash. I want you to understand that. I'm coming from the heart right now, because there's something that's happening on the inside that's causing this. She'll post a picture living my best life, but she just got finished paying the doctor $100,000 for a new body because we were uncomfortable with the first one. It's to the point that women are dying now, from this plastic surgery, for a so-called perfect body.

So I want to tell you sisters: We love you. I love you. We love you. And if you're not getting it from us, let us know. Brothers, we have to do a better job, man. Because the women and men, we're yin and yang to each other. If our sisters are doing this thing, they're telling us we're not showing them the proper attention. That's caused them to go out searching for a way to grab that attention. I'm going to leave that alone. I'm going to leave that alone for a while. But we have to do better.

Living our best life is not just traveling or going to expensive places or buying expensive things. That does not mean you're living your best life. Now if you can buy it, All Praise is Due to Allah. But you have to ask yourself, why am I buying these things? Is it for the fact that I want to show people I've arrived? Is it because I'm trying to keep up with the Joneses? There's nothing wrong with having finer things. I don't want you to think you can't have finer things. That's not the case. Because traveling is a perk of living your best life, and buying expensive things can be a perk of living your best life, but it can't be your life. Because when we're living our best life, when we're truly living out the purpose of our life, when we're really growing into the purpose of our life, Allah will benefit us even more through His blessings.

I love traveling. I honestly enjoy traveling. I went to Dubai one year, but I almost didn't come back. Why is that? Me going to Dubai, for my sports fans, was like Kevin Durant going to Golden State Warriors. Already stacked team, just won a championship. I just come in and add to the equation. What do I mean by that? I love Islam. I love what I've been taught in Islam. I love the peace and harmony and the benefits I've got from this, through that process of me learning who I am, me focusing on trying to fulfill my gifts and talents and me focusing on trying to develop my purpose in life. When I travel, I can see the blessings of Allah.

When I was in Dubai, we were in the desert I thought about the Supreme Wisdom and how we ran Yakub and his made devils from the root of civilization over the hot desert. I'm touching sand and dirt and saying, "Was it just like this?" When I got off the plane, I was away from the police brutality of America, and I was able to touch down in an Islamic country. There's peace as soon as you get off the plane.

It was the feeling of getting a deep tissue massage and you come out and you kind of floating to your car. That was the kind of peace I was getting. Then to see my sisters dressed in their modest attire. To my MGT, it was like being at Saviours' Day every day. You know that vibe you get...Sister you see that garment you got on!? Wheewwww. But then to see how the Muslims are dressed in America, being dressed modest when you have women half-naked. It was an opposite effect when I went to Dubai. When you're finding your purpose as you travel, Allah will show you things in your travels, because you're discovering who you are.

We have a certain standard in the Nation of Islam. As I'm around certain people, and they're saying, "Oh, we have to make sure we do these particular things," it was nothing to us because we already live above the standards that were given to us. So living our best life is really living our purpose in life. I want us to always remember what is really important to us.

Our dear sister Dr. Ava Muhammad was delivering a lecture. She posed more or less a question in the way she was teaching. She was asking what's more important if you're out somewhere: food, water or oxygen? And she did a breakdown. If you haven't eaten all day like during a three-day fast, and if it was time to break fast and someone came or we all went out to eat together and someone told us it's going to be about another 30 minutes before we ate and we knew we were ready to eat, we still have a bit of patience left. We can wait a little bit because we know food is coming. If we happen to be out having a long day—my brother is working outside in that hot sun—and we're trying to get some water and we go to one store and they're out, we still have enough patience to get to the next store to get water. But let's talk about oxygen for a second. If somebody cuts off your oxygen, we panic. There is no patience in that area. If somebody walks up from behind you and puts you in a chokehold, you panic! How quick your response is of I cannot breathe.

Well, who gives us oxygen? Almighty God Allah. We don't count how many breaths we take. We don't count how many times our eyes blinked to keep dust from getting in there. So that's a natural blessing from Almighty God Allah that sometimes we take for granted. I have friends who have been murdered; friends who are no longer here. And I have to count my blessings. I have to count my blessings. I was just with someone and was informed of a murder. I just had my cousin post online, his best friend's brother just died. We have to count our blessings, because once we start counting them, we become more grateful.

The Honorable Minister Louis Farrakhan said *"In the world of God and righteousness, trials are as necessary for the perfection of the human being as water is to the growth and development of life; and sunlight and air are to the nurturing and preservation and origination of life."*

What does that mean? We're going to go through trials, trying to better our lives. We're going to have ups and downs and struggles in the process of bettering our lives. But how we handle those trials will determine our level of maturity. From maturity, we can see how much we have grown over that process. And then that growth shows us another step into that level of oneness to Almighty God Allah.

The Minister also said, *"Whenever we try to establish something new, something not necessarily believed in by the many but accepted and believed in by the few, those few have to be able to withstand tremendous persecution and trials in order for the truth revealed to them to be established."*

As we make decisions to do things in our lives, and those decisions are being made, people aren't always going to have our backs. People are going to say you can't do that! They're going to turn on us. They're going to talk trash to us. They're going to make us feel little, but if we're able to withstand the persecution of that trial, Allah will show you what you had in your heart was what He wanted for you.

We have to go through that purification process, because we know that in Surah 94:5-6, it says, *"surely with difficulty is ease. And with difficulty is surely ease."*

We're going to go through hard times in life trying to live a better life, but if we can find that pocket within those trials, within those distractions, within those struggles, there is ease there, and that is the best part of the struggle for us.

The Minister also says, *"If I can rejoice in what God has given me, then I can rejoice in what God has given to others. So my thanks and gratitude for His gift to me makes me grateful for the gifts that He gives to others."* That's called patience.

As we watch other people shine and do better in their lives, we can't get upset with them. Our process might be a little bit harder, but our process might be much better at the end. Or they may have started on a process before we did. When we become grateful with all of Allah's blessings, then we don't have to have any regrets when Allah brings us much more in life. When we step out of the stresses of life to a higher thought, we will see, and we can have much more of a smile on our face during that process.

In the title, "Living Our Best Life," is the word 'living,' which means to live, right? Well, in 'live,' there's a vowel. The vowel is 'i.' That 'i' can be interchangeable, which means it can be replaced with another vowel. If we replace that 'i' vowel with an 'o' vowel, what word does that give you? Love. We have to learn how to love our life. We live a life that we have, but we don't love who we are. When we learn to love who we are, Allah will continue to bless us through that love. He will show us through the process and the progress of us loving who we are, and He will give us many more blessings.

As that happens, even though we all have regrets of things we've done in our life... I have plenty. But when we learn how to move forward and better the things that we're doing now in our life, those regrets become no longer regrets of ours; they become learned lessons.

Our beloved brother Lil Duval came out with the song Smile. Y'all don't say the rest of it. And it's called, "Living My Best Life." He said something profound to me in his interview on The Breakfast Club. He said, "I don't sell music. I sell vibes." Vibes. He was expressing that he's at a certain stage in his life. He's not concerned. Money comes, but he wants to be him. He wants to be free to express who he is. How many of you would love to be free to express who you are? I know I would. But it takes time. It's a process, a strategy. It's steps. It's figuring out "who am I," first. But the way we figure that out is by connecting ourselves to He who gave us life, Almighty God Allah. Once we connect to Him, because it goes to Allah (God), men, women, children; Allah (God), man, family, nation. That's community. We skip self a lot of times in the process, trying to give everybody else what they need, which is good, but we lose our own identity in the process.

Now, I'm not going to ask if you know who Michael Jordan is. That would be a dumb question, to be honest with you. We know Michael Jordan, and he said this. He said, *"I can accept failure. Everyone fails at something, but I can't accept not trying again."* Let that sink in for a minute.

A lot of times we say I want something better in life. I want this job. I want to start this business. I want this relationship. I want to do something, and when we fail at it, we give up. Then when the opportunity comes back around to us, we say, "Nah, I'm good. I don't wanna do that no more. I'm straight. Forget that." What we don't understand is, it could have been that it wasn't properly planned out right the first time or Allah might have been exposing us to something to see how we handled it, so we could come back into the laboratory, study what went right, what went wrong, and then go back out and conquer it. As we conquer these little checkpoints, that's when Allah will start showing us better parts of who we are, and those better parts of us at each stage of perfection is a stage of us living our best life. When we're trying to better ourselves, we're going to have failures. When we're searching for our true purpose in life, we're going to have failures.

We have to step back and enjoy the moment of failure that we had. Everybody acknowledges Michael Jordan, right? I do too, but a lot of us don't know that when he was in high school and tried out for the basketball team, he was cut his first year. The coach cut him and told him what he needed to do. Michael Jordan spent the rest of that season practicing and bettering himself to make the team the next year, and now you have Michael Jordan: the icon, the mogul. But there was something that had to transpire first. He failed. The coach said, "You're not good enough for us. You need to improve in these areas." He got advice from a proper source. Not from the homie from down the street. "Nah, man, you know you should do this right here." That may not have been the best advice. Not from the parents, who at the time may have been going through a certain struggle in their life. That may not have been the best advice. But he got the right advice from the right source, went back, got better, came back, and now we're looking at this icon Michael Jordan. It created another level of discipline for him.

When was the last time you thought about what really brings you joy? A lot of us are living our lives, but we're not happy. We compare our lives to everyone else's life. Now I'm not talking about that joy you get on the weekends when you worked a full week and you can sleep in joy. I ain't talking about that joy. I'm talking about that real joy. When you wake up, you wake up excited to do you joy.

I remember when I was in Houston, and the student minister in Houston, Brother Abdul Haleem Muhammad, used to say something like, how would you be remembered? And I would ask him questions pertaining to that. He would say, well, if something happened to you today, how will people remember you tomorrow? And it's sad. A lot of times, we don't remember our brothers and sisters until they're gone, and we're going to their funeral. But ask yourself, really think about it. What have I done in my life now that if something was to happen to me, how would I be remembered for generations to come? When we start fulfilling that part of our purpose, we know we're leaving a legacy behind.

I was talking to my brother the other day. We have a very silly, weird sense of humor type of relationship, just like most siblings have. And he was looking at the flyer for me. Here's how the conversation went:

Him: "Man, bro, you're so corny man." Now, this is funny because he would have never said that any other time in my life

Me: "Man, why you say that?"

Him: "Man, you just always smiling."

Me: There's something wrong with that? You always mean mugging. Are you not happy?

And I explained to him, I smiled, because even though I'm going through everything I go through in life, I find gratitude and gratefulness in it. I always try to find a way to make the glass half full, so it brings me joy. I mean, I've worked miserable jobs that I'm like, man, you sit in the parking lot, hour before it starts you like I might call in sick. I might just quit today. But then I find the happiness in what I'm doing, even though I got to deal with the stresses of the people. Sometimes you're driving to your destination, you get road rage a little bit, then I have to calm down, take a deep breath and say, you know what? I got to make sure I get home to my children. I almost had an incident like that yesterday. (Laughs) But I really find joy. One of the things I find joy in: helping people. I've honestly found real joy in helping people. So I get excited when I can help somebody. Like, say I was Clark Kent going inside the phone booth, going to switch out to a superhero uniform. **SUPERMAN!** I get excited, like you need help? What you need? I got you! Because when you see that joy on their face when it's accomplished, it brings me excitement.

When you're able to talk to somebody when they're in their creative genius and they want to achieve something and they get so excited about it. You're like, man, like you're happy. I want to capture that moment and just hold on to it. It brings me joy. Or when you find a brother or sister in the streets and I'm out there with my brothers with The Final

Call, and they're going through something and we stop and actually address what they're going through. They say, thank you. Or when they say, where y'all been at!? It hurts, because it's like, man, we' ain't been here in a while. But it brings me joy because they want to see us. That's telling me I'm doing something right in the purpose of my life, that people want me around them.

Proverbs 22:1 says, *"A good name is more desirable than great riches; to be esteemed is better than silver or gold."*

I've really strived to the best of my abilities to have a good name. Well, who did I learn that from? The Honorable Minister Louis Farrakhan. When you see everything he goes through, I pray on the daily asking Allah to give me the spirit of the Minister. Give me a double portion of it. Because if you looked at Aretha Franklin's Homegoing and you saw the mistreatment of our Minister, you saw a smile on his face as he sat on the stage the whole time. And it's interesting because things we already know about people, we already knew they weren't going to ask him to speak! It just got exposed on TV. We knew it already. We just get excited to talk about it. Like, I knew it. It got exposed on TV. But look at the blessing. The Minister was not concerned about that. You're talking about the man of God bringing presence to a circumstance or celebration. And when you looked at him, you saw a smile on his face the whole time. Smile. He had a smile on his face whether he spoke or didn't speak, and the blessing he gave us never came out of his mouth that day, he spoke volumes to people by his steadfastness.

All Praise is Due to Allah.

ANGELA WEISS / AFP / GETTY IMAGES

He spoke so well without opening his mouth. He spoke so well without opening it. You were watching him in the aspect of him living his best life during that moment on TV, because he was living the purpose that Almighty God Allah has given him and he was just there to show love to the family. In the process of him showing love, "I'm here just to be present," the news couldn't help but to try to create some kind of drama between him and Aretha Franklin's family. "Why is he there? Why is he front and center?" Doesn't matter. You ain't pay for this funeral. What are you worried about? But what I learned at that moment, the word of the day from that time was humility. He taught us a whole another level of humility. We know that the Minister is the best example. Patience, smiling, enjoying. He was actually engaged in every aspect of the ceremony, clapping, shaking hands, hugging and very proper, not too familiar with it.

Matthew 5:14-16 says, "*You are the light of the world.*" Are you paying attention? **YOU** are the light of the world.

A city set on a hill cannot be hidden. Nor does anyone light a lamp and put it under a basket, but on the lampstand, and it gives light to all who are in the house. Let your light shine before men in such a way that they may see your good works and glorify your Father who was in heaven. Think about that for a second.

We know the song, similar to those three verses, called "This Little Light of Mine." *This little light of mine. I'm going to let it shine.* We know the song. *This little light of mine, I'm going to let it shine.*

We work on our own self-improvement, then we bring what we're learning about ourselves to the community that we're working on together. We will become beacons of light in this dark hour we're coming into. We will become a multitude of stars in the dark hour that will guide people to the right path. But we have to be willing to shine off the dust of ourselves, the rust of ourselves. And when we do that, we will find ourselves growing into oneness with Almighty God Allah.

We must establish more faith in Almighty God Allah, and as we establish more faith in him, we have to also establish more faith in ourselves and our own capabilities. In Matthew 13:31-32 under the parables of the mustard seed, it says:

> *"The kingdom of heaven is like a mustard seed, which a man took and planted in his field. Though it is the smallest of all seeds, yet when it grows, it is the largest of garden plants and becomes a tree, so that the birds come and perch in his branches."*

We must have the faith of just a mustard seed, and if we really grow into that faith of a mustard seed, we will see how Allah will actually start showing us the better parts of ourselves. As we start fulfilling the better parts of ourselves, we will see ourselves living our best lives at that stage of development. In that process, we have to remove what's called bad habits. I can't say I want something better for myself and I'm still doing the same things that injure me from doing the better things of myself.

It takes 21 days to remove or break a bad habit. How many days? Okay, that means we have to be consistent for 21 days. It can't be on and off. It can't be like, well maybe today and then I'll come back three days later because every time we come back, we have to start all the way over. Now those habits must be substituted with good habits. If one of my habits is laziness, I replace laziness with doing good work. If one of my habits is I like to sleep a lot, I need to reduce sleep with actually doing good works that allow me to go through the process, right? If one of my habits is I smoke cigarettes or whatever it is, I have to replace that with something that's going to keep my hands busy, because I'm used to grabbing on to something to bring towards my lips.

We're going to try this again. I have a challenge for you. Don't get mad at me when I pose the challenge. Do you promise you won't get mad at me when I pose this challenge? Are you ready? If you're ready, say, "Woop woop!" I want you to take 21 days away from social media. If your mindset is "oh hell no no no no no no no!" that means you're actually addicted. Just going to be honest with you. Which means you probably need it more than you realize it, because the thing about an addict is, an addict doesn't know they're addicted to something until somebody exposes it. "Yo bro, you might want to get checked." "Get checked out for what? Man, nah bro." "You look like you're on something." "I ain't on nothing!" "You been scratching the same spot for 30 minutes bro. You addicted to something!"

If you know you wake up and you check your phone before you make prayer, you just might be addicted. I know that hurt, right? But I'm going to give you a substitution for those 21 days. Take out your cell phone. I want you to take notes for this part, because I don't want you to say you didn't know. You ready?

I'm going to give you four steps, four things to do to help during that process. If you don't do it, it's on you, trust. But one more question. Have you tried it, yet? You tried it? How did it go? How did you feel the first day? It was kind of hard, right? How was the second day? (Laughs) It shows how much we've been attached to our phones.

So here it goes. During those 21 days, I want you to reconnect with God or whatever higher being that you serve. So for my Muslim family, sometimes we miss our five prayers because we're on our phone or at work. That means we should work on catching those five prayers. That challenges us now, right? And if we find ourselves going towards that itch, take a moment to make a quick prayer. "Oh, Allah please forgive me." Keep rolling. "Oh Allah I'm tempted..." Keep rolling. We'll find ourselves making 1,000 prayers a day and not even realizing it.

Alright, step two. I want you to study yourself. I want you to study the habits we have during that time. I want us to study how we respond to "I want to get my phone. I said that. I thought like that," because as we study ourselves, we'll find out who we really are.

Number three. I want you to find something that you've always wanted in life. Well, I'm not gonna say always wanted. We'll start with want in life. We'll go there first. I want you to find something that you want in life. Examples, you might be in a hardship in your relationship with your spouse. I want you to work on that for the next 21 days. You might be trying to start a business. I want you to put that energy into that for next 21 days. Every time you would normally grab your phone, when that phone thought comes to your mind, think about your business. I want you to put that energy into the business or whatever it is in life that you want to accomplish. I want you to put that energy there for the next 21 days. Watch how Allah will use that.

This one's going to probably be one of the most important ones, because it may cause some issues with you and your family and friends, just so you know. I want you to block negative people and remove distractions. So, just as an example, I'm not on social media. I'm three days in. Your home girl hit you up. "Girl, did you see that Cardi B Nicki and Minaj fight?" "Oh, when? When was that? That's a distraction. I don't want to know about it. I'm cool. I'm busy on something right now." You don't have to tell them everything you're doing because you know, if you tell them sometimes they're going to hate on you. They don't have to know. "Know what? I'm cool. I don't need to know about that. You hold that for you. I'm focused on something right now." Because once we come out of that 21 days, we'll have a different spirit. We'll have a different energy.

So what were the four steps? To reconnect to Almighty God Allah or the higher being that you serve, to study ourselves, our habits and how we function, to find something that we want to accomplish and put the energy into that for the next 21 days, and to block negative people and remove the distractions from our lives. You got that? You can put your phone away. (Laughs)

Watch how Allah is going to manifest things for you through those next 21 days, if you commit to it. Whoever does it, I want you to connect with me after you do it because I really want to talk to you to see how it impacts your life. During this process, we're going to learn how to live the example that we've always wanted people to live for us. You're not paying attention. During this process, we're going to learn to live the example of what we wanted people to live for us.

Go and live your true purpose in life. Connect to Almighty God Allah and allow Him to guide you through the traps and distractions of life that have been in your way. And as that's happening, I want you to identify the blessings, hold on tight and acknowledge the everyday blessings Allah gives you.

The Honorable Minister Louis Farrakhan was on brother Munir's show, and he said, "Let me tell you, let me tell you something. Don't lose hope. Get some hope. But if you give up because you had a setback, you'll never win. Nobody goes forward in warfare and does not have to make a retreat. A strategic retreat to develop where they are weak"—that's a keyword right there—"to come back strong. But when you give up and punk out, there's no hope for us. Stop it. There's always hope if your hope is in God and the truth and in yourself."

When you really find yourself living your purpose, which means you found yourself living in peace and harmony with no regrets of what you're doing in life, you are now living an Islamic lifestyle. You don't know what that means. Islam is peace. Islam is the nature of a person, and when you are in oneness with Almighty God Allah and you find peace through all of the distractions of the world, through everything that's pulling towards you and you're able to stay focused, you got blinders on, and you're allowing Allah to guide you where he wants you to go, you will find peace and harmony in yourself.

Do you want to learn how to live your best life? Do you really want to start the process? Because I know some lack confidence in that area, and that's okay. But I tell you, try the Nation of Islam out for 90 days. Try us out for 90 days, and those areas that you have insecurities in, bring it to the table and watch how Allah will show you, through the Nation, how to get confidence. Watch how Allah will show you, through the Nation, how to live a purposeful life that will elevate you to another level of self that you never thought was in you. You will find the distractions that were in your way being removed, shedding off the weight like you're in the gym. I guarantee if you try us out for 90 days, Allah (God) himself will show you something different you never knew was there for you.

Do you want to live a purposeful life? Then let's live a purposeful life. Let's live our best life! And if you want to live it, come join on. I guarantee you Allah will show you something new.

10

Defending Farrakhan

"Out of the nature of our love for him, we responded to defend him—as any student would do if they love the teacher"

The Honorable Minister Louis Farrakhan

When you look at the works of the Honorable Minister Louis Farrakhan, you can see the original God manifesting Himself through him. We are watching God manifesting right now.

When you and I build confidence in God Himself, that strikes fear in our enemy. He is afraid of us building confidence in God because he knows God wants us, so he's trying to keep us away from Him. He does not want to see us grow up. Why would our enemy fear you and me building confidence in God? I'm talking about real confidence, not that I made a prayer and I went back to nothing confidence. I'm talking about I made a prayer and made action confidence. Think about it.

He fears the rise of the Messiah. He fears the rise of the Black Messiah. This started way before the 1960s; it became more prominent in the 1960s. When you were able to look at the leaders at that time and you're seeing what was happening and when you look up the FBI Cointelpro and read, you can see they were taking the preventive method to not allow the rise of the Black Messiah. They fear our mental and spiritual growth. Allah gave the Word, and the Word became flesh. Well, if He gives us the Word, we take heed to the Word of God and we just take that first step out on it, you will see God manifesting His works through our hands and feet.

What is a Messiah and why would the government and our open enemy fear that rise? Let's go to the dictionary for a moment. 'Messiah' is defined as: *the promise and expected deliverer of the Jewish people; Jesus Christ, regarded by Christians as fulfilling this promise and expectation,* which is John 4:25 and 4:26. It's also defined as *Judaism, the awaited Redeemer of the Jews, to be sent by God to free them.* To free them. *Jesus Christ, when regarded in this role, also defined as an exceptional*—an exceptional—*or hoped for liberator of a country or people.*

So you're telling me Allah will send Messengers, Messiahs and prophets for all people who are in need of one, but you have the Black man and woman of America in need and He would not send one? Or has our enemy made us blind, deaf and dumb to recognize a Messiah in our midst? When you look at the works of the Honorable Minister Louis Farrakhan, you can line him with the title and much more.

The government would look past the Honorable Minister Louis Farrakhan because their eyes were focused on Malcolm X. Their eyes were focused on Martin Luther King, Jr. They looked past the Honorable Elijah Muhammad, because he was too old in age, but they did not know that he gave birth to one and this baby would take on the throne. He was protected, shielded off, so they did not know that.

The Nation fell, and by the end of the 1970s, the Honorable Minister Louis Farrakhan had started the work of rebuilding the Nation of Islam. There were many claiming the title and saying they were the successors of the Honorable Elijah Muhammad. That's not true. By the 1980s and 90s, the rise of the Nation of Islam had become prominent.

The Minister's name became punch lines in many rap songs by Hip-Hop artists. All my brothers and sisters who listened to Public Enemy, Notorious B.I.G., KRS1, Rakim, Nas, Jay-Z, Snoop, Cube, you started hearing the Minister's name coming up in the lyrics. The Minister teaches us that when you listen to a song, it's like listening to a thousand lectures. Just the mention of his name drops a seed in the mind of the people, and it started waking them up.

The Nation of Islam started its rise. This beautiful Nation of Islam started its rise. Many looked at the Honorable Minister Louis Farrakhan like he was crazy at that time. They would bring him on talk shows to make fun of him; they would try to find a way to get him caught up in something dealing with the Mother Plane or the Baby Planes. They did anything they could to expose him, thinking that they were creating controversy, but it actually was not that. It helped.

He became comedy skits for many shows—some funny, some not funny—but one of the funniest ones was *In Living Color* when Damon Wayans played the Minister and they would do their *Star Trek* version. But what you fail to realize, by them doing that, you're putting the Honorable Minister Louis Farrakhan in the spotlight. In the 1980s to the mid-90s, media was mentioning his name on everything, trying ways to cause controversy, but it would backfire. It would create more interest in him and the Nation of Islam.

By 1995... I was in the 6th grade around that time, going into the 6th grade. He called for the Million Man March, and nearly two million men showed up and many more men and women did not go to work on that Monday, October 16th—that historical day, showing we had power. That struck fear in our enemy. That's what you call an impact.

We learn about Jesus, but the historical Jesus 2,000 years ago did not speak to no more than maybe 40 people at a time; so who is this Jesus figure we're speaking of who can speak to the masses? In Luke 14:25, it says, *"Now large crowds were going along with him."* From that Million Man March, he started striking more people, touching more people. That was a wake-up call for the enemy to see, *"Whoa...he got way more power than we thought he had."*

If you've ever seen the movie, *Malcolm X* by Spike Lee, you see F.O.I. show up to the jailhouse and when he gives his signal...*let's move out*...you see the chief. He said, "That's too much power for one Black man." They didn't say that out loud. That is what the enemy was thinking of the Honorable Minister louis Farrakhan. They went into their hiding places and said, "That's too much power for one Black man." So that's when the enemy changed up his strategy to turn you and me away from the Honorable Minister Louis Farrakhan. The enemy has been on his deen, and he's been very skillful at it. He silenced the Minister. What do I mean? How do you silence the man of God? He stopped mentioning his name on his platforms. He removed him from the comedy skits so he wouldn't be a punch line anymore. He removed consciousness from Hip-Hop and R&B. He took the roots from it so he could graft, re-graft and remake Hip-Hop and R&B into what you hear today. Then he put fear in the colleges and universities telling them not to bring the Minister on campus. Now they're scared and they turn away from the man of God.

The Minister said on Twitter, "We cannot run from being tried." The Holy Qur'an teaches us that God is going to try us with "something of fear, hunger, loss of property, loss of life and diminution of fruits, but give good news to those who are patient and steadfast under trial."

Dear Holy Apostle, you got your Nation; we are your good news. He has been under trial the whole time, to the point where people started calling him anti-Semitic. They close the doors on the Minister, but open doors for other people they would call anti-Semitic. Do you know why? They know he is that Black Messiah they fear, and they fear that if we actually identify who he is, if we attach ourselves to who he is and become who we're supposed to be, not only will you see the rise of a Black Messiah, you will see the rise of what they call Wakanda, but you will see the rise of a Nation of Islam. A nation of God's people.

Allah-u-Akbar!

By them silencing the Minister, the people thought that the Honorable Minister Louis Farrakhan was dead. They thought he was irrelevant. They thought he no longer had importance among us... until now. What I love about now is the world gets to see that the Honorable Minister Louis Farrakhan cannot be easily dismissed. They get to see that he's back on all the platforms. When he started addressing the imposer Jews, they had to speak on him. They couldn't hold back anymore, so they had to bring his name up. You start seeing clips come up on the news again about the Honorable Minister Louis Farrakhan. He's now on social media, grabbing the masses.

Let me give you some facts on that real quick. The Minister has 1,081,853 following him on Facebook as of June 17, 2018 (disclaimer: these facts were produced before he was banned from Facebook and Instagram). Allah-u-Akbar! He ain't dead! And he's not even an entertainer. He has over 481,000 Twitter followers. He's not an entertainer. He has over 436,000 followers on Instagram. Oh, you don't want to speak on him on the news, don't worry about it. He has a Farrakhan Twitter Army. He said he'll take this teaching to every nook and cranny. Well, we're going to help him get there. They got the nerve to uncertified his name as not being a public figure. That's alright, we don't need that title. We got your back Brother Minister. He has countless speeches on YouTube with millions of views and still counting. The same people who were making some real bad remarks are coming back years later saying, "I should have been listening to you. What you were saying in the 80s and 90s are manifesting right now in the 2,000s."

They tried to count us out in 2015 at the 20th Anniversary of the Million Man March, because it didn't get a million people on the floor, on the grounds of the Washington mall, but he hit over one billion people who viewed it via webcast. That's Justice or Else! They don't want you to know these facts. He touched nearly every nation that day and then you come around to his last few speeches in 2018. He spoke at the Holy Day of Atonement. He spoke at the Press Conference in November. He spoke at Saviours' Day 2018.

He spoke on May 27, 2018, and in his address, he let them know who the original Arabs are. He let them know who the original Jews are, and that caused another frenzy. They plan and Allah plans and Allah is the Best of Planners. You can't have Farrakhan! He also said on Twitter, "As sure as light banishes darkness, truth vanishes falsehood."

They've been lying for way too long, and that light is beaming on the head of people right now, so the darkness that they were living in is vanishing away. And he said, "If truth is with you, then you have nothing to fear from anyone who comes bringing darkness and falsehood. It is our duty to tell the truth." So I tell you, enemy, I let you know your attack on the Honorable Minister Louis Farrakhan is an attack on your life. Allah-u-Akbar! Because they are trying to be slick. Come on, be bold now, don't hide! He's calling you out and we want to see who you are.

These networks are trying to be very, very skillful on how they do stuff. In January and February, they just did a whole series on Waco. Why am I bringing that up? Because he called himself a messiah. He called himself a messiah, and they were frightened by that so they went and made attacks on his home and his congregation.

They just did another one, it launched on A & E, called *Cults and Extreme Beliefs*. It's hosted by a lady named Elizabeth Vargas. The most recent one they did is on the U.N.O.I., the United Nation of Islam—not the Nation of Islam—but the United Nation of Islam that started in 1978. A brother who was speaking was technically born and raised in it—which they call a cult—and his name is Elijah Muhammad. They not slick, but we have to be on our dean ready to attack when it comes, because they are trying to brainwash our people to tie us together.

The leader's name is Royal Jenkins. Well, we know that ain't the Nation, because we get rid of slave names, but the language ties into the Nation's language. He would say, "The University," or "The Nation," and if we don't know any better, we would think that they're talking about the Nation of Islam. I'm telling you off top, it's propaganda. And if you look at how they went from barely dropping seeds to now they're trying to tie us in, it lets you know the time that we're in. This is part of their last trick. So he had the nerve to be saying that he didn't like the way he was treated, and he was sent off away from his family and I'm like, we don't do that in the Nation so I ain't gotta worry about that, but I'm concerned that our people, who don't know that much about the Nation, will fall victim to it. We have to make sure you know, *"Nah, that ain't us."*

When I watched the documentary, it reminded of the Minister's speech on May 27th. He said, "Many of you don't even know me, but you have views of me because of what you heard about me." Many of them don't know the Nation, but if they happen to see this first, it would turn them off to who we really are, because this isn't us. This is part of their plan, but as I mentioned earlier, they plan and Allah plans and Allah is the Best of Planners.

You can dictate the agenda by the things that happen. It's just like if you go into the Garden of Gethsemane and Jesus is making prayer and the disciples are falling asleep. Disciples, we can't fall asleep right now, because while they're sleeping, while he's praying, the Jews are planning and they're trying to find a way to tie him into something. When they arrested Jesus, they tied him into something. They brought a case upon him and put him on charges with somebody else, and they let the people choose, but the people didn't have the real knowledge of Jesus at that time.

So I tell you, come out to the Nation, and come out to these classes. I guarantee what you will learn, you will see and be able to defend anything that comes towards you, because that man Farrakhan is the man that you want to follow.

Prophet Muhammad, may Allah's blessings be upon him, lived to be 62 ½ years old. Did you know that the Honorable Minister Louis

Farrakhan had been preaching in America for longer than the Prophet has lived? Think about that. With all of their attacks and plots, he's still standing. That's because he's backed by God. They can't touch him, and he keeps calling for them and while he's calling for them, we have to be prepared for that attack.

He said, "Troubling times in life is what makes us who and what we are. Seek assistance through patience and prayer and you will find your troubles will diminish." Sometimes, we're afraid to make a move or we're afraid to stand up because we have ties with the enemy. We may not purposefully have ties with the enemy, but the enemy found us slipping up at some point in time in our lives; so we're afraid to stand up, that we will be exposed. But I tell you, take the exposure. We got you; we understand that you have shortcomings. I have shortcomings. But speak that truth to falsehood and we got your back.

God has brought us all to the earth to face one difficulty after another, and it is the facing of these difficulties and the overcoming of these difficulties that improves our character and improves ourselves. Our submission to do the Will of God is our admission to become a god. All we have to do is submit to His Will and walk with this man, Farrakhan. He has never misguided us. Any misunderstanding is different than misguidance, and if we submit to do the will and follow his instructions, watch how God will manifest in you and me. When the Minister decides to go see the Father, they will be so fearful because you will see a whole bunch of Farrakhan's running the streets. Allah-u-Akbar.

Today is Father's Day. Happy Father's Day, my brothers. The Honorable Minister Louis Farrakhan is the father to the fatherless. He is the Jesus to Lazarus, if we really understand who he is. So to my mothers who are raising children with absent fathers, I tell you this: Line yourself up with this man, Farrakhan. His wisdom and guidance is an extended hand in the home. He will help better the development of your children. Don't stress yourselves out. If the father is not in the home, bring the Teachings of the Most Honorable Elijah Muhammad in the home and watch how that will raise your young son up to be a man, and then line him up with these men and make all men and boys join the F.O.I. They will be better fathers than their father was to them. Allah-u-Akbar.

The Minister said, "Feeling unworthy of God's eminence, grace puts our mind in a state of humility and deep gratitude for that grace."

If you keep that state of mind, you will continue to grow in strength. To my brothers, the Minister said, "There is a need in our community for a universal change, and it starts with the man. Being a man of God means being a man possessed of the knowledge, the spirit and the power of God, anointed to do His Will. To build a people, you first must make man. Every man, no matter of his color, no matter of his race, every man—in order to be a man—he must be a man of God or he's not a man at all. Let us make man. Man. There will always be an obstacle in any great desire that you and I have, but it is the overcoming of the obstacle that brings joy to the accomplishment of our desire."

The Honorable Minister Louis Farrakhan makes men and women. He made me, and that's why I'll give my life for that man. He is our last hope. He is our last chance. So I tell you, grab a hold to Islam, follow the man—the Honorable Minister Louis Farrakhan—get in tight, hold on tight, get a tighter grip amongst the brotherhood and sisterhood and watch how Allah will manifest Himself in you and me.

11

WHY I WALK WITH FARRAKHAN

"Jesus The Christ: The anointed of God to crush Satan and take his world out of existence. Can you walk with that Jesus?"

The Honorable Minister Louis Farrakhan

I want to talk about why I walk with Farrakhan. Sometimes we can get deep into scriptures and find ourselves out in the galaxy somewhere, and the people who are reading have no idea where they went, where they're at and how they get back home. But when I think about the Honorable Minister Louis Farrakhan, I think about a man who has given nearly 60 years of his life for the salvation of a people. We're coming on 40 years in absence of his father, the Honorable Elijah Muhammad.

Minister Farrakhan teaches that your love will renew your spirit to continue your labor until you reach your goal. Your love for what you do must be deepened. I was born and raised in the Nation of Islam. That itself is an honor. Sometimes you don't realize how blessed you really are. I have family—my mother, my father, my uncle my aunt—who were part of the rebuilding of the Nation of Islam. I'm speaking of the absence of the Honorable Elijah Muhammad.

They attended at a place in the area of Arizona State University. And I see it on some of the faces of the ones who were around during that time. During that time, there really was no structure like you see now when it comes to the Nation of Islam. Really, as long as you believed that Master Fard Muhammad was God, the Most Honorable Elijah

Muhammad was the exalted Christ and the Honorable Minister Louis Farrakhan was the divinely guided one, that was all you needed.

During the rebuilding, access to the Honorable Minister Louis Farrakhan was so easy. He didn't have security, then. It's just like, when you plant a seed in the dirt and there's no one else around you. You alone have to do the work to get it to sprout out of the dirt. My parents told me the same story at different times. I was in Houston once, and my father told me this story. I laughed, like you're over-exaggerating. About a few months later, my mother and I are talking, and she tells me the same story. And I'm like, okay, maybe this is accurate. During the rebuilding, before we had the National House back, as the Honorable Minister Louis Farrakhan traveled across the country, he didn't stay in hotels. He stayed with the believers who said that they wanted to help rebuild this Nation of Islam.

I'm a privileged young man, because my parents' home was one of the houses he would rest that. There was a time when they were at the coffee table, sitting down dialoguing. And my parents told me I came up off the couch and crawled under the coffee table and bit the Minister on his ankle. I'm just saying I always wanted some of the juice. From that day, I've been connected to this man. I'm serious. From that day, I've been connected to this man. I wanted what he had. I wanted to be like this man because he, for many of us, is a spiritual father. Even once we got the National House, the family was so accessible. I remember spending the night at his son Joshua's house when him and sister Marie were still married. And growing up with Malia and Josh and Elijah and Lewis and Fard and Muhammad. Muhammad was still a baby. I remember the time we would play at the National House. That beautiful home you see right on 20th or 21st and Violet. But as you elevate, you have to tighten up and get security.

I'm going to show you why I walk with this man. In November 1984 after my oldest brother made his transition, the Honorable Minister Louis Farrakhan delivered his eulogy. He's never been too big of a man to come down to the little people.

I walk with Farrakhan! I remember being in elementary school and I had to do an essay. And I went to my mother and said, "I want to interview the Honorable Minister Louis Farrakhan." And I probably called him Uncle Louie back then, because everybody was an aunt and uncle to me. When Minister Jabril would come by the house, he was Uncle Jabril. And he would greet me "As-Salaam Alaikum chief," and I'm like, "Walaikum Salaam sir!" And my mother told me I would reach out to him and see what I can do.

A few days later, Brother Jabril comes to the house while working on my project. He greets me "As-Salaam Alaikum chief," and I'm like, "Walaikum Salaam sir." And he goes to tell me, "Well, I spoke with the Minister and he will not be able to come in to help you with this project. But he did tell me to tell you any questions you have, you can ask me." But you know I'm young. I got upset. "I don't want to interview you. I want to interview the Minister." I'm being honest. Now, after some pleading from my mother, we're gonna say it nicely. Because it wasn't that kind of pleading. "Boy, you better get your butt in there." But after getting some stern words from my mother, I found myself sitting down asking questions to Brother Jabril.

I always looked at Brother Jabril as just Uncle Jabril. I never looked at him in scripture. As a child, I always looked at the Honorable Minister Louis Farrakhan as Uncle Louis. I didn't look at him in scripture. But I've always had a connection to this man. As I started growing up, I attended the mosque.

Around 1994, the Minister went on a Stop the Killing Tour to help stop Black-on-Black violence, Black-on-Black crime, because we were killing one another. The president at the time did not have that kind of clout. Jesse Jackson did not have that kind of clout. But the Minister has that type of cloud that he could call for 1 million and nearly 2 million show up not on a Saturday. You have two peak days in the week, Monday and Friday. He called us out on a Monday, and we came.

I wasn't there, but I wanted to go so bad that when the brothers went, I was there too. I remember being at my mother's house as the brothers came by before they left. At 11 years old, I drew a picture of the National Mall with many people in the audience and the Minister mounted at the rostrum. And a little bubble sign said, "Get him. Stop him." I don't know what I'm getting into; I just know we have to protect this man. But what I'm not knowing is at this time, the Minister is so prominent in America that Notorious BIG is mentioning him in his rap songs, that Public Enemy is mentioning him in their rap songs and that all through hip-hop, as hip hop is evolving, they're mentioning the Minister and the Million Man March through their music. The music is being utilized to wake up the masses.

Following that lecture on October 16, 1995, established as the Holy Day of Atonement, the enemy went into full effect. They did not want you and I to know who the Honorable Minister Louis Farrakhan was, so they went on a campaign to damage and tarnish his name, It was to the point where if he did any good, and that's the only thing he does, you would not hear of it in any media outlet.

By the time we get to '99 and the 2000s, that music that you grew up to, the music you enjoyed listening to had completely changed. It was no longer Black consciousness. It was, "Shake it fast, watch yourself." It was, "Oochie Wowee." It was, "Drop down girl get you." Don't act like you don't know music. It's okay. It became very hyper-sexual, and every song has something related to sex in it. They may not have it like when you had Genuine, Pony, Jump on it. You had R Kelly Bumping and Grinding. We stopped having conscious music at that point in time.

As media ignored the Nation of Islam, they still saw that the Honorable Minister Louis Farrakhan had a pull on the people. So September 11, 2001, known as 9/11, two towers get hit, and the Pentagon gets hit. And then from there comes the war on Islam. See, we think that war was abroad, but it was a war on two fronts. It was really a threat for us here in America, because at the end of the day, they don't care about them there. They want the Minister off the streets, so the Minister, being who he is, had the men of the Nation of Islam remove their bowties and start wearing straight ties. The signature bowties would cause us to separate ourselves from our peers, so he had us blend in with them. That was a chess move to save our lives. We started wearing bowties again when we really started seeing the celebrities wearing them.

As a teenager, I'm going from a black and white understanding to a gray understanding, but I'm not quite there yet. When you read scripture or books as a child or when your parents give you instructions, you only know what's right and what's wrong. During my teenage years, I started parting away from the Nation of Islam and my spiritual father, the Honorable Minister Louis Farrakhan. It became challenging for me. It was challenging for me to be able to look at us when I'm told we do things this way but I see the opposite being done. When you see your mother do one thing, but she tells you another; you see your father do one thing, he tells you another; you see the believers tell you one thing, they do something else and you see the community doing whatever they see pleasing to them. So I parted ways.

I started partying. Some of the brothers I grew up with and I used to be in the club, in the house parties, on the west side and Scottsdale. Whew! We found ourselves away from the guidance of the Honorable Minister Louis Farrakhan, but there is a saying that raise your child up in the way it should go and when they get old, they will not depart. So no matter what I tried to do to fit in with this world, I still stuck out like a sore thumb. My peers would say, "You're very mature for your age." "What do you mean?" "Well, you know too much. You're always talking about this here. We're trying to party." "Well, you know I don't drink. I'm just not into it." "Well then we're trying to get tipsy." "I'll roll with ya'll. I'll drive, how about that?" I feel safer.

Even though this was going on, I was still attached to my father. So while I was still in high school, I would still attend Saviours' Day. Don't ask me to come to the mosque though. I'm good. Because at that age, I was bored out of my mind. And I'm putting that out there for a reason. Because there's a certain age that teenagers, your children, get to where the mosques and study groups across the nation, even the churches across the nation do not address them at their age. As children, it's easy. Put em in the back, have somebody watch them, give them some pen, paper and cutting utensils and let em have some fun. But as you start coming up into your teenage years, sometimes you don't want to sit in the pews and listen to somebody lecture all day. So I parted ways.

The next thing you know, I'm in Houston, Texas attending college. At this point in time, I'm so far out there. But one of my sisters by the name of Nicole wound up attending the same school as me, and she fell right into the mosque in Houston. "Hannibal, you gotta go." "Nah, I'm good. You have fun. Tell me how it was." Because at that point in time, I did not want to know. I didn't want to hear nothing about no mosque. I wanted to enjoy the world. It was so enticing. But periodically if I heard the Minister was speaking, I would find myself at Muhammad's Mosque Number 45. When the Minister had Saviours' Day and I couldn't make it, I would be at Muhammad's Mosque Number 45. When Holy Day of Atonement would happen, I would be at Muhammad's Mosque Number 45 or TSU when they held it at a public venue. No matter how far away I tried to park myself from this, I couldn't get away. When I would hear my father speak, it would resonate me, but it would not be enough for me to move forward yet. And at that point in time, the gap had started to increase and I didn't even know it.

Sometimes when seeds are planted, you don't know they're being planted. I didn't know there were seeds already planted in me from being in the womb of my mother and from going to the mosque every meeting. Man, even at the times when Muhammad's Mosque No. 32 did not have a building, the meeting was conducted at my mother's house, so I couldn't even run from the mosque. I remember when they would have MGT class at my mom's house. Man! Couldn't sleep in. "Brother, go out there and make sure the cars are parked right." Sister Dorianna would bring Joelle and Jamil over. I had to watch them. "Let's go play Mortal Kombat." "Nope, y'all making too much noise, let's go outside." Like, it's the middle of the summer, 115 degrees and you got us in the sun during MGT class.

I was such a savage. I want you to understand this. No, seriously. I would wake up basketball shorts on, no T-shirt. They in the middle of MGT Class and I would go in the kitchen and make a big old pan of pancakes and be in there trying to flip it. And the sisters would walk in and say, "Brother, that smell good. What you making?" "Pancakes. You want some?" My mom would come in there in a captain-type way and curse me out without cursing me. "Boy, you better get yo butt back in that room. Go put your shirt on. Why you in here cooking? Quit playin!" "Ma, I'm hungry." But I don't know I'm such a savage at the time. I was so disrespectful. I was ignorant. I knew not of my ways.

But what I do know now is that there were seeds planted within me. So while I'm in Houston, these seeds would try to germinate. They would try to activate within and sprout. But I had so much filth on me that they would not come out. The next thing you know, I'm telling you, I stayed close, and they didn't realize how close I tried to stay to the father. Because in 2005, I'm still a savage in my own ways. But my father called me, "You're coming to Washington for the 10th Anniversary of the Million Man March." I went to the National Mall in Washington, D.C., and I enjoyed the lecture. I got a chance to take my stepbrother back to Hampton, Virginia. What I don't know is that the seed in me is trying to come out, but that just wasn't enough yet.

A whole year passes by and I'm still asleep. By the time December 2006 comes around, it happened. The seed pushed through. All Praise is Due to Allah. I find myself in my room in a two-bedroom apartment. My best friend lived right down the street from the National House. We were roommates. But at that point in time, he parted his way, and one of my friends moved into his room. I'm lying on the bed. It's the middle of the night. And I hear a voice. "Hannibal. Get up." I'm like, "Yo bro, what you want man? It's early dude, what's wrong with you?" "Hannibal get up." "Dude, for real. If I get up, I'mma punch you in the chest. Leave me alone. I'm sleepy." "Hannibal get up. Pray." "Whoa! Did you just say pray?" And then I recognized, "Partner's not here anymore. Who's this man's voice I'm hearing?" I'm lying in the bed like I'm in a horror movie. I pulled the sheets over my head. I was a punk. I ain't gon' lie. I was like, oh no. If I'm gonna die, I'm thinking death, now. If I die, I at least want to know who killed me.

The voice says, "Get up. Pray!" Next thing I know, I'm at the foot of my bed on the floor, tears running down my face. I am apologizing to Almighty God Allah for my flaws. "Oh Allah, forgive me. I'm sorry. I should have been came home. Oh, please forgive me. Oh Allah, I promise. I promise if you let me go, I'm coming home." I called my mother. She didn't answer the phone. I called my father. He didn't answer the phone. I'm going through it at this point in time. I'm crazy out my mind now, right? She finally answers the phone. Anytime I called my mother in the middle of night, this how much of a savage I was. Anytime I called my mother in the middle of the night, her first response was, "What's wrong? Who did you get pregnant?" I'm serious. "Nah ma! Nah, nah, I didn't get nobody pregnant? Nah ma, I'm good. I'm good. I'm good."

I'm crying. I mean I'm boo-hooing. I'm like, "Ma, grab the Qur'an." She knew something was wrong then. "Ma, grab the Quran. Please grab the Qur'an." "Boy, what's wrong with you?" "Please grab the Qur'an, mom. Please grab the Quran." "What do you want me to read?" "I don't know. Just open to something. Start reading." I still don't know where she went. All I know is she started reading the Qur'an to me. "Is that good?" "No, keep going, keep going." And she kept going, kept going, kept going. Then I was like, "I'm good." "What happened?" Then I tell her the same story. She says "So what are you going to do?"

As far away as I tried to go, for some reason I could not get past the shore. Muhammad's Mosque Number 45 is right off of 4443 Old Spanish Trail. I was about to get the zip code, but I couldn't remember it. I lived less than a mile and a half from the mosque. I kept trying to run from it, but I did not go far away from it. I would come up with every excuse to not go there. "Where are you going to go?" "I'm going to the mosque." "When?" "Right now." "What time is it?" "I don't know like six in the morning."

I pulled up to the mosque. I saw the sanctuary, the building where meetings are held. There were no lights on. I saw another building, which happens to be the school and the kitchen. I started walking over there because I saw lights on, and a sister was on the phone. She caught my attention. "Brother, you need some assistance?" There are children already on campus. I'm a threat to security at this point in time. I don't know this. "Yes, ma'am. I'm good." You would have thought I was on crack. I'm serious. I'm shaking. I'm like, "I need to see the FOI." She's like, "Brother, you okay?" "Yes, ma'am. Yes, ma'am." She's like, "Hold on, brother." She calls her husband. I love the FOI. She calls her husband, Brother Sylvester, who happened to be my first lieutenant. "My husband said give him a call. His name is Sylvester." This is why I love the FOI. I called him and told him what's going on. He says, "Yes sir. Okay, this is what I want you to do." This is happening on a Thursday or Friday. "This is what I want you to do. I want you to come to the mosque on Sunday. The meeting starts at 10am. I'll talk to you at the mosque."

He literally fished me into the mosque. Me, a savage at the time. "Yes, sir." I go to the mosque that Sunday. I planned it. I shut everything down. I was trying to avoid it. I shut everything down. I swear to Allah. That day, Student Minister Abdul Haleem (formerly Student Minister Robert) spoke. "Brother, I know what you're going through." When he asked for acceptance, I said, "Yes, sir!" Then, I walked up to the front. He asked, "Brother, what's your name?" I say, "Hannibal Muhammad." He said, "Brother, you know what your name mean?" I said, "Yes, sir." He said, "Well brother, you got a lot of work to do." And from that day, I picked up my cross and started walking with Farrakhan. All Praise is Due to Allah.

Now, during this time period, I'm so eager that I would literally run to the doors. You couldn't slow me down. I was moving so fast they thought I was going to be one of those six-month brothers. See, the ones in the Nation know what I'm talking about. The ones who come in going real hard and you try see how long they're gonna last. Then that six-month mark comes, and they go boop! They fall straight out, but they ain't know I have something on my shoulders. See, when I was on that floor praying to Allah, I made a covenant with Him that day. I made a promise to Him that day. And I told Him I was going to give my life to this. I was so afraid of being disobedient to Him. I was afraid that He would take my life if I fell out. I ain't talking about going out the mosque. I'm talking about physically taking me out of this world.

I was rockin a purple suit with purple candy-colored gators on. I had locs in my hair. I love locs. I wish I could still get them, but I had locks in my head. That was me. You dress like a pimp. You know what I'm saying. That was me. You want to be that fly. Next thing I know, I'm coming around 2007. My mother flew me in to Detroit, Michigan for Saviours' Day. This is the same year they were wondering if the Minister was going to make it. This is the same year the Minister was on his deathbed. Me not knowing a few months earlier, I'm on my bed making a covenant to Allah to come help this man who's going to soon be on his deathbed. I'm telling you, I've always been attached to this man.

So next thing you know, I return. I'm here. But the thing that excites me the most, what people don't know and I never told my mom this. When I moved to Houston, I took her book *This Is The One*. I hope she wasn't looking for it. For some reason, every blue moon I would pick up the book. I would just want something to read, and I'll start reading through it. See to me, Brother Jabril was just Uncle Jabril who's a writer. That's how I looked at him. Oh, Uncle Jabril, he's a writer. He writes great books. By the time I came into the Nation, the book *Closing the Gap* was being introduced. I'm not knowing at this point in time that I have a gap. I'm closing myself to Almighty God Allah, to the Messenger and to the Minister. Now I start reading this book, and I'm looking at the questions that Bro. Jabril is posing to the Minister. And I go from yeah, Jabril, Gabriel, Jabril, oooooo, Michael, hold on. I know who you two are.

Now I'm really digging deep into my scriptures, because I'm really loving this. I'm having fun. If you open Closing the Gap to pages 39 and 40 and you go to Phoenix, Arizona, I'm blessed to know these names. Brother Britton Muhammad, back corner. Brother Bobby

Muhammad, Brother Carlos Muhammad, Sister Edith Muhammad, Brother Gary A. Muhammad, Brother Gary C. Muhammad, Brother Hakeem Muhammad, Brother Hannibal Muhammad. When I came into the mosque, they were my brothers. "You wrote this book with Brother Jabril?" "No, no, no. My father helped in that." I realized they started asking me questions about Brother Jabril. Brother, how's he doing? When was last time he talked to him? I'm like it's Uncle Jabril? I didn't even read the book yet.

As I started going into the book, I started fighting harder to close that gap with my spiritual father. One thing I know about the Honorable Minister Louis Farrakhan, on page 47 of Closing the Gap it says: *"For Allah God so loved the world that he gave his only begotten son. He gave, he sacrificed him, and his son was willing to be sacrificed. Minister: I have no life of my own. My life is for the redemption of a people. And that is pretty hard. However, that is the necessary requirement to affect resurrection, redemption, restoration and reconciliation of the soul that is loss."*

And he said in conclusion, *"When a person is like that, he has no sin. He has shortcomings for sure and he may commit sin, but by his long suffering and continuing to pull on the good nature of Allah, God and the people to make them better and better and better, Allah, God just wipes away sin, that he has and throws it in the sea of forgetfulness, and forgives his sin, because of the work that he does of redemption. This is why Jesus is looked at as absolutely perfect and sinless."*

That's why I walk with Farrakhan, because he has no life of his own, and the sins that he may commit, they're thrown into the sea of forgetfulness, because he gives his life for us every single day. If you go on and read this book on the life of the Minister, he lost his job a few times. One time he lost his job because he saw something happening to a person. The police beat them up, picked them up and drove off with this person, and he went chasing after the police car, abandoning his job because he wanted to make sure nothing happened to that person. This is a man of humility.

Did you know he had humble beginnings? When he and his wife, Mother Khadijah, were coming up after they got married and had children, the grocery store and the marketplace would be closed, and they would pick through the groceries that were thrown out in the street so they could go home and feed their family.

That man gives his life for us every single day. He had one suit. He had one pair of shoes. He was giving a demonstration in the men's class, and during this demonstration, the men saw that he had holes at the bottom of his shoes. He didn't complain about that.

This enemy attacks his name every single day. If you go to social media every day, someone's attacking his name. If you go to Google search every day, someone's writing an article trying to tarnish his name. Even with all that has been thrown at him and all of the attacks he goes through, this man still prevails. That's why I walk with Farrakhan. That taught me, no matter what people do or say about you, you should not allow it to keep you from what Allah has placed on your heart to achieve. Fight through the adversity. Fulfill your purpose in life, because that's what he's doing every day for us. When you walk with Allah, he will show you the hands of the enemy. He will also show you your helpers. He will show you who your enemies are. He will show you who the hypocrites are. You just gotta walk with him. He will protect you from the front. He'll watch him back. He'll guard your sides.

What a friend we have in the Honorable Minister Louis Farrakhan, who guides us on the straight path every single day. He makes decisions we may not agree with because of our little understanding. He sees prophecy, so he puts things in place so that we can be guided to it. But we want to fight and be disrespectful to the man who's guiding us. That's why I walk with Farrakhan. I want you understand who you're looking at. If something happened to Barack Obama today, they would swear in Biden, the current vice president, to be the president. I want you to know, when you're looking at Farrakhan, that's not who you're looking at. Minister Farrakhan died years ago. And I stand on that. When you look at Farrakhan, you weren't looking at the Honorable Elijah Muhammad!

You have to understand, the Honorable Elijah Muhammad put this man in his chair. He said, "No, brother, not there. You sit here in my chair." Let's go to John 16:28: *"I came from the Father and entered the world; now I am leaving the world and going back to the Father."*

How about 6:38: *"For I came down from Heaven, not to do Mine own will, but the will of Him that sent Me."*

14:31: *"But that the world may know that I love the Father, as the Father gave Me commandment, even so I do. Arise, let us go hence."* That's him guiding us.

5:19: *"Jesus gave them this answer: 'Very truly I tell you, the Son can do nothing by himself; he can do only what he sees his Father doing, because whatever the Father does the Son also does.'"*

10:30: *"I and the Father are one."* When you look at him, you are not looking at Louis Farrakhan! You are looking at the Honorable Elijah Muhammad!

John 10:15: *"Just as the Father knows me and I know the Father—and I lay down my life for the sheep."*

John 15:10: "If ye keep My commandments, ye shall abide in My love, even as I have kept My Father's commandments, and abide in His love."

And in Matthew 26:39: *"Going a little farther, he fell with his face to the ground and prayed, 'My Father, if it is possible, may this cup be taken from me. Yet not as I will, but as you will.'"*

* * *

You do not want to be unclear when it's time to put the Lamb's blood on the top and the side of your doors when Allah's plagues come.

Because what you're seeing with the weather right now is just a small comparison of what's going to be. These signs are just warning signs for us to clean ourselves up.

The Honorable Minister Louis Farrakhan is a divinely guided man. He's so divinely guided that he led us to Dianetics. We're not part of the Church of Scientology, but there is a tool in the Church of Scientology called Dianetics, and he led us to this tool to help clear up some of the pain and struggles of our past. Our enemy attacks us through our pain struggles, and emotions, so as long as we're emotional, they have us locked into their grip. He needs us to be clear-minded.

In the Supreme Wisdom, in the Rules of Instructions to the Laborers, it says, "According to the Holy Qur'an, 59:7 the Muslims were very poor when they first started to teach Islam. And all contributions were given to Allah's Apostle for him and his family's support. And what the Apostle could spare he gave to help take care of the poor Muslims that were unable to help themselves. And the other part was given to those who were confined to the labor of Islam."

The Honorable Minister Louis Farrakhan writes checks all the time helping families. He doesn't run around bragging 'look who I gave a check to, look who I donated to.' A few years ago, Haiti got hit and they needed a water purification system. I think it costs over $50,000. I know they got a water purification system in Haiti now. We don't run around talking about "where's the news cameras. We need to do a press conference. Look what we're doing." This man sacrifices and gives to the ones who need it. He pays for funerals. He gets people out of debt. He pays for school for people to go through.

He gave us a 58-week lecture series, The Time and What Must be Done. In one of the broadcasts, he talked about the shadow government who holds secret from the presidents. He's exposing a shadow government that we don't know nothing about. You say he ain't divinely guided. He ain't no leader. All right. He gave us the Divine Instructions this past Saviours' Day, and in those divine instructions, he gave 35 commands and instructions. What came of that was the 10,000

Fearless. In the past, you could not get to the Minister once his security evolved, which means he's being exalted. Anytime you have a question for the Minister, he's assessable to you through social media. now. Nearly every day you see a post come up through Twitter or Facebook, even Instagram, from the Honorable Minister Louis Farrakhan of divine guidance.

This is why I walk with this man. And it's an honor to walk with this man. It's an honor to bear witness to the man of God. This man has saved my life! That's the least I can do. He's built confidence in me. You know how hard it is to walk around with the name Hannibal as a child? Hannibal the cannibal. Hannibal lector, what you eatin' today? You got brains on the plate? Hey, Claris. I mean, I got it all. I'm serious. But me bearing witness to him and what he goes through builds confidence in me to endure those challenges. When I was a child, I didn't want to be called Hannibal. You know what the most popular name to be called was back then? Michael. You had Michael Jordan. You had Mike Tyson. You had Michael Jackson. Mom, can I change my name to Michael? I requested it.

I was vegetarian way before being a vegetarian was popular. Born and raised vegetarian, before it was popular. Born and raised vegetarian. It's popular now. So my name is Hannibal, and I don't eat no meat. I got it all growing up. No, I've never had a steak before. No, I've never had ribs before. And no, I've never had pork chops before. No pork on my plate. And no, I don't know what I'm missing, because I've never had it. All Praise is Due to Allah.

That takes me to this point. On social media, a sister put out a little meme, a little video. She posed a question to the Nation of Islam. She said she has a friend. She has a question. She was talking about the Black Muslims in America, especially Nation of Islam. When the Muslim start eating pork? She has a friend, she's a comedian. She's having fun. She said, "It's Tuesday and he was out eating. He was like, yeah, let me get this pork, this pork that" and she was like "I thought you was Muslim." And he was like, "But I'm good on Tuesdays and Thursdays." "Tuesdays and Thursdays? But I thought y'all don't eat pork?" "Nah, we good on Tuesdays and Thursday. "Y'all have part-time Muslims?"

No ma'am! We don't eat pork. When you walk with Farrakhan, you put that down? When you walk with Farrakhan you throw that poison away. The first time you see the video when you see some pork and the worms start coming out, you go in your refrigerator, freezer, and you start tossing it out. No ma'am, and tell that brother to call me. We need to have a conversation, and to any brothers and sisters who's eating pork, get off it. Get off it. Even the pork by-products. Get off it. They already poison us with everything else. Let's not give them any extra. No ma'am, we don't eat pork and tell Amad Ahad or whatever his name was to holla at me. We got to have a conversation because he's making the Nation look bad. I gotta talk to the brother.

But I'm serious. The Honorable Minister Louis Farrakhan has saved my life. And I'm pretty sure if I look at some of your faces, he saved your life too, and even the ones who are coming into this knowledge for the first time. He saved your life, even if you don't know it. Because when you see the 60s and they talk about being pro-Black, that came from the Nation of Islam, first. We were still being called Negro. No, we are Black, because Black is universal. There's no ending to darkness.

I guarantee that you were influenced in some way by the Nation of Islam and the Honorable Minister Louis Farrakhan. When you see Colin Kaepernick, who took a knee, he's a birth child of the Minister. That comes from the Minister's era of rebuilding the Nation. We don't stand up for the National Anthem. My whole childhood was you better sit down. I used to get in trouble in school. "Boy, you better sit down." "But Mama." "Boy! We don't play that." You want us to stand and put our hands on our heart for anthem that does not represent us. Come on, man.

The Honorable Minister Louis Farrakhan has been influencing this world for a long time. He does not go out and say, hey, look at what I have done. This is the man who's gonna carry us on his shoulders across the river, across the Red Sea. He's gonna get us to the other side, and he ain't gonna brag on it. He's gonna say look what Allah has done! All Praise is Due to Allah!

He saved my life. He's the reason why I'm married today. I told you I was a savage. I told you when I called my mom, she'd be like, boy you're gonna get somebody pregnant. He taught me the value of woman, because I was trying to see the value of women. He said, "No, brother, the value of one woman, singular." Singular.

When he teaches you the value of marriage, you could see it coming out of him. He and his wife Mother Khadijah just made 63 years. Takbir! (Allah-u-Akbar!) That just simply means God is the Greatest!

He taught me the value of community and family. He taught me the reason for mental, spiritual and physical security. He made me want to secure and take care of my family, because me taking care of my family helps me to produce and take care of a proper community. If I'm not taking care of my wife and children, how can I help take care of a community at large? And I'm so thankful to that. They got 63 years. I need my years times nine because this December, my wife and I make seven if it will be the will of Allah. That comes from the science of mating. Our enemies don't teach us that. They teach us the science of having sex and jumping on the next one, like we used to do through slavery.

I'm telling you this man will save your life. He has transformed lives. Some of us were drug dealers. Some of us were strung out on drugs. Some of us were alcoholics, gangbangers, hustlers, thieves, prostitutes. Not anymore. We all have a story we can tell of how the Life-Giving Teachings of the Most Honorable Elijah Muhammad through the guidance of the Honorable Minister Louis Farrakhan has transformed our lives.

This man is a surgeon with wordplay. He drops it on you in a way that it doesn't hit you too hard, but it's a seed. Then when it's time, it pops up and you're like, "Man, I don't want to do that no more. I'm good. I'm trying to change my life."

I've been blessed, and you have, too. When my wife gave birth to our second child, Eiliyah. Eiliyah was a home birth. We didn't go to the hospital. We delivered that child in our house because we didn't want to be part of that. We didn't want them trying to force vaccinations in our child. But during February of last year, I reached out to the Minister and I asked him if he would be willing to name our child. And he was trying to work it out between delivering the keynote lecture and getting time for us. But we always have a plan B, just in case. So we named our Eiliyah. Then we printed up little birth announcement cards with a picture and stuff on it, and it got to him. And someone within the family informed me that he took the card and he kissed the baby. He then lifted it up in the sky, and he made a prayer for this child. I'm a blessed man.

When this child was born, she was still in the sack, which is rare. That does not happen often. That's coming through the science of mating, walking with a man who will guide you the right way. That when my daughter walks in the room, she lights it up. That's the believers like oh my God, I love her. She has a certain vibe about her. When she smiles, you can look in her eyes and tell she knows something. I'm waiting for her to talk so she can tell me what she knows, too.

I'm a blessed man. Early this year, in January or February, I was at work when the Minister came in and sat down in my office. I got a chance to talk to the Honorable Minister Louis Farrakhan one-on-one for about 30 minutes. You know how hard it is to get that close to the man of God? And during our conversation, he said, "Brother, I pray"—and I'm paraphrasing—'that Allah gives you what you need this year to make it one of your best years. And that whatever you have on your heart, Allah allows you to handle and be able to move forward with those endeavors." That conversation resonates in my mind every morning when I wake up. I'm constantly thinking about my future. I can't wait 'til next Sunday to be in full effect, where we'll see the Honorable

Minister Louis Farrakhan in person at the 21st anniversary of the Holy Day of Atonement, the Million Man March!

They still trying to take this man off the planet. They plan and Allah plans and Allah is the Best of Planners. You can't touch him. Try if you want to. The Minister will be breaking down our future and the future of America with these two candidates running, Lucifer and... excuse me, Hillary Clinton and Donald Trump. My bad, my bad. Which way you wanna go? You want Lucifer or Satan? He's gonna help us prepare for our future. To my youth, to my young ones who are able to vote now. You think voting is the way. I tell you, it is not the way. You can give them whatever power you want to give them. They're not going to do anything for you and I. The power is in us. The power is in our unity. As long as we come together, we don't need their votes.

Go to the Asian community. I wonder if they vote? They're like, we don't need them. We got our own community. I wish a police officer would roll through their community. What you want? I wish you would. They said to study them. Why do we study Asians? Why do we observe Asians and how they function? Minister Farrakhan says, you can rise above any condition you're in with knowledge.

One of the problems we have is we're beating down on the young people. Why do you beat down on the young people when Minister Farrakhan said this generation of youth are the greatest? Farrakhan does not fear the youth. He sees the importance in them. It seems that we fear our youth. We teach them. We say we want them to be better than us. We give them everything we couldn't have so they can go beyond us. And as soon as they challenge our level of thought, we want to push them back down instead of allowing and helping them to exalt their greatness, so that they can carry us on to the other side. The Minister says, Black youth, you have something to offer to the world. But if you simply get in where you fit in, you will not make a contribution. The youth are the future leaders, the future thinkers. They are the future heirs of the throne.

So to my youth 16 to 35. Youth can be a spiritual thing, but we're talking about physically. I think 16-35s works. Since I'm 32, I'll take claim to that. Deuteronomy 31:6 says, *"Be strong and courageous. Do not be afraid or terrified because of them, for the Lord your God goes with you; he will never leave you nor forsake you."*

If you ever played any sport before, whoever is the starting quarterback, the starting basketball player, point guard, shooting guard, center, and you come on that team, they're not going to just give you that position. You have to fight for it. You think Peyton Manning just want to give up his spot? You think Tom Brady just wants to give up his spot? You got to come and earn that spot. If you want that position, go and take that position. Work for that position. Because if you're not willing to fight for it, why should you have that position? But that's not enough. Let me keep going.

Galatians 6:9 says, *"Let us not become weary in doing good, for at the proper time we will reap a harvest If we do not give up."* Let me read that again. Let us not become weary, exhausted, in doing good for at the proper time, the time and what must be done, we will reap a harvest. We will reap mature crops, mature mental crops, mature spiritual crops, mature physical land and crops if we do not give up.

Sometimes we have to nag like children if you really want it. If you see the starting quarterback on the field and you want to get in, you don't go sit on the bench somewhere. You go stand next to the coach and you wait your turn. Every time a coach turns left, you turn left too; coach turn right, you turn right too. If he runs out to the field, you run out too. You want him to know you are ready. You have to nag like a child in a candy store or a child in a store going down the candy aisle and anybody got children to know how that feels. They're persistent about that aisle, and you try to avoid it. You are not like "NOPE, I AIN'T GOING DOWN THAT AISLE!" The rest of the time in that store, what's that child going to do? "Mom, dad for real, come on, please. Please, I just want one." They gon' nag you the whole time. So you're gonna let them hold it. You might pull it out before you go through the line or you're gonna let 'em take it to the car with you but you have to be willing to put that kind of effort in if you want to manifest it.

To my youth, I want to tell you are great. Yes, you are the Joshua Generation of this time. You are the ones to bring in the hereafter. You are the ones to bring the change this world desires. Never give up and never lose the fire to fight for your future.

12

Greater is He That is in Me

"I want to share whatever my Teacher taught me with you so that the mind of God that's in me will be in you. Paul said, "Let this mind be in you, the same that was in Christ Jesus." Jesus was offering you God's mind."

The Honorable Minister Louis Farrakhan

Allah has put on my heart to take on a subject, titled "Greater is He That is in Me." Greater is He that is in you. Greater is He that is in us. Well, who is the 'He' that is in me? Who is the 'He' that is in you? And who is the 'He' that is in us?

That He is the same person Jesus is striving to instill in us. That He is Almighty God Allah. He is the Creator of the heavens and the earth. He is the being of all beings. He is the reason for our existence.

We read all through the scriptures, but for some reason, we don't see ourselves in it. But in the scripture it says that God made us in His image and likeness. So who is it speaking of? We call ourselves dog but we forget that if you turn the words around and put the g in front of the d and reverse it, it says, god. God is trying to instill in us what He is to us, our Father. And if He is our Father, then what does that make us? The son of God, the son of man. That means that we ourselves have the potential to live up to what our Father has set forth for us.

When Allah gives us something, He also gives us law and structure. When we deviate from law and structure, we are deviating from Allah Himself, which disconnects Him from you and I. In the Nation of Islam, which I'm so thankful to be in today, we are given something called the Restrictive Laws of Islam. Restrictive Laws of Islam. The Restrictive Laws are designed to keep us connected to Almighty God Allah.

Restrictive Law No. 1: *"Worship no God but Allah, the one the Messenger represents to us."* Worship no God but Allah. That means do not be polytheistic to Almighty God Allah.

Restrictive Law No. 2: *"It is forbidden to commit fornication or adultery."* If Allah has given us men and women and through men and women, we bring a union together, that union is what produced you and me. But when we commit adultery and fornication, we have caused problems in the union Allah has produced for us.

Restrictive Law No. 3: *"It is forbidden to commit indecent acts on another (sodomy)."* Why would we insert things into the anus of a person when the male part and the female part are already designed for that connection? If you're in electricity, you learn you have a male part and a female part that connect, which brings you the proper energy like understanding to produce progress.

Restrictive Law No. 4: *"It is forbidden to eat pig or its by-products."* If you're a Christian, I know you probably like, "Come on, bro. Really? You know I had my bacon this morning." Allah did not design the pig for us to consume. It was designed because there's a medicine that can be used for White people. When we consume the pig, there are things and viruses within that pig that also impacts our thinking, our operations. That's why we become sluggish. We become down in tune. We are no longer living to the potential of God, because we are taking toxins into our bodies.

Restrictive Law No. 5: *"No stealing."* When we steal from one another, we lose trust. When you lose trust, you lose unity. And because we have done ourselves wrong for so long, it's hard for us to build trust and unity with one another. If I find a man in a house with my wife, how can I trust that man, if he has stolen something from me?

Restrictive Law No. 6: *"No gambling of any kind (numbers, dice, cards, games of chance)."* I understand Power Ball, trying to get those couple of mills. We've been struggling our whole lives. But look at it from this angle: We do not believe in the game of chance. We are taught that Islam is mathematics and mathematics is Islam, and they can be proven in any unit of time. We have to work the mathematical equation through our lives. As we learn the variables through our lives, we can put the calculations together, and through those calculations we will find peace and harmony. We will find the connection to Almighty God Allah.

Restrictive Law No. 7: *"No smoking of any kind (reefers or cigarettes, cigar or pipe)."* We do not do drugs. We do not smoke. When we consume tobacco or weed, it can cause us to become imbalanced, which clouds our mind from what God might be trying to show us. If you look at the drugs today, they're being laced with things that are not even pure anymore. And that's why you see us doing crazy acts after we inhale one time. That lacing is so bad that the one time we do it, we might have been that person everyone looked up to, but now we're that person everybody looks down on.

Restrictive Law No. 8: *"No drinking (wine, whiskey, beer, ale, alcohol or other intoxicant."* When we find ourselves wanting a little sip of alcohol, as soon as you take it, it takes the purity out of yourself and it throws you into an imbalance. It throws us into an imbalance of our own thinking. That's the major reason why when you see accidents, the first thing they're looking for is, is this person intoxicated? It takes away our clear thinking. If we're not thinking clearly, how can we see the signs that Allah gives us?

Restrictive Law No. 9: *"No dope (heroin, cocaine or any other)."* No crack, no cocaine. To my young generation, no Molly. None of those prescribed drugs that we are taking; no inhaling on the spray paint; nothing that can take away what Allah is trying to show us.

Restrictive Law No. 10: *"Do not associate with those in bad standing or out of the mosque."* We do not associate with those in bad standing. We do not want to be caught up in their drama. If you're trying to stay pure in an impure world, which is hard to do, when we find ourselves associating with those who are not following that same path, that same law that we're striving to uphold, that standard, either you're going to raise the person up, or they're going to bring you down.

Restrictive Law No. 11: *"Kill no one whom Allah has not ordered to be killed."* When you come to the mosque, you go through a search procedure. We are checking your mind to see what your mental condition is, but we are also checking you physically to make sure you don't have anything on you that's harmful. If you know about any member of the Nation of Islam, we do not carry weapons, not even a pin knife. But for some reason, this open enemy who says so many negative things about us has not been able to destroy the Nation of Islam.

Restrictive Law No. 12: *"Do not commit acts of violence on ourselves or others."* We are never to be the aggressor. We walk in peace and in harmony with one another. We go into the hood where our brothers and sisters are hurting at. We know who we're walking with. We understand what the situation is, and we understand where we came from. So we go back to the homes that we came out so that we can extend our arm down and lift our brothers and sisters up. All Praise is Due to Allah.

Restrictive Law No. 13: *"Do not deal with the hypocrite or show sympathy towards them."* **HYPOCRITE**, that's a word we don't play with in the Nation of Islam. If we sniff it, we already removing you from the equation. You say, "I love the Honorable Elijah Muhammad," but then you go behind closed doors and speak negatively of the man. We don't play with that.

Restrictive Law No. 14: *"Insubordination is forbidden."* We are taught that we obey authority unless it conflicts with our religion.

Restrictive Law No. 15: *"Slack talk and gossip is forbidden."* When we find ourselves backbiting we lose the credibility of ourselves. Not only are we losing credibility of the person who's looking at us and we're engaging with, we lose the credibility of Almighty God Allah. We've put him to the side of the equation. How can we be pure with Him if we're backbiting about our brother or sister who we're taught to settle on the best part of, which is settling on the best part of their being?

Restrictive Law No. 16: *"Do not feel, rub or pat sisters."* I'm going to say that again. We do not feel, rub or pat sisters. We are not going to send any mixed signals. Now come on. Tell me when have you seen God rubbing and patting on a woman? Getting his Donald Trump on? Come on, man! What you see happening in America right now with Donald Trump is in the Holy Qur'an. It's in the Holy Qur'an, what you see happening right now. In the Holy Quran 27:82 it says, *"And when the word comes to pass against them, We shall bring forth for them a creature from the earth that will speak to them, because people did not believe in Our messages."*

Let me break that down just a little bit. When the word comes to the person, and it passes against them, it rubs against them. Word is coming to you right now. Depending on how you take it will determine how the outcome works out. *"We shall bring forth for them a creature from the earth that will speak to them, because people did not believe in Our messages."*

We're upset with Donald Trump being president. That was a sham. But look at it from this angle: If we had listened to the Honorable Elijah Muhammad from the 1930s to the 1970s, we would not be in this place. If we were listening to the Honorable Minister Louis Farrakhan from 1977 up until now, we would not be in this equation. So when Allah gives you a messenger and he puts a word on you to guide us and we don't follow suit to those words, then what happens is God sends a counter move to force us to His side. All Praise Is Due To Allah.

That counter move is the winds that are blowing to shake up the dry bones. We are the dry bones. We have become complacent in our own beings. Look at the impact of the election of Donald Trump. Because of his election, you had a Woman's March take place, and stats shows it was an estimate of 2.9 women that covered the streets across this country. I just finished discussing in the Holy Qur'an, how Allah will use a grossly materialistic person and bring them up from among us to force us right into Allah's hand. These women are trying to tap into the "greater is He" that is in them, even if some do not know that at this point of time. We must remember, there were women surrounding Jesus during the time of crucifixion. In every war, in every battle, in every major move that's done as a people, as a nation, the women are always involved. And if you look at the condition that we live in right now, the women have always taken the forefront.

Now, as men, how are we going to let our women go out and run the streets and have to make things happen and we not be by their side to make sure that they're secure? Ask yourself that question, because we have to answer to Allah if one of them gets harmed.

Here's something to think deeply about. The Honorable Minister Louis Farrakhan said some suffering is to accomplish the will of God. Some of us are suffering by Donald Trump becoming president. Before the 2016 election, you had Blacks, Latinos, and Native protesting. After the election, you had Caucasians protesting. That's suffering. But it also shows we are coming into zen. We're coming into unity. We're coming into a like mind right now. We all have a common disagreement. We don't like the condition that we're currently in.

Today's the day that we tap into our God power. I took on this subject for many different reasons. One of them was, I was looking at the state of our condition. Another reason was our fear and dissatisfaction of America's new president, Donald Trump. One last reason I was thinking on was leaving 2016 in 2016 and doing something different in the future.

We have a problem right now. Our problem is this: We forgot whom we belong to. When you know whom you belong to, you know what He desires for you. But if we don't know, then what are we going to do except wander and not understand why things are happening. What He desires for us is freedom, justice, equality, peace and harmony. We've lost track of where we are going. When we know where we're going, we will figure out how to get there.

In a few weeks, members of the Nation of Islam and communities and organizations across this country and world will be traveling to Detroit, Michigan for our annual Saviours' Day Convention.

I know where I'm going. The question becomes, how do I get there? Am I going to walk? That's too far. Am I going to ride a bike? You're measuring what's the best method to achieve your goal. Am I going to drive? I never drove that far in my life and I don't plan on doing it anytime soon. Am I going to catch a train, or would I catch a plane, which might be the most feasible move to make?

Have you seen the movie Hidden Figures? Taraji P. Henson played one of the main characters in the movie. There was a what and a how to get into space and back. They had to figure out: How do we get to space? That was the goal of America and Russia: Who will be first to get to space? There's a lot of underlying reasons that goes with it, but the goal was who could get to space first with the least amount of casualties?

In the process, they had to engineer a rocket ship. They had to test it against different climates to figure it out. They had to also run a mathematical equation that was never done before, to figure out how to launch. What's the distance? What's the circumference? What's the area that it needs to go to so that it can make it out of the atmosphere and into the orbit? While it's out there, it has to circle around. How and what time can we calculate this equation, where it could turn and fall right back into the Earth's atmosphere?

We deal with these equations mentally every single day of our lives. The question becomes, are we doing the right equations to keep us connected to God? Or are we doing the equation to keep us connected to our open enemy and our oppressor?

The problem is, we don't know who God is, They paint false pictures on our walls and in our churches, telling us God looks like this particular person. But for some reason, He does not look like you and I, so we don't connect to this Jesus figure. We don't connect to this Moses figure. We don't connect to Almighty God because if He made Jesus and Jesus is His son and Jesus seems to be White... The brown germ is the recessive germ to the black germ. We are not going to connect ourselves to Him.

That's where the X variable comes into our lives. If you think about our beloved brother, May Allah be pleased with him, he was once called Malcolm Little. He got registered in the Nation of Islam and took on the variable X. Well, X is an unknown variable. Solving for X means "I don't know who I am at this point in time, but I'm in the process of figuring out who I'm going to be when it comes to the right hand of God." That's our mathematical equation. That's the reason why we find ourselves stagnant and non-productive in our life, because there's an X variable sitting in front of us and we're not working out the equation. We just wander here in North America, going to work, working at a job we don't like, saying hi and being pleasant to people we disagree with instead of taking the time to drive our true purpose that Allah has given us.

Matthew 25:14-13 is the parable of the talents. There were three men who God gave gifts and talents. Two of them doubled their gifts and talents. The third one was dissatisfied, not knowing how easy it is when you only have to deal with one gift rather than 10. He took it and buried it under a rock. We do that every day of our lives when we don't challenge ourselves to do better. We bury our Self-Accusing Spirits. We bury our connection to God. We bury our connection to the true and living Jesus. And we find ourselves saying I gave you back what you gave to me.

Because we don't know who He is, we don't identify with the signs that God has given us. In the beautiful book the Holy Qur'an, Surah 18:60-82 is titled, *"Moses travels in Search of Knowledge."* It says:

> *And when Moses said to his servant: I will not seize until I reach the junction of the two rivers*—that's a decision that has to made in our lives when we have two things that are trying to pull us—*otherwise I will go on for years. So when they reached the junction of the two (rivers), they forgot their fish, and it took its way into the river, being free. But when they had gone further, he said to this servant: Bring to us our morning meal, certainly we have found fatigue in this our journey. He said: Sawest thou when we took refuge on the rock, I forgot the fish, and none but the devil made me forget to speak of it...*

That's a lie. That's a lie. That was being afraid to admit I did something wrong, so he planted the blame and played the victim.

> *"...and it took its way into the river; what a wonder! He (Moses) said: This is what we sought for. So they returned retracing their footsteps. Then they found one of Our servants whom We had taught knowledge from Ourselves. Moses said to him: May I follow thee that thou mayest teach me of the good thou hast been taught." He said: Thou canst not have patience with me. And how canst thou have patience in that whereof thou hast not a comprehensive knowledge?*

How can you have patience if you don't have an understanding of what I'm doing?

He said: If Allah please, thou wilt find me patient, nor shall I disobey thee in aught. He said: If thou wouldst follow me, question me not about aught until I myself speak to thee about it.

So they set out until, when they embarked in a boat, he made a hole in it. (Moses) said: Hast thou made a hole in it to drown its occupants? Thou hast surely done a grievous thing. He said (to Moses): Did I not say that thou couldst not have patience with me? He said: Blame me not for what I forgot, and be not hard upon me for what I did.

So they went on until, when they met a boy, he slew him. (Moses) said: Hast thou slain an innocent person, not guilty of slaying another? Thou hast indeed done a horrible thing. He said (to Moses): Did I not say to thee that thou couldst not have patience with me? He said: If I ask thee about anything after this, keep not company with me. Thou wilt then indeed have found an excuse in my case.

So they went on, until, when they came to the people of a town, they asked its people for food, but they refused to entertain them as guests. Then they found in it a wall which was on the point of falling, so he put it into the right state. (Moses) said: If thou hadst wished, thou couldst have taken a recompense for it. He said: This is the parting between me and thee.

We deal with this our whole lives. Allah will give us signs in our life, but we don't have the patience to see through what Allah is putting in front of us. Because we don't have the patience for what Allah is putting in front of us, he ends up parting ways from us, and we walk right into the hands of our oppressors.

Now I will inform thee of the significance of that with which though couldst not have patience. As for the boat, it belonged

> *to poor people working on the river, and I intended to damage it, for there was behind them a king who seized every boat by force.*

The wise man damaging the boat ensured that the king would not injure or hurt the people, thus saving their lives.

> *As for the boy, his parents were believers and we feared lest he should involve them in wrongdoing and disbelief.*

This reminds me of why we ran Yakub and his made devil from among us.

> *So we intended that their Lord might give them in his place one better in purity and nearer to mercy.*

> *And, as for the wall, it belonged to two orphan boys in the city, and there was beneath it a treasure belonging to them, and their father had been a righteous man. So thy Lord intended that they should attain their maturity and take out their treasure—a mercy from thy Lord—and I did not do it of my own accord. This is the significance of that with which is thou couldst not have patience.*

We're going to go through trials and tribulations in our lives. We're going through them right now, but if we don't have the patience to stay steadfast as God is guiding us through, because through difficulty comes easy and with difficulty is ease. But if we do not stay connected to Him, we're constantly questioning, "Why are you doing this to me?" If we're constantly being a victim of asking, how about we ask this question: "What do you want me to learn from this?" If we rearrange the question, we can actually get the proper guidance, because we have opened ourselves up to see the connection of why it happened.

There are times when we might be in a hurry to be somewhere and someone cuts us off and we wound up having to slam on the brakes, but they kept going through the intersection and they wound up in a car accident. That was a sign from Allah, if you look at His mercy.

It reminds me of a single mother telling you to love your father who you never met, because many of us never met our fathers before. But imagine your mom saying love your father, even though you don't know who this man is who laid in the bed with your mother. How can we say we love our father when we don't even know who our father is? So what do we do? We start asking questions. Who is this man? So how can we love God, if we do not truly know nor understand who God is?

We've been robbed of our being. He, the enemy of God, has destroyed our connection to our God to keep us from speaking the language. We were taught to pray to our God, and when that disconnect happens, then we lose the true nature of understanding who God is.
The woman is taught to breastfeed and nurture the baby, to bring it close to them. There are studies that show that if the mother brings the baby close to her through breastfeeding, they develop a connection. It's a natural energy that instills confidence in that child. But when you disconnect the child from the mother and you give them a bottle, there's no longer a relationship there between the mother and the child, and the child grows up with insecurity. If we don't know who God is, how are we going to be confident in ourselves?

That is why our enemy has ruled over us. That's also the reason why we look to him and everyone else but God for acceptance. We have made him a god beside Allah, which means we are currently practicing polytheism. We are praying to multiple gods, and we don't even know that because he has confused us and clouded our thought process. We don't see the "greater He that is in us," because we're looking to someone who is not trying to instill the true essence, the true understanding of who God is. But I tell you who a man is that's doing that: His name is the Honorable Minister Louis Farrakhan! All Praise is Due to Allah!

In the beautiful book called *The Supreme Wisdom*—in order to get a copy, you have to be a registered member of the Nation of Islam, which means you have to accept Islam. You have to go through the registration process and acceptance to get what you call your X, your holy name.

There's a part in the book that deals with the 85 percent, the 10 percent, and the 5 percent, which adds up to 100 percent. The question is asked, "Who is the 85 percent?" Answer: "The uncivilized people, poison animal eaters..." I mentioned the pig earlier. "...slaves from mental death and power. People who do not know the living God or their origin in this world, and they worship that which they know not what, who are easily led in the wrong direction, but hard to lead in the right direction."

Who's the 10 percent? The rich. You know some rich people? I'm not rich. I think our president is rich. He was rich coming into office. The rich, the slave maker of the poor, who teach the poor lies to believe that all-mighty true and living God is a book and cannot be seen by the physical eye. Otherwise known as the bloodsucker of the poor.

I've worked in banking. If you look at the way the taxes are set up, why is it that the middle class pays the highest taxes but the higher class pays the lower taxes and they also get exempt from taxes? That is taking advantage of the poor.

Who's the 5 percent? The poor, righteous teachers who do not believe in the teachings of the 10 percent, and are all-wise, and know who the living God is, and teach that the living God is the Son of Man, the Supreme Being The black men of Asia, and teach freedom, justice, and equality to all human family of the planet earth.

When we fall in love with the wrong person, we give power. We give them power over us. Since we have been here in America since 1555, we have been living in the valence of our oppressor. We have been living in the mindset of our oppressor to the point where you can say we're made in America. Donald Trump and like-minded people represent the mind of 1555. And what did Jesus say in John 8:44?

> *You belong to your father, the devil, and you want to carry out your father's desires. He was a murderer from the beginning, not holding to the truth, for there is no truth in him.*

He has been lying ever since he was inaugurated. Whenever he speaks, he lies. He speaks from his own nature. It's in their nature to lie to us. He is a liar and the father of lies!

Because we are now made in America, we have two beings in us. We have the good and the bad, our oppressor and God, so we find ourselves acting other than ourselves.

Who are we going to give our attention to? Who have we been giving our attention to? If we sit back and reflect for a moment and ask, "Am I where I want to be at currently in life?" what would our answer be? Then the next question should become, "Why? What is preventing it? Who am I giving my power to?" So the question also is, who will win our hearts?

Either we're going to be on the right-hand side of God or we're going to be on the left-hand side of God. I know when scripture speaks about Jesus coming with a sword dripping with blood, I know I don't want that to be my blood! So we have to ask ourselves, whose side are we on? The Honorable Minister Louis Farrakhan teaches us, don't tell me we don't have the power. We have just never used it wisely. Allah has given us the power to exercise. We just do not realize we have the power, so we're using it wrong.

One of my dear brothers in the city, Brother Tremikus, wrote this on social media: "You - talking about us - are the only god your children know."

Remember that. You are the only god your children know. How can we say we love God who we've never seen but hate our brother, our parents, our children, who we see every day. When a child is born, their first words are not God. They ain't running out saying, "Allah-u-Akbar!" They ain't saying, "Allah." They ain't saying "God." What is their first word? "Mama. Dadda." When they're crying out because they need something, they ain't saying God come help me. They're calling on a mama and dadda. To them, we answer their prayers. When that baby is crying and they need milk, who goes to get them milk? Who goes the changes their diaper? Who goes to comfort them? Allah has made us as an example for the children, which means we are little gods to God.

All Praise is Due to Allah!

Striving to grow into good company with God makes me nervous. I'm constantly asking Him to use me as an instrument. That's all I can do. I have to die so he can grow in. We have to die so he can grow in us. I am not talking about a physical death. I am talking about killing my old ways. I am talking about killing the things of me that are not in line with what God desires of me. Parenting is one of the best times to practice. That is one of the best times to practice and exercise the "greater is He" that is in us. If we do not use the He that is in us, then we are losing the potential of becoming that god that He has set forth for us to become. We talked about being an image and likeness. If God is our Father, what does that make us?

How do we tap into our God powers? One, keep God at the center, which keeps the bad from rising from in us. Two, desire. We must have the desire to want him in the center of our being. We must have a desire to push forward in our lives, walking that path. We must have the will to stay consistent in the efforts to be better in life. Three, determination. We must have the determination to make the decision and stay steadfast with it. Four, discipline. That's our big issue right there. Having a little gut, that's a lack of discipline. Did you know when you're running late to work, that's a lack of discipline? You know we didn't get dinner ready for the children. That's a lack of discipline. We have failed short in that. We must stay disciplined to not deviate as we exercise and grow into our God powers.

Five, making our word bond, which is also important. If our word ain't bond, we're not credible. In the same book, *Supreme Wisdom*, it says, "*Have you not learned that your word shall be bond regardless of whom or what?*" The answer is, "*Yes, my word is bond and bond is life. And I will give my life before my word shall fail.*" If we can't keep our word, that goes back to trust. That goes back to credibility. Six, is trust. Why should I work with you and why would I want unity with you if you can't keep your word with me? If we say we're going to do something, we make sure it gets done. And if we know we're not able to, we communicate that well enough in advance so that they know we're not purposely breaking our word.

Oh, this is the one we deal with personally. Seven, the Self-Accusing Spirit. Oh! Oh! Oh! The spirit! That's the time when you're at the house and it's National Fast weekend and you had your last meal on Thursday. And you're like, "I ain't eating." But for some reason it's Saturday and you don't have to work and you standing there going back and forth to the refrigerator. You're looking in the cabinets. You looking like Martin when he was leaning over for Thanksgiving, trying not to touch his mama's biscuits.

That's when we say we're going to purify ourselves, and we find ourselves at those two junctions, like Moses and the wise man. That's when we find ourselves having to question ourselves and our intent. "Can I do it?" That's when you say, "Oh Allah, please help me. I found myself in a position and I'm about to deviate." That's when you pull out your Qur'an and your Bible. And that's when you start reading through the scriptures. That's when you find yourself calling your best friend saying, "Girl, I almost went to his house! I said I wasn't gone' do it!" That's when you call your best friend and you're like, "Bro, I'm telling you. I'm about to head to the bar. She working my nerves," and he says, "Don't do it! Come over to my house! Let's talk for a minute." That's that Self-Accusing Spirit. Every time we deviate, we kill it. Every time we deviate, we kill the angel that lives within us, which prevents us from tapping into the "greater is He" that lives within us.

Number eight, prayer and meditation. We have to find time throughout our day to keep Him in the center and say thank you, Allah. When I wake up in the morning, I say thank you Allah for my eyes. I can see. Thank you for my fingers. I can touch. Thank you for my feet. I don't count but you do. Thank you for the blinking. Oh Allah, thank you. I know I had a hard time getting out the bed this morning, but you allowed me to get up. You allowed me to open my eyes. I can still breathe. You allowed me to still be able to move. Allah, thank you! Oh my God, thank you for my wife. Thank you for the children. I'm glad they opened their eyes this morning. Thank you for the believers. Thank you for the people. Thank you for everything you put in front of me. Thank you for this house that I could easily lose, but you gave me comfort under you, as long as I'm in your bosom.

We pray, but you also have to meditate. That's when you find yourself at peace. That's when you clear your thoughts, because we run through a chaotic day, trying to break us down. There was a study that went out and said if you work at eight o'clock in the morning, it's actually designed to break your system down, man. I was like, can I switch my shift?

But all that won't count for anything if we do not find ourselves fasting. That's one of the most important components of Allah. All through the scriptures, we read about fasting. The importance of the fast is it allows those toxins to be removed from our system. We find ourselves consuming stuff all day long. We find ourselves taking in mental things all day long that jacks up our psyche. We have to push out those toxins. But after we finish our fast, we don't run up to McDeath. We don't go to Taco Hell. We don't go to Jack in the Crack. We have to find a nice, wholesome and healthy meal. We have to learn How to Eat to Live.

We need that meal that's going to help bring comfort to us, but I ain't talking about that normal church comfort. I ain't talking about when the sister was like, "I got the chitlins', the greens, the beans, the meat." I ain't talking about that one, because that's that high cholesterol, the pork. "I'm going to the doctor next week, because I might be dying in a few." No! I'm talking about that nice wholesome bean soup, that whole wheat bread, that raw milk. I'm talking about one meal a day. We've been prescribed how to eat. We eat between the hours of four and six because that's when our body starts to calm down, and sometimes you need that boost to get it back up. We don't eat late. When you eat late, you start getting that Hannibal belly.

You want to eat between four and six. We don't eat heavy meals. You eat the right meal. You eat one meal a day. It keeps you from being sluggish. We constantly find ourselves eating. Then we find ourselves at work with the itis. You know that Thanksgiving itis? Well, we got the itis every day. We sluggish every day. We find ourselves walking in like this. Nah! We have to be fast-moving, right down to the modern time. That's why when you see the FOI on the block, we in ranks. We're moving, because we know we've been taught. We move fast. We have a purpose. When you eat right, it helps with that.

Veganism has now become the popular thing, but we've been taught in How to Eat to Live to be a vegetarian since we've been in existence in the Nation of Islam and since we've been here in the wilderness of North America. It's very nice.

I see all these healthy habits and all these healthy ways of eating, but we've been teaching that. Somebody owes us some dues. We're owed some dues right now. People been taking our stuff saying, "Woo, I'm about to market it." We owe the Honorable Elijah Muhammad.

We're taught it takes 21 days to purify ourselves and break bad habits, so that means while we're going through this, we have to look and say, "What is a bad habit I have?" We have to ask ourselves that question. I loved being in banking because I ask the question, "What's your credit look like?" "I don't know." If you don't look at your credit, you don't know if you need to improve it. Well, if we ain't looking in the mirror, we don't know if we need to cut back a meal. If we ain't studying, we don't know how well our advancement is. So we have to go on that 21 days of purifying the toxins out of us—mental, spiritual and physical toxins. All Praise is Due to Allah.

All that counts for nothing if we do not exercise. We have to exercise not just physically with weights, but the same practice, the same regimen we have, we have to exercise mentally. We have to pick up a book and challenge our train of thought, to open up that infinite mind that we have. We open up a book to learn more, and then we grab another book to reference what we were studying. It takes us to another level of thought, and we find ourselves digging deeper, brushing off the dirt, not just off the bookshelf, but the dirt of our mind. And as we find God going deep within us, we spark gold!

That's when you see God rising and feel that light, that beam, coming within you, and you see yourself removing negativity. If you don't know you're in a negative environment, how are you going to remove it? But if you find yourself walking a path, you will see the negativity miles away, and they're throwing stones at you. While they're throwing stone, you look like ah! Hypocrite! Ah! Agent! Ah! I ain't with you, and as you move them out the way, you see God right in front of you. As you continue to study the Supreme Wisdom, the Bible, the Qur'an, and the books of the Most Honorable Elijah Muhammad you will see things start lining up and the picture and the words are dropping off the pages. You'll say, "Oh Allah! Thank you." All Praise is Due to Allah.

As we remove negativity, we start seeing the natural beauty of what Allah has put in our presence. I want you to try this tomorrow. When you get out of the house and you get in your car, you walk to the bus stop, or you wait for your Uber or Lyft, whatever it may be. I want you to look up at the sky and just look at how the clouds are arranged. Look at how that sun is beaming.

13

Put on the New Man

"Put on the new man, take off the old man. This is the Will of God. There must be a transformation in our lives."

The Honorable Minister Louis Farrakhan

The Honorable Minister Louis Farrakhan said, "The House of God is not determined by walls or pews. The real church is not made of stone. The real house of God is the people. It's people united in the bond of love."

The New Testament says, "We could tell that we have passed from death into life because we **love** the brotherhood." The death that is upon us is the death of self-hatred.

Did you know that Almighty God Allah personally picked you? You are personally picked by **God!** We don't believe we are the chosen ones because if we really believed we are the chosen ones, we would stand up and walk with this man Farrakhan.

When you attend a mosque meeting for the first time, it's not that person who you ran into on the streets that brings you. It's not that lecture that you may have heard that brings you. Through the annals of time, we're taught that we write our history 25,000 years in advance. Allah has put things in place for us to conquer, starting with the wombs of our mothers.

When we were sperm, there were multi-billions of us in there, but the day our mother and our father wanted to engage in biological interactions, on that day, we said, "I'm not sitting here no more." No matter where we were placed in that race going **upwards**, going against gravity, we maneuvered through everyone to beat our counterparts to the egg.

Once we got to the egg, we existed in secret. Our own mother did not even know that she was going to be conceiving a child. We became a clot. We attached ourselves to the **placenta**. We started **pulling** all of the nutrients from our mother, and whatever was on the mind of our mother would go into our hearts and the mind of our DNA. We were already manifested for greatness. And the next thing you know, you're here today.

We were going through things in our personal lives, but something brought you this book. And our psyche knows we need a new man. This old way ain't working for us no more. We tried every religion! But when we got here, it stuck to us. The Minister said, "God allows you..." He allows who? He allows **you** to get hints of your powers. In those hints of our powers, as we develop them, the true manifestation is we're being made to help this man, FARRAKHAN!

We're being made to help the Messiah and the Christ, because this man Farrakhan, he's pregnant with a nation. When we were in the womb of our mothers, studies say that a 40-week term of pregnancy is considered full-term. Pay Attention. I said in 40 weeks, right?

The Honorable Minister Louis Farrakhan has been rebuilding this Nation for just over 40 years. When a child goes past their term within the womb, it becomes life or death for that child **and** that for mother if the mother does not give birth to the child. This is why C-sections have become so popular. Well, that is some of the reasons why C-sections have become so popular. They're afraid that the child may defecate within the womb, releasing toxins to the child that can kill the child within the womb.

If The Honorable Minister Louis Farrakhan does not give birth to this Nation, it becomes intoxicating for him and us. It becomes health challenging for him and us as babies. In order for us to become better helpers to him, we must come out of the womb. Let me say that again. In order for us to become better helpers to **him**, we must come out of the womb.

What a wonderful thing to be given an assignment to help a man whom God has given the hardest job of any man that has ever lived. We have to grow into a new man. The mind that Jesus offers us is the mind of God. In order to accept this mind that is offered to us, we have to permit the overthrow of the mind that is in us now! God is calling for a regime change. Your mind. Your mind.

The Honorable Elijah Muhammad was talking to The Honorable Minister Louis Farrakhan, and he told the Minister: I want you to align your mind with my mind. And our beloved Minister was talking to Minister Jabril Muhammad and then asked him a question. "Well, how do you do that?" "Brother, that's easy. You will have to go through what **he** went through."

Check this out. The Honorable Minister Louis Farrakhan is striving to give us his mind. He wants us to align our mind with his mind, because when we align our mind with his mind, that gives us the direct connection through him to the Honorable Elijah Muhammad. Well if the Most Honorable Elijah Muhammad was taught night and day for 3-1/2 years, whose mind does he have? So if we're connected to his mind, that means we're connected to Almighty God Allah's mind who came in the Person of Master Fard Muhammad. Allah-u-Akbar!

The Bible says there is a way that seemeth right unto men but the ends thereof are the way of death. What kind of death? Once human beings live in a flesh rather than in the spirit, they become dead to the real power of self.

In order to come into this new man, we have to remove the attractions of the flesh. We have to grow from our lowest desires to the highest of desire, which is the desire to be next to God.

I love the Holy Qur'an. And the Minister recently brought something out to us from it in Surah 18 dealing with Moses walking with the Wise Man.

Do you mind if I pull a few words out? I want to take it from Surah 18 verses 65 through 70. It says:

> *Then they found one of Our servants whom We had granted mercy from Us and whom We had taught knowledge from Ourselves.*

So this is an ally, but he's not just a normal ally. Then it goes on to say:

> *Moses said to him...*

and that person that we're speaking of is this wise man.

> *Moses said to him: May I follow thee that thou mayest teach me of the good thou hast been taught?*

The Wise Man said to Moses:

> *He said: Thou canst not have patience with me.*

How do we grow into a new man if we can't have patience with the man guiding us? And he says:

> *And how canst thou have patience in that whereof, thou hast not a comprehensive knowledge?*

So, let's break that down right there. The **comprehensive** knowledge. When they say comprehensive knowledge, he's really talking about **experiences**. He's talking about your own personal experiences.

We all came from a past that we don't agree with. We all at some point in time in our development *shunned* our past. We were upset on the way we did things to the point that we wanted to forget it, but that experience that Almighty God Allah allowed us to go through in our past makes us the men and women we are today. If we do not go back and research our past—Supreme Wisdom—history is best suited to reward our research. If we do not go back and study our past, we won't understand how to walk without a doubt with the man we follow.

Look. I speak a lot about some of my past. I used to beat myself mentally and spiritually because of my past. And one day I was making a prayer to Allah asking why would you allow me to do the things in my past? Then it clicked! "Well, brother, if I didn't allow you to go through this, how could I use you to get your brothers and sisters who are currently going through this?"

We couldn't walk in patience because we didn't understand our own past. When we come across our past, we get nervous. "Oh, nah. Nah. Nah. No." Because we haven't strengthened ourselves up yet. So then Moses said:

> *He said: If Allah please, thou wilt find me patient nor shall I disobey thee in aught.*
>
> *He said: If thou wouldst follow me* ...this is the wise man talking to Moses. Let me bring it to layman's terms. This is The Honorable Minister Louis Farrakhan talking to **us**. ... *question me **not** about aught until I myself speak to thee about it.*

In order for us to grow into this new man, we must first go back and look into our history so that we could see the mistakes and errors that we have made in our past. And as we study these mistakes in our past, we learn how to maneuver through the present to prepare for a better future. And as we're going through this process, that's what allows us to grab on to a brother, grab on to a sister who is going through a similar struggle. We can now provide guidance on how to walk into Christ.

Allah-u-Akbar!

The Minister said stop complaining. We have a lot of those nowadays, right? He said stop complaining and start learning how to be grateful. Grateful for what Allah has given to us all.

Now pay attention to this. He finishes off by saying nobody gives like Allah. The last part of the verse of Surah 110, Al-Nasir, The Help, says: *"Surely Allah is ever returning to mercy."*

I have a question for you. Why do people come to the Nation of Islam? I mean, there are so many spiritual places out there, but they come to the Nation of Islam. Well, the Nation of Islam has what I will call an impeccable track record. The Nation of Islam is known for this, ready? Are you ready? The Nation of Islam is known for transforming lives.

People come in and even if they seem to fall out, don't worry, because the little bit that they did get will help increase and help heighten the Self-Accusing Spirit, that no matter what they go through, their life is still transforming. They just need to reconnect to the spiritual process. The Minister also said Allah is involved in our purification and we have to let Allah purify our hearts.

Then he says there is nothing that happens in life that you can't win over if you go in the name of God. What's the challenge? What's the challenge? The challenge now is we must release and remove the self-doubt. The enemy gives us **nothing**. He fed us poison when we were babies. So we have self-doubt when we look up to him. We must remove our own personal self from the equation. We must be willing to mentally and spiritually die so He can fill us up with all of Himself.

That takes time because we know we don't want to just give up everything yet. "I don't know brother. I like this part of me." Sister, she loves that part of her. But as we're going through that process, if we unite together and work cheerfully hand in hand, Allah will purify us together.

It will feel like the womb. It will feel like when we have Jummah prayer. When we all come together and we pray together, but imagine that prayer turning into work together and we're working cheerfully and we're not getting jealous that this brother's in line in front of me or this sister's in line in front of me because I know I'm next. I'm next on that purification! I'm next for Allah to put a new man in me! Oh, Allah!

Allah is with us if we are with Him! We're going to win because it is Allah's Will that we triumph over evil **and falsehood**. Allah-u-Akbar!

2 Corinthians 5:17 says: *Therefore, if anyone is in Christ, the new creation her come. The old has gone, the new is here!*

That's not easy, but it's easier than we think because we have a lot of distractions in our way. But are these permitted distractions or self-afflicted distractions? If we remove the distractions, we will find ourselves with more time being dutiful to Allah. We will find ourselves with more time working cheerfully with Allah. We will find ourselves with more time building his Kingdom. Oh Allah!

Ephesians 4:24 says: *And to put on the new self, created to be like God in true righteousness and holiness.* The Honorable Minister Louis Farrakhan is making new men today! He is making us into himself today! All we have to do is stay tight to him. When he speaks we listen. When he moves, we move. When he says stand up, we stand up. When he says go get the people, we go get our people! Allah-u-Akbar!

We've been given a challenge this season, because sometimes we get self-righteous. We find ourselves irritable sometimes. But the Minister said this season, not last season but this season, he wants us to go and do acts of kindness. What is he teaching us? We're taught that the Minister was with the Messenger, the Honorable Elijah Muhammad, one day. And I believe they went to a dentist's appointment. As he was leaving, he was giving out $100 bills to people while he was there. And the Minister asked him a question, why was he doing it. He wanted to let them know when they start talking about

Muhammad, they'll be like not **that** one! That one has done so much for me!

The Minister told the Believers in Houston after Hurricane Harvey that Allah is using them to get to the people. He spared them so they could work cheerfully. When they attacked the mosque, Temple #7 in New York, when the Minister was there the people stormed all around the building going blocks out. You can't have this man. They had to ask for permission to get in and out. I'm talking about the police.

He said acts of kindness. The greatest gift that you can give is right within yourself. It's your ability to love yourself, love your family and love your people. That's a gift, and that's the best of gifts. "Aww, man. You can have the parking spot, brother. It's okay. We're not going fight over it. You know. And I need to walk. I need to exercise anyway."

The Minister says our unity will win the battle. "Our" means a collective effort. Our unity will win the battle. Our dear brother David Banner has a video clip on social media. He spoke about how he was with the Minister and the Minister said to him, "Brother, I'm not asking you to join the Nation or be Muslim." And that puzzled him because he was surprised to hear that. He said they don't know what you are. They don't know if your Jehovah's Witness, Christian, Muslim, Jew, but what you teach is what people need to hear. He is creating people and sending them out there to make friends for us.

Not one of us will have to raise a sword. I know we got some brothers and sisters who can't wait to put those fists up, can't wait to drop one. But what I'm saying is since we don't go in front of the Minister, the Minister said not one of us will have to raise a sword! Not one gun will we need to fire. The first cannon that will be fired is our unity. Our unity is the best. Why are you afraid to unite? That question came from the Honorable Elijah Muhammad.

Colossians 3:12-14 says:

Therefore, as God's chosen people, holy and dearly loved, clothe yourselves with compassion, kindness, humility, gentleness and patience. Bear with each other and forgive one another if any of you has a grievance against someone. Forgive as the Lord forgave you. And over all these virtues put on love, which binds them all together in perfect unity.

We find ourselves on social media bashing. Uh oh. We find ourselves at our family members' house bashing. I was in banking for nearly 10 years, and I was in sales for even longer. In sales, you learn how to find an agreement. If you're trying to win someone over, you don't win them over by bashing them. You win them over by finding an equal agreement, and then you slowly work it in. It's like when you get a massage. I'm telling you I get some sometimes because I enjoy mine, but it starts off soft and then it goes to a deep tissue massage.

Well, the Minister is saying, "Hold on brother! Hold on sister! You're throwing dirt in the water right now. I need them to drink from this." So we need to take another approach. We're not going to kill them with kindness. We're going to win them with kindness. Oh Allah!

When they look up and they see the ranks of men and the ranks of women and they see us there and they are like "Ahhhh, I don't wanna try you," but yet we do an imbalance to ourselves. We ain't just giving away everything. That means you still have to take care of yourself. But we're taking a different approach, so let us not find ourselves arguing in this season with our brothers and sisters.

Let's find ourselves in an equal agreement with them so that we can win them over, because we're winning their souls over to Allah, anyway. We remove ourselves from the equations and we hand them over to this man.

We have been given a great opportunity, we have been given a great chance and we've been given the direct connection of who Almighty God is. Let's find ourselves working cheerfully. Let's find ourselves **studying**. Let's find ourselves connecting to The Honorable Minister Louis Farrakhan so he could make us into new men and new women.

14

Allah's Saviour in Our Midst

"A Universal Saviour was produced by the longing of the whole planet to be delivered from the pain of a world of sin and evil and war and bloodshed."

The Honorable Minister Louis Farrakhan

I am excited and nervous at the same time, because I always ask Allah to challenge me to go further than I normally would go. I plan to bear witness to this chapter that's titled, *Allah's Saviour in Our Midst.*

Let me first define a few words in the title so we can have a clear understanding of the title. The first word is 'Allah' with an apostrophe 's.' In grammar school, we learn that an apostrophe 's' means 'possession of or belonging to.' For example, *that's Hannibal's car - I pay the note on that.* Allah's Saviour, not ours. He's in our midst for us, but he belongs to Almighty God Allah.

Let me define the word 'saviour.' The word 'saviour' is a noun that means 'a person who saves, rescues or delivers.' Within that same definition, it says, 'a title of God, especially of Christ.' A Saviour. The title is, *Allah's Saviour in our Midst.* Our. That's you and I, brothers and sisters.

The last word I want to define in the title is 'midst'. It is also a noun, and it means the 'position of anything surrounded by other things or parts or occurring in the middle of.' It goes further to say, 'a period of time, course of action, usually preceded by *the*,' and it gave an example:

a familiar face in the midst of the crowd; In the midst of the performance.

Allah's Saviour in our midst.

1 John 4:10 says, *"This is love: not that we loved God, but that he loved us and sent his Son as an atoning sacrifice for our sins."* We are talking about Allah's Saviour in our midst.

In the *Final Call Newspaper*, on February 17, 2015—which was our Saviours' Day convention—the Honorable Minister Louis Farrakhan delivered a lecture. The article in the *Final Call* is called, *God Will Send Saviours.* God will send Saviours. That's plural. In the article, the Minister says, "One is God Himself sending 'a great one' to be a *savior*; and that one is making *many saviours* to send them to save a people distressed and oppressed. The question is: Who is the 'he' that is going to make 'a great one' and make him a 'savior?' And who is the 'them' to whom this Great Grace of Salvation is being offered? There's a specific 'them,' and a general 'them.'"

In our salutation, we say I bear witness that there is no God but Allah, Who came in the Person of Master Fard Muhammad, the Great Mahdi. Then we go on to say, I bear witness that the Honorable Elijah Muhammad is the Exalted Christ, Living Messiah. We continue on in the salutation saying, I further bear witness that the Honorable Minister Louis Farrakhan is the Divine Reminder in our midst.

Check this part out. Master Fard Muhammad came and made himself known in Black Bottom Detroit. He is the 'Comer by Night' that we've been waiting on. He took the Most Honorable Elijah Muhammad, who came to him and identified who he is. Master Fard Muhammad hushed him and told him not to go any further into that because "everyone doesn't know that yet." He taught little Elijah, who did not go beyond the fourth grade. The Honorable Elijah Muhammad was the son of a preacher. His father was a preacher, so he came from a lineage of studying the Bible.

Master Fard Muhammad gave Elijah his mind for over three years. I'm not talking about the mind of this system. I'm talking about a man who was taught by God Himself, and after 40 years through this process, the Most Honorable Elijah Muhammad told the Honorable Minister Louis Farrakhan to line his mind with him. If he is lining his mind with the Most Honorable Elijah Muhammad, he's lining his mind with Master Fard Muhammad, Who is the Supreme Being in our midst.

Jesus said to the disciples, "When you see me, you did not see the father? Because the Father and I are one and the same." We must die and be reborn again. Well, Farrakhan will release himself, that the Most Honorable Elijah Muhammad can fill him up with his mind.

Saviours' Day 1954, the Most Honorable Elijah Muhammad delivered his Saviours' Day speech, and in his speech, he asked for a helper. Then in 1955, Allah blessed him with a helper, the Honorable Minister Louis Farrakhan, as a Saviours' Day Gift. This man, Farrakhan, ever since he has joined the Nation of Islam, he has sacrificed his life for the betterment of Black people and all of humanity.

We all have made sacrifices and I don't want to take away from your sacrifices, but today I want to focus on this man, Farrakhan, because his sacrifice is much different and divine than our sacrifices. We don't understand. In February 1955, at that Saviours' Day Convention, when he's on the second level listening to the Honorable Elijah Muhammad, getting his commission, he was only 21 years old; barely into adulthood. Think about what you were doing at the age of 21. This man is more valuable than gold and silver. He is more valuable than pearls and diamonds, and he has dedicated his whole adulthood to the resurrection of a people.

He has been standing up for over 65 years as a true gift to the Honorable Elijah Muhammad. It's been over 42 years since he started the rebuilding process of the Nation of Islam. I'm in my 30's, and I feel like I have a hard life. This man has given all of him! He didn't get the chance to play catch with his children; he didn't get a chance to go to the recitals for his daughters, because the whole time, he was giving us himself.

The Honorable Minister Louis Farrakhan was a poor man. I want to put that on the record. Because we look at what you would call the final product, but we don't understand the sacrifices he went through in life. He was giving a demonstration in our men's only class and had holes at the bottom of his shoes. He wore the same suit every time he came out because he only had one suit. He and his family were so poor that they would go to the market after it was closed to pick through the leftovers to feed their family. Some of us are spoiled today.

He was commissioned to run New York as the Minister after Malcolm X. Now, I want you to understand, this is after Malcolm X, because everybody in the world knows who Malcolm X is, so you're talking about big shoes to fill. But he put in so much work that during that time, New York was number one in the *Muhammad Speaks Newspaper*. During this time, he was establishing Mosques and Study Groups, or Temples, all through New York to the point that they had 7V. Whoa, let's run that number. What is 7V? 22. 22 Mosques and Study Groups in New York. 22! And he still had to manage his home life.

This man, Farrakhan, has dealt with prostate cancer. He has met death's door three times. Not just once, not just twice, but three times, and every time he came out, all he wanted to do was see the people. This enemy has run high radiation into his body, burning his insides. They can't kill Farrakhan! How many people can you say they could have been through that and not wavered from their post? We get banged up a little bit and we're like, "I ain't coming to work today, boss." If we catch a little cold, "[cough, cough], I can't come in."

This man has sacrificed his life. In the '90s, I know we got some young people reading, but if we go back to the '90s, gang activity was at an all-time high. He went on a "Stop the Killing" tour. He's done three World Friendship tours. This man Farrakhan has thousands and thousands of lectures on every subject. If he never opened his mouth again, we have enough to feed on for generations.

Allah's Saviour in our midst.

He has and continues to feed the masses with his words. He had nearly two million in attendance at the Million Man March. A lot of us don't really understand that even if we never joined the Nation of Islam, the way we move with what has saved us from situations in life is really this man, Farrakhan. During the Million Man March, he asked the men to step back up and be men. From the Million Man March, he talked about the educational system, and more Black charter schools started popping up, saving the minds of the youth. From the Million Man March, men went out and women went out and started adopting Black children from this system that is designed to kill them. Allah's Saviour in our midst. Twenty years later from the Million Man March takes us to October 10, 2015, with the subject, *Justice or Else.*

I'm going to paraphrase something from the Most Honorable Elijah Muhammad, but he told the Minister that with modern equipment, he would be able to reach the masses with the click of a finger. Well, people are learning about him on Facebook, Twitter, Instagram, and TikTok. Isn't that the click of a finger? Don't they broadcast the lectures from Mosque Maryam in Chicago, Illinois with the click of a finger? Don't people go onto YouTube and click their fingers and search Farrakhan's lectures?

I had to reach out to my big brother, Abdul Qiyam Muhammad (formally Known as Jesse Muhammad). I said, "Brother, I need the stats real quick from 10.10.15." We are talking about a man who has reached the masses?

10.10.15 statistics: #JusticeOrElse reached, are you ready for this number? 1.5 billion people worldwide—1.5 billion people, worldwide. And on that day, you didn't hear about any fights; on that day, you didn't hear about any gun activity. Now check this part out. Over 15 different hashtags were being used. With people worldwide, in D.C. and watching online, #JusticeOrElse trended number one, nationally and worldwide, on Twitter for over 15 hours straight! That's powerful.

Allah's Saviour in our midst.

The hashtag #JusticeOrElse reached over 400 cities worldwide and 92 nations. You all know we have the United Nations, ninety-two nations. #JusticeOrElse trended number 1 and number 2, nationally and worldwide, on Facebook for four consecutive days.

This man, Farrakhan.

#JusticeOrElse was a top trending topic on Instagram and Snapchat. Now, check this part out. Due to outrage by those angry at BET—we might as well not even call it Black Entertainment Television no more—for not airing the gathering, a boycott was launched on Twitter, which caused the BET Hip Hop Awards to lose over one million viewers compared to last year.

Brother Qiyam said, "Over one million was in attendance, according to what the Honorable Minister Louis Farrakhan said to me on a phone call last year. That was the first time I was told that stat."

In the Scriptures, it said Jesus spoke to the masses.

This man, Farrakhan.

He stood up over 65 years ago and joined the Nation of Islam, and he has never sold us out. Never sold us out. It's a lot of people out there who've sold us out. He has integrity. He has morals.

Outside of the Jesus in the scriptures, Minister Farrakhan is the only one who has withstood such a long-running attack by the Jewish community. This man, Farrakhan, has lost and gained friendships due to him not wavering in his stance. The Honorable Elijah Muhammad told him, "I will get my people through you." There's a reason why you are reading this. Even if you don't realize it, there's no coincidence in this. Allah is using us, even if we don't realize it.

The Minister said on January 22nd, 2019 via Twitter—yes, he's on Twitter; @LouisFarrakhan, hit follow, hit push notifications, so you can get your daily hadiths because he's on Twitter. He tweeted, "When you are in the place of a redeemer of your people, there's a price you've got to pay. God made Jesus a Redeemer, a Saviour and if we're following such a man, how could we flee from the price of redemption?"

Well, they use this man, Farrakhan, as a litmus test, and if we look at the track record of all these Black leaders, they all seem to fail that test when it comes to us. They may pass it for them. Jesse Jackson, in the 80s, had to deal with the litmus test when he ran for the presidential election. Barak Obama dealt with the litmus test, in his first election. Their whole focus is for people to denounce Farrakhan. Denounce Farrakhan. Condemn him. And the Minister expressed to us, "I didn't want to go public because I didn't want to interrupt his race, and I could see the people really wanted him to win, so I said, I'm going to give them that time." Then he came back and said, "But, now, it's my time." They're were running our beloved sister, Tamika Mallory, through the litmus test. As she was promoting the Women's March on Washington, everywhere she went to promote it the conversation was, "You said Farrakhan was the G.O.A.T. You won't condemn him?" She said she wouldn't

Some of us may not agree with the way she went about it, but I will say this. Family have disagreements. She said she doesn't agree with everything he says. That's fine, because you can tell she's still dealing with the litmus test, because everywhere she goes, the Jewish community pops up saying she ain't gave us enough. So, she's still going through this litmus test. But that's still our sister. And if our father, our spiritual father, the Honorable Minister Louis Farrakhan, is rocking with the sister, we protect the sister. Any time there is a Black person rising in the eyes of Black people, they make sure to have them denounce Farrakhan. Denounce Farrakhan. Just go look. And if they don't denounce him, they try to wiggle out of it some kind of way.

I was in an interview dealing with something at one of the schools, as I'm striving to set up a Nation of Islam Student Association on campus, and this Jewish guy tried to bring up some rhetoric about the Minister. That's incorrect. He had the nerve to say, "So you're not going to condemn him?" Emphatically, no! I stand with whatever Minister Farrakhan says and does because he is my leader.

They misunderstand Farrakhan, and they keep our people blind to understanding Farrakhan. Why is that, is the real question though. Why do they bow to them and turn their backs to Farrakhan? Are we still afraid of this enemy? Are we still seeking to be in their social equality? We still desire to integrate with them, that's what it is. That's what it is. I'm okay with you beating that brother over there if I can still integrate with you.

Wow. Them turning their backs on Farrakhan reminds me of the scriptures when Jesus was coming into the Passover. As he came into the city, the people were screaming out, "Hosanna, Hosanna!" and then by the time he was placed on trial, they gave him an option and the people yelled out, "Crucify him! Crucify him!" We are at that time. So we love this man and we will quote this man and say I stand with this man and put a fist in the air for this man until we are under some pressure. Then we turn our backs on Farrakhan.

There's a reason why they apply pressure on us. There's a reason why they don't want us to be attached to this man, Farrakhan. The rulers of this world are still afraid of the rise of a Black Messiah. The rulers of this world know that if we connect our self to that in which Allah has given us as a gift, we will rise from the ashes like the Phoenix bird. Once we rise, in our rising we start removing the plague of this world. Our mindset changes. Our spirit changes. Our action changes. The way we move from being sluggish to fast-moving, right down to the modern time, changes.

They don't need a woke black man and woman today because they know if we wake up, they are the plague. So, they judge this man, Farrakhan, out of context, and they word it so swiftly that we fall in line and say, "Yes, Massa; yes, boss. I won't listen to that man, Farrakhan."

They still fear the coming of the man, but the thing is, they know who the man is. They don't want you and I to know who this man, Farrakhan, is. So they keep us entertained with things that will not build up our conscious and our spiritual realm. Then they feed us foods that create plagues to our bodies, so our mind is messed up. We can't think clear no more. And then you wonder why the Honorable Minister

Louis Farrakhan makes statements about anti-termites; because they are not just eating at the foundation of the world, but they are eating at the foundation of us.

They know something, and the Minister keeps placing something out there for us, testing to see how well we're paying attention to move out on something. Because if we go back to Holy Day of Atonement, which is the Million Man March, a year after 10.10.15, in Atlanta, Georgia; the Minister said, "This is really the Messiah standing in front of you today." But it went over a lot of our heads. So I just want to remind us, go back and catch that lecture. I'm pretty sure it's on YouTube. Click of a finger. And you can look up the true meaning of Messiah.

There will be one prepared for you and me by the Lord of the worlds. It was hard for many people to accept Jesus, his role and his connection to God. Well, it's hard for people to accept the Honorable Minister Louis Farrakhan, his role and his connection to God. It is hard to believe the man we've been yearning for is right here in front of us. Because the sad part is this, when he goes away, the enemy is going to come out and say, "That was your Saviour." And we are going to look stupid as hell, excuse me.

Allah's Saviour in our midst.

He sits in the chair of the Honorable Elijah Muhammad, who was taught by God, Himself. And we can be disrespectful to a man, not even knowing we're being disrespectful to him. If we were to look up in scriptures, all of the prophets, warners, and messengers were placed upon the people as the Saviour for the people. It's hard to know a man who may have flaws, like we all do, and be comfortable with identifying with who he is.

I was at Arizona State University one day and a guy said, "Farrakhan like any other leader." Ooh, wee. I almost had to throw on some boxing gloves. Don't do that. Don't do that. It ain't a lot of them who didn't sell out. And the Honorable Minister Louis Farrakhan, this man, loves people so much, he loves us so much that he will take what Allah is giving him and he would instill it in us, that when I gave you that title earlier, we'll be able to say God sent saviours after His people. Right now, he is the lead student in front of us, as he's preparing us to go into our spiritual realm of understanding and allowing us to grow step-by-step, with his patience with us; and he has been very patient with us. Oh, he has been patient with us. The Honorable Minister Louis Farrakhan said on January 21st, 2019 via Twitter, "When God says, love me with all your heart, you don't know what all is until He stretches you. Until you are willing to be stretched, God would not give you a commandment that He knew you couldn't fulfill."

If we open up our hearts to this man; if we open up our minds to this man—he's not an arrogant man; he honestly doesn't even like getting credit. What I love about this man, what he does when he teaches is he's actually sending you to Elijah, because he knows he's a vessel of Elijah. The Most Honorable Elijah Muhammad said in the book *Our Savior Has Arrived,* "The dawn of a new day has arrived to seek our place in that which is new." We must have a guide. Allah, God, has always provided guides for those who seek to walk in His path. The guide, right now, is the Honorable Minister Louis Farrakhan. Oh, man, a Saviours' Day gift for our Christ.

We know next month many of us will be traveling to Chicago, Illinois, sitting in the seats at the United Center, waiting to hear a historical lecture of guidance from the Honorable Minister Louis Farrakhan. I have a request for us. The Honorable Elijah Muhammad asked for a helper, and he was given a Saviour's Day Gift; but we, as Muslims, have a Saviours' Day Gift requirement that we give to the Honorable Minister Louis Farrakhan. Do we want to see this man working a 9 to 5 when there are things going on in the world that he needs to tackle? *"Oh, dear Apostle, I ain't got it?"*

Not only do we give our financial support to him and his family for their 65 years plus of sacrifices for us, but how about we be a gift to the Honorable Minister Louis Farrakhan by being helpers in this cause of Islam, for him, that he can fashion us up properly to be saviours for our people. We should be focusing off of Surah 110, where it says:

> *"In the Name of Allah, the Beneficent, the Merciful. When Allah's help and victory comes, And thou seest men entering the religion of Allah in companies, Celebrate the praise of thy Lord and ask His protection. Surely He is ever Returning (to mercy).'*

How about we be Allah's help at this time and we help this man, Farrakhan? It's going to take a little sacrifice, but what are you willing to give to get into the Kingdom of Allah? What are you willing to give to be on the right side of Allah? What are you willing to give?

Oh, brothers and sisters, this man, Farrakhan, is Surah 53 of the Holy Qur'an; He is Al-Najm, the Star; he is the bright star of no equal. He is the Son of Man; he is the great wonder in Revelations 12, where it says *"clothed with the sun and the moon under her feet and upon her head, a crown of 12 stars."* Oh, this man, Farrakhan. He has sacrificed himself for us; he's willing to give up his life for us, but are we willing to give up our lives to help him, because he's pregnant right now. He's pregnant with a Nation, and he had to give birth to this Nation. Oh, brothers and sisters. Through the Honorable Minister Louis Farrakhan, Allah will make saviours for this Nation, and that is you and I.

Romans 8:38-39 says:

> *"For I am convinced that neither death nor life, neither angels nor demons, neither the present nor the future, nor any powers, neither height nor death, nor anything else in all creation, will be able to separate us from the love of God that is in Christ Jesus our Lord."*

We must attach ourselves tight right now. And in Matthew 8:18-22:

> *"When Jesus saw the crowd around him, he gave orders to cross the other side of the lake. Then a teacher of the law came to him and said, 'Teacher, I will follow you wherever you go.'*

Jesus replied, 'Foxes have dens and birds have nests, but the Son of Man has no place to lay his head.' Another disciple said to him, 'Lord, first let me go and bury my father.' But Jesus told him, 'Follow me, and let the dead bury their own dead.'"

We are alive today; we must find ourselves doing living things. We must find ourselves following the one we have in our midst today. Through this man, Farrakhan, Elijah will get all of his people. Follow him and we will all be victorious. Allah's Saviour is in our midst today, and he is willing to give his life for us. We must be willing to give our lives for him. Us giving our lives, is us being willing to follow his lead, because he said he needs 10,000 Fearless who are willing to go and stand between the guns and the gangs and to work peaceful resolutions. With just a little study and a lot of application, we can find ourselves growing more in oneness with Allah, God, if we follow His Saviour in our midst.

The Honorable Minister Louis Farrakhan met with brothers and sisters of the 10,000 Fearless at the 10,000 Fearless headquarters. He was pleased, but he knows we have much more work to do in our community. All we have to do is stand up and be willing to give ourselves, and Allah will reward us by us giving up ourselves to Him. You are so important to Allah. Be the best you can be and watch how Allah will bless you abundantly.

DEDICATION

This book was in the making years before the transition of my father. His transition has shown me one important thing in life: You never know when your time is up, and you should accomplish whatever desires you have before your time expires.

I dedicate this book to my father, Hannibal Yusuf Sirboya Muhammad. A warrior of love. A wise workaholic always willing to help others, even if it's an inconvenience to him. A straightforward man with a great, one-on-one personality and sense of humor, telling the funniest of stories.

My father helped build the stage at the monumental 20th anniversary of the Million Man March, "Justice or Else" held on October 10, 2015. He was a man who didn't seek praise or a spotlight, and he was a hard-working servant from behind the scenes.

Not only is he a survivor, but he has left a major impact on the Nation of Islam and the nations of the earth. He was sent off with a forever memorable Janazah service conducted by the Honorable Minister Louis Farrakhan.

I pray I've made you proud, father.

Doing what he enjoys

In 2016 visiting Southern Regional Student Minister Abdul Sharrieff Muhammad and the 10,000 Fearless Headquarter in Atlanta, GA

In 2016 visiting siblings and father.

2016 Ramadan Retreat in Georgia

Embracing his brother Student Minister Joel Muhammad at his 80th birth anniversary in Phoenix, AZ

In 2015 behind the scenes helping to build the stage for the 20th Anniversary of the Million Man March – Holy Day of Atonement in Washington, DC

In 2015 behind the scenes helping to build the stage for the 20th Anniversary of the Million Man March – Holy Day of Atonement in Washington, DC (Continued)

In 2012 wearing his hoody in honor of our little brother Trayvon Martin and pointing at picture of his father Big John White (former sparring partner of Heavyweight Champion Joe Lewis). Photo taken in Phoenix, AZ

With his big brother and mentor Minister Jabril Muhammad in Phoenix, AZ

2013 embracing his big brother and mentor The Honorable Minister Louis Farrakhan at the National House (Palace) in Phoenix, AZ

May Allah bless you!!!! October 5, 2019 in Phoenix, AZ

ACKNOWLEDGEMENTS

THE HONORABLE MINISTER LOUIS FARRAKHAN .... CHICAGO, IL

MOTHER KHADIJAH FARRAKHAN .... CHICAGO, IL

JABRIL MUHAMMAD .... PHOENIX, AZ

LATANYA MUHAMMAD .... PHOENIX, AZ

HANNIBAL MUHAMMAD .... PHOENIX, AZ

CHARLENE MUHAMMAD .... LOS ANGELES, CA

DONNA MUHAMMAD .... MEMPHIS, TN

ANISAH MUHAMMAD .... MACON, GA

DEANDREA MUHAMMAD .... PHOENIX, AZ

NUR AL-HUDA MUHAMMAD .... PHOENIX, AZ

EILIYAH MUHAMMAD .... PHOENIX, AZ

JABRIL NAIM MUHAMMAD .... OAKLAND, CA

MARCUS W 2X HILL .... BALTIMORE, MD

HILARIO MUHAMMAD .... PHOENIX, AZ

JAHLEEL MUHAMMAD .... DETROIT, MI

MICHAEL T MUHAMMAD .... ATLANTIC CITY, NJ

JOY TRICHE .... PHOENIX, AZ

ABDUL QIYAM MUHAMMAD .... HOUSTON, TX

INDEX

A

action · 89, 100, 106, 107, 109, 154, 217, 281, 288
Allah · 3, ii, iii, iv, 1, 2, 3, 5, 9, 21, 22, 24, 27, 30, 31, 34, 35, 37, 39, 40, 41, 42, 43, 45, 50, 51, 52, 54, 55, 56, 57, 58, 59, 60, 62, 63, 64, 65, 66, 67, 68, 70, 71, 72, 73, 76, 77, 78, 79, 80, 81, 82, 83, 84, 86, 87, 89, 91, 92, 93, 95, 96, 97, 98, 99, 101, 110, 111, 112, 113, 114, 115, 116, 117, 118, 119, 121, 122, 125, 126, 127, 128, 130, 132, 139, 140, 144, 145, 146, 148, 151, 153, 154, 155, 156, 157, 159, 160, 161, 162, 163, 165, 168, 173, 175, 176, 177, 178, 179, 182, 184, 185, 186, 187, 188, 189, 190, 192, 193, 194, 195, 196, 197, 198, 200, 201, 202, 203, 204, 205, 206, 207, 210, 211, 212, 213, 214, 215, 216, 217, 218, 221, 222, 223, 224, 225, 226, 234, 236, 237, 238, 239, 241, 243, 244, 245, 246, 249, 250, 251, 252, 253, 254, 255, 257, 258, 259, 260, 261, 263, 264, 266, 267, 268, 269, 270, 272, 274, 275, 276, 277, 279, 280, 281, 282, 284, 285, 286, 288, 289, 290, 291, 292, 293
America · iii, 1, 2, 3, 9, 23, 61, 62, 123, 135, 162, 174, 182, 203, 218, 224, 230, 231, 243, 246, 253, 255, 256, 257, 263, 268

B

believe · 15, 62, 63, 64, 76, 77, 84, 90, 99, 149, 165, 251, 253, 254, 262, 270, 277, 289
best · 18, 25, 30, 35, 39, 40, 41, 47, 50, 51, 54, 64, 78, 83, 92, 97, 107, 140, 145, 154, 165, 168, 174, 175, 176, 177, 178, 179, 180, 181, 182, 183, 184, 187, 189, 190, 191, 192, 194, 196, 198, 199, 200, 201, 202, 203, 204, 205, 207, 208, 210, 212, 216, 234, 246, 253, 256, 264, 266, 274, 278, 293
Bible · 32, 42, 90, 127, 266, 269, 273, 282
biological · 35, 271
Black · iii, 1, 18, 19, 20, 21, 22, 46, 47, 49, 50, 61, 66, 82, 90, 123, 129, 217, 218, 220, 221, 230, 243, 247, 281, 282, 284, 285, 286, 287, 288
book · ii, 8, 21, 42, 61, 62, 63, 68, 81, 87, 90, 92, 102, 106, 126, 128, 136, 138, 142, 158, 168, 176, 193, 196, 237, 238, 257, 261, 262, 265, 268, 271, 290, 294
boys · 27, 30, 137, 226, 260
breastfeeding · 261

C

celebrities · 168, 181, 231
celebrity · 168
child · 3, 5, 6, 11, 12, 15, 17, 18, 22, 23, 25, 26, 32, 33, 34, 35, 36, 39, 40, 41, 42, 44, 45, 92, 94, 98, 100, 113, 118, 119, 133, 148, 155, 174, 176, 178, 194, 198, 229, 231, 232, 242, 244, 245, 246, 248, 261, 264, 271

Christ · iii, 53, 76, 85, 120, 144, 153, 218, 227, 228, 249, 271, 275, 276, 280, 281, 290, 292
circumstance · 56, 72, 97, 210
Cointelpro · 217
corrupt · 147, 154, 160

D

DEFENDING · 5, 298
desire · ii, 29, 49, 68, 93, 94, 97, 99, 104, 106, 126, 166, 187, 226, 265, 273, 288
determination · 91, 93, 94, 265
devil · 8, 50, 61, 62, 78, 91, 95, 102, 110, 115, 142, 152, 153, 166, 258, 259, 263
Dianetics · 94, 155, 241
Dua · 65

E

Elijah · ii, iii, iv, 21, 35, 55, 57, 59, 60, 62, 63, 64, 65, 66, 67, 68, 70, 71, 72, 73, 75, 76, 77, 78, 79, 80, 81, 82, 86, 87, 110, 134, 136, 137, 139, 142, 143, 144, 157, 158, 165, 182, 218, 219, 223, 225, 227, 228, 240, 245, 253, 254, 268, 269, 272, 277, 278, 281, 282, 283, 285, 286, 289, 290, 291, 292
enemy · 3, 9, 17, 18, 23, 25, 29, 40, 64, 90, 91, 95, 97, 100, 102, 123, 126, 132, 145, 162, 178, 217, 218, 220, 222, 225, 230, 239, 241, 252, 256, 261, 276, 284, 288, 289
environment · 19, 29, 91, 110, 118, 133, 148, 149, 155, 156, 269
envy · 67, 81, 152, 153, 159
exalt · 152, 165, 247
exercise · 264, 265, 268, 278

F

Facebook · 14, 103, 196, 221, 242, 285
Fard · iii, iv, 87, 132, 144, 165, 228, 272, 281, 282
Farrakhan · ii, iv, v, 1, 2, 16, 19, 29, 30, 35, 40, 53, 55, 57, 59, 64, 65, 67, 71, 73, 77, 78, 79, 82, 87, 89, 90, 97, 101, 106, 111, 122, 125, 126, 129, 133, 137, 141, 142, 144, 145, 157, 160, 164, 165, 168, 173, 176, 181, 182, 186, 190, 191, 192, 198, 200, 204, 210, 215, 217, 218, 219, 220, 221, 222, 223, 224, 225, 226, 227, 228, 229, 230, 231, 232, 236, 238, 239, 240, 241, 242, 243, 244, 245, 246, 247, 249, 254, 255, 261, 263, 270, 271, 272, 275, 277, 279, 280, 281, 282, 283, 284, 285, 286, 287, 288, 289, 290, 291, 292, 293, 294
father · iv, 4, 7, 12, 18, 22, 27, 33, 34, 35, 36, 37, 39, 40, 41, 42, 48, 53, 71, 78, 79, 82, 87, 112, 113, 119, 130, 153, 155, 225, 227, 228, 231, 232, 233, 234, 238, 260, 263, 271, 282, 287, 292, 294
FBI · 217
fear · 3, 29, 74, 97, 98, 99, 100, 110, 111, 145, 155, 161, 173, 189, 190, 193, 217, 218, 220, 221, 222, 247, 255, 289
Final Call · 62, 64, 90, 105, 209, 281
focus · 22, 81, 144, 195, 201, 282, 287
FOI · 102, 235, 267
foster · 23, 24, 29
fun · 14, 43, 109, 119, 176, 189, 219, 232, 237, 243

G

gift · 54, 70, 110, 130, 145, 206, 257, 278, 283, 288, 290, 291

God · iii, iv, v, 1, 3, 4, 5, 7, 9, 10, 22, 24, 27, 29, 30, 32, 33, 34, 35, 36, 37, 38, 39, 40, 42, 44, 51, 52, 53, 54, 55, 57, 58, 59, 61, 63, 64, 66, 67, 70, 71, 74, 75, 76, 77, 78, 81, 82, 83, 84, 85, 88, 89, 90, 91, 96, 97, 98, 104, 111, 113, 114, 115, 116, 117, 120, 122, 123, 125, 126, 127, 128, 132, 139, 140, 141, 144, 145, 147, 148, 151, 152, 153, 154, 155, 159, 160, 161, 162, 165, 166, 168, 175, 182, 185, 186, 187, 189, 194, 195, 196, 198, 200, 204, 205, 207, 210, 211, 213, 214, 215, 216, 217, 218, 220, 221, 224, 225, 226, 227, 228, 234, 237, 238, 242, 244, 246, 247, 249, 250, 251, 253, 254, 255, 256, 257, 260, 261, 262, 263, 264, 265, 266, 269, 270, 271, 272, 273, 274, 276, 277, 278, 279, 280, 281, 282, 286, 289, 290, 292, 293
Great · iii, 281
guest · 87
guidance · 5, 36, 44, 52, 65, 145, 158, 159, 225, 232, 242, 245, 260, 275, 291

H

Hannibal · 3, 30, 31, 66, 80, 99, 101, 131, 149, 232, 234, 236, 237, 242, 267, 280, 294
heart · 9, 35, 55, 80, 96, 145, 162, 164, 182, 194, 198, 200, 201, 202, 205, 239, 244, 246, 249, 290
holy · 4, 74, 85, 262, 278
Honor · 33, 39
Hosanna · 288
humble · 65, 83, 140, 239
husband · 23, 37, 38, 40, 131, 235

I

illusion · 104, 114, 162, 175, 178, 179, 181, 198
interactions · 146, 271
internal · 38, 91, 95, 97, 102
Islam · 1, 5, 60, 62, 63, 65, 66, 78, 84, 88, 94, 102, 134, 135, 137, 138, 164, 166, 168, 173, 174, 196, 203, 215, 216, 218, 219, 221, 223, 226, 227, 228, 231, 241, 243, 244, 250, 251, 252, 253, 255, 257, 261, 268, 275, 282, 283, 284, 286, 287, 291, 294

J

Janazah · 58, 81, 112, 131, 294
Jesus · iv, 35, 36, 52, 53, 55, 60, 76, 77, 79, 85, 116, 120, 128, 152, 153, 161, 173, 218, 220, 224, 225, 227, 238, 240, 249, 254, 256, 257, 263, 272, 282, 286, 288, 289, 292
journey · 3, iv, 68, 89, 122, 127, 145, 258

K

Khadijah · 40, 182, 239, 244

L

life · ii, 3, 4, 6, 7, 8, 9, 10, 15, 16, 18, 21, 22, 27, 29, 33, 36, 38, 43, 44, 52, 53, 55, 56, 57, 64, 68, 72, 73, 76, 78, 87, 90, 97, 98, 103, 104, 105, 106, 108, 110, 111, 112, 113, 116, 117, 118, 119, 120, 123, 125, 126, 129, 130, 131, 132, 133, 138, 141,142, 146, 147, 149, 150, 154, 157, 158, 160, 161, 165, 166, 168, 174, 175, 176, 177, 178, 179, 180, 181, 182, 183, 184, 185, 186, 187, 188, 189, 190,

191, 192, 193, 194, 195, 196, 197, 198, 199, 200, 201, 202, 203, 205, 206, 207, 208, 209, 210, 214, 215, 216, 220, 223, 224, 226, 227, 236, 238, 239, 240, 242, 243, 244, 245, 256, 257, 259, 263, 265, 270, 271, 276, 282, 283, 284, 292, 294
live · ii, 8, 9, 10, 22, 23, 24, 32, 33, 63, 80, 110, 111, 119, 150, 154, 156, 174, 177, 178, 179, 184, 187, 188, 189, 190, 192, 193, 195, 198, 200, 203, 205, 206, 215, 216, 249, 254, 273
love · iv, 4, 5, 7, 18, 20, 21, 22, 23, 24, 25, 27, 29, 30, 31, 33, 35, 36, 39, 40, 44, 45, 46, 52, 54, 55, 56, 73, 79, 80, 94, 114, 115, 116, 118, 122, 130, 132, 133, 134, 135, 137, 143, 145, 154, 156, 160, 162, 168, 170, 181, 182, 183, 185, 186, 190, 191, 194, 200, 202, 206, 207, 211, 217, 221, 227, 235, 237, 240, 246, 253, 260, 262, 264, 270, 273, 278, 281, 288, 290, 292, 294
lust · 153

M

MAN · 5, 158, 298
manifest · 83, 127, 129, 155, 158, 164, 186, 190, 215, 225, 226, *menifesting*, *menifesting*
March · 18, 84, 124, 125, 219, 220, 222, 230, 234, 246, 254, 284, 287, 289, 294
meditation · 266
mental · 67, 177, 217, 244, 248, 252, 262, 267, 268
Messenger · iii, 21, 39, 51, 59, 63, 64, 79, 81, 137, 138, 148, 182, 237, 250, 277
messiah · 223
MGT · 135, 203, 233
mirror · 16, 17, 25, 27, 91, 92, 95, 96, 97, 105, 155, 201, 268
modus operandi · 146

Moses · 53, 78, 192, 256, 257, 258, 259, 266, 273, 274, 275
Muhammad · 3, ii, iii, iv, 21, 33, 35, 39, 44, 47, 51, 55, 57, 59, 60, 62, 63, 64, 65, 66, 67, 68, 70, 71, 72, 73, 75, 76, 77, 78, 79, 80, 81, 82, 86, 87, 95, 106, 110, 132, 135, 136, 137, 139, 142, 143, 144, 155, 157, 158, 159, 165, 182, 191, 195, 204, 208, 218, 219, 223, 224, 225, 227, 228, 232, 233, 235, 236, 237, 240, 245, 253, 254, 268, 269, 272, 277, 278, 281, 282, 283, 285, 286, 289, 290, 291, 294, 298
Muslim · 50, 62, 65, 84, 94, 120, 135, 136, 173, 213, 243, 278

N

Nas · 153, 219
natural · 22, 90, 154, 204, 261, 269
nature · 40, 52, 58, 90, 151, 160, 177, 215, 217, 238, 261, 263
New · 54, 55, 56, 57, 58, 59, 124, 181, 270, 277, 283

O

Original · v, 50, 60, 72, 73, 89, 90, 106, 123, 168
orphan · 260
outside · 7, 12, 13, 22, 23, 29, 31, 58, 128, 146, 148, 154, 204, 233
overseas · 174

P

parent · 11, 12, 15, 22, 33, 34, 40, 98, 112, 118, 119, 155, 176, 198
Passover · 288

patience · 12, 22, 51, 132, 204, 206, 224, 258, 259, 260, 273, 274, 278, 290
people · iii, 1, 3, 8, 10, 13, 14, 15, 16, 20, 24, 26, 28, 29, 35, 43, 51, 52, 53, 54, 59, 61, 62, 66, 67, 71, 72, 73, 74, 76, 77, 78, 79, 80, 81, 83, 85, 86, 93, 95, 97, 98, 99, 101, 103, 105, 116, 117, 118, 119, 123, 124, 131, 132, 133, 135, 136, 137, 138, 141, 142, 143, 144, 146, 149, 150, 156, 158, 159, 160, 162, 163, 164, 166, 168, 170, 171, 173, 174, 175, 179, 180, 181, 182, 183, 185, 189, 191, 193, 196, 198, 199, 202, 203, 205, 206, 208, 209, 210, 211, 214, 215, 218, 219, 220, 221, 222, 223, 224, 226, 227, 229, 230, 231, 237, 238, 239, 241, 247, 250, 253, 254, 257, 259, 262, 263, 266, 270, 275, 277, 278, 281, 282, 283, 284, 285, 286, 287, 288, 289, 290, 291, 292
physical · ii, 19, 79, 244, 248, 262, 264, 268
plan · 20, 100, 106, 168, 222, 224, 245, 246, 256, 280
point · 1, 2, 3, 4, 5, 6, 7, 10, 12, 16, 17, 42, 46, 48, 55, 68, 72, 73, 79, 80, 89, 100, 126, 130, 139, 147, 174, 175, 188, 191, 197, 202, 221, 225, 230, 231, 232, 234, 235, 237, 243, 248, 254, 257, 259, 263, 274, 283
potential · 10, 19, 90, 124, 158, 167, 174, 249, 250, 264
practice · 20, 73, 77, 96, 97, 106, 264, 268
pray · ii, 30, 54, 59, 65, 79, 103, 110, 194, 196, 200, 201, 210, 234, 246, 261, 266, 276, 294
president · 45, 230, 240, 254, 255, 262
produce · 61, 64, 67, 80, 98, 103, 106, 133, 143, 178, 194, 244, 250
productivity · 141, 143
purification · 93, 100, 150, 157, 205, 241, 276

Q

Qur'an · 42, 52, 66, 93, 126, 127, 143, 165, 220, 235, 241, 253, 254, 257, 266, 269, 273, 291

R

read · 2, 3, 8, 11, 41, 42, 63, 65, 79, 81, 87, 91, 96, 102, 107, 112, 128, 132, 158, 159, 165, 176, 193, 217, 231, 235, 237, 238, 248, 249, 267

S

Sahirah · 32
same · 4, 5, 6, 9, 10, 13, 16, 17, 22, 33, 36, 40, 47, 52, 68, 81, 91, 94, 98, 101, 103, 105, 108, 110, 120, 121, 125, 137, 138, 146, 147, 148, 149, 153, 154, 163, 176, 177, 179, 182, 189, 212, 213, 222, 228, 232, 235, 237, 249, 252, 265, 268, 280, 282, 283
Satan · 3, 10, 45, 78, 90, 115, 124, 127, 142, 147, 151, 152, 158, 227, 246
save · 2, 3, 24, 29, 80, 114, 231, 245, 281
Saviour · 63, 280, 281, 284, 285, 286, 289, 290, 291, 292
scripture · 84, 152, 229, 231, 249, 263
Self-Accusing Spirits · 257
sex · 9, 20, 230, 245
slave · 48, 123, 128, 192, 223, 262
Social media · 11, 15, 178, 179, 188
spirit · ii, iv, 38, 64, 77, 85, 94, 111, 112, 113, 116, 117, 118, 120, 166, 177, 210, 214, 226, 227, 265, 273, 288
steadfast · 46, 111, 129, 221, 260, 265
step · 27, 62, 87, 88, 102, 105, 108, 110, 128, 136, 141, 151, 153, 154, 165, 166, 187, 190, 196, 205, 206, 207, 213, 218, 284, 290
stress · 13, 14, 94, 131, 174, 225

study · iii, 1, 6, 21, 26, 33, 34, 57, 73, 79, 80, 98, 102, 106, 132, 143, 144, 154, 156, 159, 160, 192, 196, 207, 213, 214, 232, 247, 266, 269, 274, 275, 293

T

talent · 69, 70, 88
travel · 55, 92, 101, 132, 174, 184, 203
Twitter · 16, 88, 97, 103, 196, 220, 221, 222, 242, 285, 286, 290

V

variables · 92, 97, 104, 110, 251
Veganism · 268

W

wife · 20, 23, 35, 43, 44, 92, 101, 102, 127, 131, 156, 182, 239, 244, 245, 251, 266
wisdom · iii, 225

wise · 259, 262, 266, 273, 275, 294
work · iii, 2, 3, 15, 16, 17, 18, 21, 22, 23, 24, 25, 27, 39, 41, 42, 43, 52, 54, 56, 60, 67, 70, 72, 77, 79, 80, 81, 83, 84, 85, 86, 88, 92, 94, 97, 99, 103, 104, 105, 106, 107, 110, 112, 123, 128, 131, 134, 135, 136, 137, 138, 139, 140, 141, 142, 144, 149, 152, 156, 161, 164, 174, 180, 185, 187, 188, 189, 192, 193, 194, 211, 212, 213, 214, 218, 219, 228, 236, 238, 245, 246, 251, 257, 265, 266, 267, 276, 277, 279, 283, 284, 292, 293
world · iv, 1, 6, 27, 36, 40, 42, 43, 45, 52, 53, 63, 65, 81, 91, 92, 99, 100, 109, 111, 114, 116, 119, 124, 132, 141, 142, 145, 152, 159, 160, 162, 166, 175, 176, 177, 192, 194, 204, 211, 215, 221, 227, 232, 236, 238, 240, 244, 247, 252, 255, 262, 280, 283, 288, 289, 291

Y

youth · 1, 2, 3, 4, 5, 6, 7, 10, 19, 23, 24, 118, 246, 247, 284

www.ingramcontent.com/pod-product-compliance
Lightning Source LLC
Chambersburg PA
CBHW050102170426
43198CB00014B/2434